HOT CORN
LIFE SCENES
IN
NEW YORK
ILLUSTRATED
N. ORR Sc.

I0754270

HOT CORN:

LIFE SCENES IN NEW YORK ILLUSTRATED.

INCLUDING

THE STORY OF LITTLE KATY,

MADALINA, THE RAG-PICKER'S DAUGHTER,

WILD MAGGIE, &c.

WITH ORIGINAL DESIGNS, ENGRAVED BY N. ORR.

BY SOLON ROBINSON.

"Bid that welcome
Which comes to punish us."

"A beggar's book outworth's a noble's blood."

"Of every inordinate cup beware,
Or drink, and with it misery share."

NEW YORK:
DE WITT AND DAVENPORT, PUBLISHERS,
160 & 162 NASSAU STREET.
1854.

W. H. TINSON, Stereotyper, &c.,
22 Spruce Street, New York.

R. CRAIGHEAD, PRINTER,
53 Vesey st., N. Y.

TO

HORACE GREELEY,

AND HIS CO-LABORERS,

EDITORS OF THE NEW YORK TRIBUNE;

The Friends of the Working Man; The Advocates of
Lifting up poor trodden-down Humanity; The Ardent Supporters of, and Earnest
Advocates for the Maine Law;
The Wishers for Better Rewards for Woman's Labor,
And All Honest Industry,

This Volume is

RESPECTFULLY DEDICATED,

BY YOUR FRIEND AND FELLOW WORKER,

THE AUTHOR.

INTRODUCTION.

THE growing taste for works of this kind—works intended to promote temperance and virtue, to lift up the lowly, to expose to open day the hidden effects produced by Rum, to give narratives of misery suffered by the poor in this city—has induced the Publishers to offer liberal inducements to the author to use his powerful pen, and words of fire, to depict his "Life Scenes," and embody them in a volume, which, we are satisfied, will prove one of the most acceptable to the moral portion of the community, ever published. It is a work of high tone, that must do good. The peculiar style of the author is as original as the tales of truth which he narrates. It is unlike that of any other author, and every page is full of fresh interest and thrilling narrative.

As a temperance tale, it has no equal. As such, we hope it may prove but the commencement of a series. As an exposé of life among the poor in this city, it will be read with deep and abiding interest, in all parts of this country. It is a work for the fireside of every family; a book that commends itself to the heart.

No one who has read the "HOT CORN STORIES," as they appeared in the *Tribune*, but will rejoice to have the opportunity to possess them, and many more like them, all complete and connected, in one handsome volume, such as we now offer.

To a moral and religious public; to all who would promote

temperance; to all who would rather see virtue than vice abound; to all who have a heart to feel for other's woes; to all who would have their hearts touched with sympathy for the afflictions of their fellow creatures, "Life Scenes," as depicted in this volume, are respectfully commended, by

THE PUBLISHERS.

AUTHOR'S PREFACE.

"OH, pshaw," says pretty Miss Impulsive, "I hate prefaces." So do I. Nobody reads them; that is, nobody but a few old fellows with spectacles. I would not write one, only that some folks think a book looks not well without. Well, then, I have written a great deal in my life—travels, tales, songs, temperance stories, some politics, a good deal upon agriculture, much truth, and some fiction, always in the newspapers, never before in a book. I know that many, very many, have read what I have written with pleasure, or else "this world is awfully given to lying," for they have said so. Will they read my *book?* That we shall see. If they do, they must not criticise too closely. Remember that some of the most thrilling sketches were written amid the daily scenes and avocations of a city editor's office, for the paper in which they first appeared, without any thought or design on the part of the author of making a book;—that was the thought of the publishers. They read the first sketches, and judged, we hope rightly, if enlarged and embodied in a neat volume, it would be appreciated as one of the best efforts, in this book-making age, to do good.

If they have judged rightly,—if it *does* have that effect,—if the public *do* appreciate the volume as they often have my fugitive effusions,—then shall I be rewarded, and they may rest assured, whenever they buy a volume, that a portion of the purchase money will go to ameliorate the condition of the poor, such as you will become acquainted with, if you follow me in my walks through the city, as depicted in this volume, which I offer most hopingly to all who do not know, and most trustingly to all who do know him, who has so often signed himself

Your old friend,

SOLON ROBINSON.

NEW YORK, *November*, 1853.

CONTENTS.

CHAPTER I.

CHAPTER II.

CHAPTER III.

CHAPTER IV.

CHAPTER XII.

CHAPTER XIII.

CHAPTER XIV.

CHAPTER XV.

HOT CORN.

LIFE SCENES IN NEW YORK ILLUSTRATED.

CHAPTER I.

OUR TITLE.—THE STORY.

"How hard it is to hide the sparks of nature."

It is a queer title for a book; what can it mean?" is the exclamation of those who open it for the first time.

Visit this city—walk with me from nine o'clock till midnight, through the streets of New York, in the month of August, then read the first interview of the author with little Katy, the Hot Corn girl, and the story of her life, and you will not ask, "What does it mean?" But you may ask, what does it mean that I see so many squalid-looking women, so many tender children, so many boys, who with well directed labor might work their way to fortune; or crippled men, sitting upon the stone steps along the street crying, "Hot corn! here's your nice hot corn—smoking hot, smoking hot, just from the pot!" Your heart, if it has not grown callous, will be pained as mine has been at the sights of misery you will meet with, and you will then exclaim, "What does it mean that I see these things in the very heart of this great commercial city, where wealth, luxury, extravagance, all abound in such profusion? Surely the condition of the people, the ways and wants of the poor, cannot be known, or they would be improved. Why does not somebody write a book illustrating these "Life Scenes in New York," whose every page shall be a cry, startling as this of 'Hot corn, hot corn!' now pealing in the midnight air?"

So thought I; and so straightway set about the work, with ample material at hand, and more accumulating at every step. In writing a book, the first thought of the author is, what shall be my title? What better could I have than HOT CORN, since that was the inciting cry that waked my pen to action, to paint these life scenes in vivid pictures, for the world to look at and improve?

If, in my daily walks and midnight rambles, I have seen revolting sights, the details of which are harrowing to your soul as you read, so much the more need that they be opened to your view. Wounds must be seen to be healed. Old sores are often pronounced incurable, simply because they are old.

First, strip off their dirty covering, then probe and wash, and then apply the healing balsam. If not already gangrened from long neglect, you may save the patient's life, and at all events, ease his suffering, and smooth his road to the grave.

Be mine the task to strip and expose, and yours to wash and heal.

Of just such life scenes as I depict, there are enough transpiring every night to fill a volume.

Come, walk with me, of an August evening, from the Battery to Union Square, and you shall see all the characters of a romance.

'Tis concert night at Castle Garden. Stand here a short half hour, and look at the gay and smiling throng. There is material for many a tale.

Three thousand robes of fine cloth, silks, gauze, and lace, pass the Battery gates in one night, fluttering to the open sea breeze, without one thought from those who wear them for the poor little girl that sits shivering by the path, crying hot corn, or vainly striving to beg one penny from the overflowing purses that freely give dollars for amusement, and less than nothing to misery, or for its annihilation. Little do they think that this child has a mother at home, who once counted one in just such a thoughtless throng.

Here might a chapter be written, but let us on; we shall find plenty of subjects. If we stop to write the history of that little girl and her mother, we shall fill our book before we start.

The Philadelphia boat has just landed her passengers at Pier No. 1., North River, and the crowd are coming up Battery Place. Here is a picture of American character. Every one is pushing forward as though there was but one bed left in the city, and to obtain that he intended to outstride and overreach all his fellow travellers. Take care, little hot corn girl, or you will be run over, and your store trampled underfoot. Bitter tears for your loss will run down your hollow cheeks, but they will gain you no sympathy. The only answer that you will get, will be, "Why didn't you get out of the way, you little dirty brat—good enough for you." Yes, good enough for you, that you have lost your entire stock of merchandize; what business had you in the way of commerce, or path of pleasure?

"But, sir," says benevolence in a drab bonnet, "you have hurt the child."

"What if I have? she has no business in the way. She is nothing but a hot corn girl; they are no better than beggars and often are little thieves. Why don't she stay at home?" Sure enough. Simply because necessity or cruelty drives her into the street. Now your cruelty will drive her home to be beaten by a drunken father, for your act of wanton carelessness.

Stand aside, my little sufferer, or you will be run over again. Here comes a little dark skinned, black-eyed, black-haired man, with life and death in his very step.

What magic power impels him forward. He is a Jew—a dealer in second-hand clothes. Surely his business cannot be so important that he need to upset little children, or step on the gouty toes of slow-going old gentlemen, in his hurry to get forward.

It is Friday night, his Sabbath has already commenced, he can do no business—make no monish—to-night. He is not in a hurry to reach the synagogue, that is closed, what then? He has a Christian partner, and he wants to arrange a little speculation for to-morrow. He has just received information of a shipment of yellow fever patients' clothing, which will arrive to-morrow or Sunday, and he wants his Christian partner to look out on Saturday; on Sunday, the Jew will watch the chance to buy the infected rags, which both will sell on Monday at a hundred per cent profit.

"What, at the risk of human life? Oh, I can believe that of a Jew, but certainly no Christian would do it."

There spoke the Christian reader. The Jew will say the same, only reversing the character. No good Christian or Jew either will do it; yet it will be done, and little beggar girls will be run over in the hot haste to meet the coming ship.

Walk on. The side-walks are crowded, and the street between the curb-stones full of great lumbering omnibuses and carriages, that go up and down all night for hire; but there is a melancholy stillness in all the houses where wealth and fashion, in our young days, lived in lamp-lighted parlors, and diamonds flashed down upon the listener to music which had its home in these gay dwellings, where happy looking faces were seen through open windows. Iron shutters close them now, and commerce wears a dark frown by gas light.

On the right is Wall street, where fortunes are made and lost as by the turn of a card, or rattle of a dice box. It is very thronged at noon day. It is very dull now. A few watchmen tread slowly around the great banking houses, working for a dollar a night to eke out a poorly paid day, by guarding treasures that the owners would not watch all the live long night for all the watchman is worth. But he must watch and work; he has a sick wife at home, and four little girls are growing up to womanhood and city life. God knows for what!

A few express wagons, and more of these ever-going ever-coming omnibuses, are coming out of Wall street to join the great Broadway throng. And a pale-faced little girl sits upon the steps of the Bank of the Republic, adding to that constant cry, "Hot corn! Hot corn!" Now here comes the Cerberus of this money palace. What possible harm to his treasures, can this little poverty-clad girl and her sickly looking little beggar boy brother do, sitting here upon the cold grey, stone steps, with an appealing look to every passer-by to give a penny or buy an ear of corn. Does he think they are merely using their trade to plot mischief and schemes to rob his vaults of their stores of gold? One would judge so by the way he growls at them.

"Clear out, you dirty brats—away with you, lousy beggars —home to your kennel, young thieves. Don't come on these steps again, or I will throw your corn in the gutter."

Are these the words to work reform? They are such as fall every day and night upon the ear of just such specimens of the young sprouts of humanity, that vegetate and grow a brief summer in the city, dying in some of the chill winters of neglect, that come over their tender years, blighting, freezing, killing. How little of the gold, Cerberus guards, would serve to warm these two young children into useful life. How little those who guard or use it, care for those they drive unfeelingly away from their door steps—for what? They have made it a place of convenience for their nightly trade. Tired of walking, carrying a heavy pail between them—heavy to them—it would be light, and were it all gold, compared with that within—they have sat themselves down, and just uttered one brief cry of "Hot corn, here's your nice hot corn!" when they are roughly ordered to "clear out, you dirty brats." Yes, they are dirty, poor, and miserable, children of a drunken father—who made them so? No matter. They are so, and little has that gold done to make them otherwise.

"Clear out—get off these steps, or I will kick you off."

They did so, and went over to the other side of Broadway, and clung to that strong iron fence, and looked up three hundred feet along that spire which points to heaven from Trinity church. Did they think of the half million of dollars there piled up, to tell the world of the wealth of New York city? No, they thought of the poor, wretched room, to them their only home, a little way down Rector street, scarcely a stone's throw from this great pile, in a house, owned and rented to its poor occupants by that great land monopoly, the Rectory of this great church.

"Bill," says the girl, "do you see that gal? how fine she is tittivated up. Don't she look like a lady? I know who she is, Bill. Do you think when I gets a little bigger, the old woman is going to keep me in the street all day and half the night, peddling peanuts and selling hot corn? No, sir-ee. I will dress as fine as she does, and go to balls and theatres, and have good suppers and wine, at Taylor's, and lay a-bed next day just as long as I please. Why not? I am as good-looking, if I was dressed up, as she is."

"Why, Sal, how will you do that? You ha'n't got no good clothes, and mother ha'n't got none, and if she had, she wouldn't give 'em to ye."

"I don't care, I know how to get them. I know the woman that owns every rag that street gal has got on her back."

"Them ain't rags, them's silk, and just as good dress as them opera gals had on, that went stringing along down Broadway a while ago. I don't see how you can get sich, 'less you prig 'em. I'd do that if I had a chance, blessed quick. How'd she get 'em, Sal?"

"I knows, and that's 'nuff."

Why should she not know? She had been to school long enough to learn, and would be a very inapt scholar if she had not learned some of the ways of the street, in thirteen years. In thirteen years more she will be a fit subject to excite the care of the Moral Reform Society, or become the inmate of a Mary Magdalene asylum; perchance, of Randall's Island.

There is a history about these two children and their parents, which you may read by and by. We cannot stop, now. Let us walk on. Iron shutters—bolted, barred, and strong locked doors, what piles of treasure lie just within.

At Maiden lane on the right, and Courtlandt street on the left, more omnibuses come up, crowding their way into an already overfull "Broadway."

Oh! what a scream. It is a woman's scream. A cry of

anguish—of horror, that chills the blood. It comes from the apple woman at the corner, and yet she is not hurt. No one is near her, the crowd is rushing to the centre of the street. What for? An omnibus has run over a drunken man. This is always enough to excite the sympathy of woman, and make her cry out as with pain. It is pain, the worst of pain; it comes from a blow upon the heart; worse than that, in this case, for the man is her husband. He has just left her, where he has been tormenting her for an hour, begging, coaxing, pleading, promising, that if she would give him one shilling, he would go directly home and go to bed, as soon as he got something to eat. "Something to drink." No. Upon his word, he would not touch another drop the blessed night. She well knew the value of such promises. She well knew that the corner grocery, where he would stop to buy the loaf of bread, which he promised to share with the two children, kept a row of glistening glasses and decanters upon the same shelf with the loaves. "The staff of life," and life's destroyer, side by side. She knew his appetite—she knew the temptation to which he would be subjected, she knew he could not resist, she knew the vampire who dealt in life and death, would suck up that shilling, if with it came the heart's blood of him, her, and their two children. She knew her husband, he could not resist the temptation. Once sober and he could keep so, if the means of intoxication were kept out of his sight. Once drunk and he would keep so, as long as he could obtain a shilling to pay for the poison. His last resource was to beg from his wife's scanty profits, by which she mainly supported the family, who often went supperless to bed, for the rent must be paid. Landlords are inexorable. Hers was worth so many millions that the income was a source of great care, how it should be disposed of. Her rent was coming due, and every shilling looked to her of tenfold value to-night. Her children are in the street, filling the night air with an appealing cry, "Hot corn, hot corn, who'll buy my nice hot corn?" her husband was begging for one more shilling to waste—worse than waste—to close an ill-spent day. Oh, what a contrast between this and their wedding day!

She resisted his importunity until he found 'twas no avail, and then he swore he would upset her little store in the gutter, if she did not give him the money. What could she do? She would not call an officer to take him away. No, she could not do that, he was her husband. She could not resist him, could not have an altercation in the street, that would draw an idle crowd around her, spoil her trade, and worse than that, let the world know that this bloated, ill-looking, miserable remnant of a man, was her husband. Shame did what persuasion or fear could not: she gave him the shilling, and he started to cross the crowded street. He heeded little of danger—he had often crossed when more drunk than now—he heeded not the tripartite crush of carriages coming up and going down these streets, all meeting in a sort of vortex at that point. He heard, or heeded not, the drivers, "hi, hi, hi, get out of the way, you drunken son of a ——." and down he went among the horses' clattering feet, upon the slippery stones, and the wheels passed over him, crushing bones—human bones, and mangling flesh, and mixing human blood with street dirt.

The omnibuses turned aside, the passengers shuddered as the poor wretch was lifted up, covered with blood and dirt, and inquired, "Is he dead?" the drivers looked down coolly from their high seats, with a consoling remark, that, "it's nothing but a drunken man," yet, that drunken man was that woman's husband; him who, fourteen years ago, walked the streets as well dressed, as proud, as sober as any in the crowd who now gaze carelessly upon his bruised form, and hear the remark, that he, "is nothing but a drunken man."

Fourteen years ago—yes, this very night—that woman walked this very street, arm in arm, with that man, and heard him, for the first time, call her wife. It was a happy time then, and "all was merry as the marriage bell." Little thought they then—less thought they a year afterwards, while rocking the cradle in their own happy home, that the time would come when he would raise his hand in anger to strike that loving wife, or that child would be driven, with kicks and curses, into the streets, or that he would lie bleeding upon the pavement he had so often and so proudly trod before, a poor mangled drunkard.

Oh how those words—joyous words—first rung in that happy mother's ears, when the proud father said:—

"Have you got a baby?"

"Yes, Willie, *we* have got a baby."

How these words have rung like electric sparks through many a happy heart.

"Have you got a baby?" said a little girl to a gentleman riding out of Boston. It was a queer question, arising as it did from a child he overtook on the road. How his city friends would have laughed at him if they had heard the question—"Have you got a baby?" No he had got no baby, yet he was a man full forty years of age, and looked as though he might have been a father, and so thought the little girl. Yet he had no baby. Why? He was a bachelor! So he had to answer, "no, my pretty miss, I have got no baby." "Oh la, haven't you? Well *we* have. We have got a baby at *our* house!!"

This was not interesting to a bachelor. How different it would have been if he had married Lucy Smith, whom he intended to a dozen years ago, but he was too busy then—too intent upon making money enough, to support a wife before he got one. Nonsense! How little he knew of the sweet music of the words, "have you got a baby?" How her heart would have leaped up and choked her utterance if she had now been riding by his side as his wife, instead of his "old flame," Lucy Smith! Lucy Smith, still, for she had never heard those words touchingly applied to her, "have you got a baby?" nor had she ever heard a sweet little girl say of her, "we have got a baby at our house!"

How many a mother's heart has leapt for joy, at that question, when she could answer it, "Yes, I *have* got a baby!"

THE NEW-YORK FIREMAN.—*Page 30.*

How many a father's heart will be touched with emotion when he reads, "Have you got a baby?" for he will think as I do, of a time when, returning from a long journey, he meets just such a little cherub of a girl at his own gate, who does not stop to ask him how he does, nor climb his knee for the accustomed kiss, so exuberant is her joy—so anxious is she to possess him with the secret that wells up and fills her very existence to overflowing, so that she must speak or burst, and hence she watches for Papa, and runs out to meet him at the gate with such a smile—such a joyous, glorious smile, and cry of "Oh, Papa, we have got a baby!!" How many a mother's heart will swell and throb, and how the warm tears—tears of joy and gladness—will flow as she hears that husband's footstep approach, for she knows he will say, "*Have* you got a baby?"

But there is no such joy now for that mother's heart. Yet that is the same father—fallen, trampled, dying, and she rushes to the rescue.

Two police officers bear him to the side-walk and lift him, lifeless as he is, upon a hand-cart. How the idle crowd push and jostle each other to get a sight of the wounded man. What for? To administer to his wants; to give, if need be, something to minister to his relief? No. To gratify curiosity —morbid, idle curiosity.

How this woman pushes and struggles to break the circle, crying, "Let me in, let me in; let me see him." How little the crowd heed her. They think it is curiosity, too, nothing but curiosity, that impels her, as it does themselves.

Why don't she say, "It is my husband?" and then they would give her room, or the officers would make them. Why! why don't she say it? She is ashamed to tell unfeeling hearts how low she has been sunk in the world since first she called that man by that name, or heard those heart-touching words when their first child was born.

Husband was a sweet word once; it is a bitter one now; yet it must be spoken, for they are about to bear him away to the hospital. Whether dead or alive she knows not, and she rushes madly forward, seizing the policeman, with a cry of, "No, no; not there, not there; take him home, I will take care of him—nobody can take care of him so well as I can. Oh, let me take him home! Do let me take him home." What could she do with him in her one room, the home of herself and children. She could not stay to nurse him day after day, for then her trade would be lost; somebody else would take her stand; there would be no income, all would be outgo, and all would soon be exhausted; nothing to buy bread, nothing to pay rent, and then out must go the whole, sick or well; they must go in the street if they fail to meet that dreaded periodical—the rent day. There is no help for it. All this is hastily considered, and there is no other way; he must go to the hospital. 'Tis a blessed institution—a noble honor to the city, charitably sustained, to give relief to—who? A thousand just such subjects as this; made drunk, covered with gore, maimed with broken limbs, by a legalized traffic in hell's best aid on earth. A trade that fills jails, thieves-dens, and brothels, and furnishes subjects like this for hospitals.

"He must go to the hospital."

"Then I will follow and nurse him there."

There spoke the wife, as, ever since that holy name was known, the wife has spoken—can speak alone.

How can she go?

Something clings to her dress and pulls her back. She looks around upon a little boy and girl—it is the hot corn girl, just driven from the banking-house steps three squares below.

"Mother, mother, do speak to us; it is Bill and me. Is father dead? What killed him?"

Rum! She did not say so. She only thought. She thought, too, of her helpless children, and what would they do if she went to take care of their father. She did not think of the blows, the kicks, and cuffs, and curses, received from him during long bitter years, for they were given by—not by him—not by her husband—but by the demon in him—the devil engendered by rum. She thought nothing of the cruel neglect and poverty and suffering of herself and children, for that was a sequence of the other. She did think of this night, fourteen years ago. She did think of the night when this girl, now clinging to her dress and convulsively crying, "Mother, is he dead," was born, for then she was a happy wife and mother. Then that father took that child in his arms and kissed and blessed it—then he took her in his arms and kissed and loved her, and called her his dear wife. She did not think of the night when that little slender boy, now ten years old, was born, for then a devil—not a husband—dragged her by the hair, while in labor, from her poor cot, and bid her go out in the pitiless storm to fill his bottle for him. No, she did not remember that; she only remembered that he was her husband; wounded, dying husband, in need of some kind hand to make his bed and smooth his passage to the grave, and she would leave all without a thought to follow him to the hospital. She was his wife. Now there is a struggle between duty and affection—between husband and children. She cannot go with both. One must be neglected; which shall it be? Had the husband been what he was when that girl was born, the heart of many a wife would give the ready answer. She looked upon her and remembered the time when she first heard these words, "Have you got a baby?" She looked upon her, and all intervening time faded from memory, and she thought and felt as she would have felt if he had been struck down that night. She tears herself away from the grasp of the little girl, telling her to pick up the apples and go home, she must go with father.

Another hand clings to her dress, and looks up with such an appealing look and says:—

"Don't go, mother; they will take care of father. Don't leave us."

She looked upon her sickly boy, and thought of the night he was born. Why does she start and turn round? Did some one pull her by the hair? No, it was only fancy. A sort of magnetic influence, linked with thought. That twinge decided her. That twinge decided his fate, and saved her childen's lives. She went home with them, and tired nature slept in spite of mental agony. At four o'clock the bells rung for fire; it was long before she could wake sufficiently to count the eight strokes which told it was in her district. Dreamily unconscious of danger, she moves not till she hears a crash and sees a light through the small rear window, when she springs up, opens the door, looks out in the direction of the stairs, and meets a burst of flame and smoke coming up. Back, back to the bed, closing the door—a thin pine door—the only barrier between the fire and her sleeping babes, she drags them out and up to the window. Will she throw them down upon the pavement below, as the only hope of saving their lives, for the fire is fairly up the stairs and rattling at the door behind her? If it enters all is lost. The window is opened, and the little boy first—he is the darling—poised upon the sill, in the bewildered amazement of half-awaking consciousness.

"Oh mother, mother, don't throw me out! I will be a good boy, mother. I never will tear my jacket again. Indeed I could not help it. It was a big boy that pulled me. Oh, mother, mother, don't, pray don't."

He screams with fear, as he hangs convulsively upon his mother's neck, and looks down upon the gathering crowd, crying, "Throw him out, throw him out; we will catch him." And a hundred hands are outstretched, a hundred noble hearts would prostrate themselves upon the pavement to save, to break the fall of a beggar boy whom they would have kicked out of their path the day before. Now a mother appeals to her fellow men to save her child. She had oft appealed before, but then the house was not on fire; the fire was in his father's mouth—and that they heeded not. No bells rung, to call the engines with copious streams of water to put it out—they are ringing now. And now see the outstretched hands, each ready to risk its own life to save that of a child.

"Let him go—throw him out—you will all burn up in five minutes more—this old wooden house burns like tinder."

She looks behind her; the flame is sending serpent tongues under the door. Her dress upon a chair is on fire—now the bed. They must jump, naked too, down among those men, or die.

"Hold on! hold on! Way there—give way there Hurrah, men! lively now!"

Oh, that was a sight for that mother and her two children. A ladder company thundered down the street with their cry of "Way there!" for they have caught the sight of a woman and children in distress; and oh! how they do press forward, shouting, "Way there! lively now! Hold on, we will save you!" How quick, after they reach the spot, a ladder is loosened and off the carriage, with one end on the ground and the other going up, up—"Up with her now!" and so they do. Before it has found a resting-place, a man, active as a cat, is halfway up. Now he is at the top; now—hurrah!—how the shouts rend the air, for he has the boy in one arm and the girl in the other, and tells the mother to follow. She hesitates. What for? The noble fireman sees at a glance, stops a moment, pulls off his coat and throws it to her—"now"—down they go—now they are safe. Safe with life—

not a thing else on earth but her two fatherless children, her only covering a fireman's coat. Where is her husband now? Where he will never see them again; for while his attendant slept he tore the bandages from his wound, and then slept himself—a sleep that one voice alone will awaken. Judge him not harshly; he was the victim, not the criminal. He is dead now, tread lightly upon his grave.

Look to his wife and children. It is they who need your sympathy. Raised in the worst school on earth—the streets of this city, some of the Life Scenes of which I aim to depict—the boy has already learned to "prig;" and, so he shared the proceeds with his father—that father, or rather the monster who made him a devil, would encourage the boy to be a thief. What could the mother do to counteract such deleterious influence? All day she must stand at her corner, selling fruit, pea-nuts, and candy, to make bread to feed her else starving offspring, and to keep her husband out of the prison or alms-house.

You have already seen the effect of the street education upon Sally; the sight of her playmate, Julia Antrim, dressed in silks and laces, although borrowed—no, furnished, by "the woman," on hire, for a purpose more wicked than murder, for murder only kills the body—has already tempted her towards the same road—to that broad path to woe; not in the future, but here present with us every day; and she has already determined that she will follow it as soon as "she gets big enough."

Who shall rescue her?

The danger is still more imminent now. Houseless, naked, starving in the street, how shall she live? One step, one resolution, will take her to the clothes-lending harpy, who fattens upon the life-blood of young girls, whom she dooms to the fate of Ixion for the remainder of their lives; for her garments are the shirts of Nessus to all who wear them.

She feels that she *is* big enough now—big enough to begin. Younger girls than her are night-walkers. Julia is no older, and but little bigger, and she has often stopped in her walk to eat hot corn or pea-nuts with Sally, and show her shining gold, trying to tempt her to go and do likewise. She has an interest, too, in the temptation, for she has told Mrs. Brown of her old playmate, Sally Eaton, and how good-looking she was; and Mrs. Brown has been to see her, has bought her merchandise, and spoken words of soul-trapping flattery, and promised Julia a present of a new silk dress—that is, just as good as new, it had just been bought by a girl whom she turned out of doors because she could not pay her way—if she will coax Sally to come and live with her.

And so she has been sorely tempted. Eve was so, and fell.

These tempting words are now running through the brain of Sally, as she stands in the crowd, wrapt in a blanket, kindly lent her, with her mother and little Willie, looking at their home and every earthly thing going up in flame and smoke heavenward. Her mother weeps, for the first time in long years. Long, long, had she steeled her heart against such indulgence; its pent up fountains burst now. Not for grief; no, they were tears, such as she shed when that girl was born.

How she cried, and thanked God, and pressed the hand of the fireman and thanked him for saving her children's lives, dearer to her than all her household goods.

How little he thought of the noble act. He almost repulsed her and her gratitude.

"There, that'll do, old woman. You had better be getting in somewhere."

Somewhere! Yes, somewhere! Where?

That is the question. The crowd shout at the heroic deeds of the firemen, and would carry them in triumph through the streets, or bring out baskets of champaigne to drink libations to their honor, for saving two helpless children from the flames. Saved for what? To stand naked in the street! No. Let them go to their friends. They have none. Yes, they have, but not relatives. A few dollars are put into the mother's hand, but who will take her in? who will give her a home? One that three years ago had no home himself. One who had been more drunken than Bill Eaton—had been drunk for forty years. He is sober now—you shall hear directly how he became so.

A man advanced in years, say more than half a century, followed by a tall, fine-formed, well-dressed, bright-eyed girl, about one-third her father's age, press through the crowd to where the widow and her children stand, take them by the hand and lead on, with the simple words, "Come with us."

It needs but few such words, spoken in such kind tones, to the afflicted to lead them into paths of peace, and hope, and joy.

2*

The mother went forward with a sort of mechanical motion of the limbs, unaided by any impulse of the mind. Willie followed, as the lamb follows the ewe, whether to green fields or the butcher's shambles.

Sally was more independent. She was on the point of being entirely so, but a moment before. Now she clung to her girlish companion, as the wrecked mariner to hope. Had hope come one minute later, she had been led by the tempter that was gnawing at her heart-strings, to slip away from her mother, and in one hour afterwards, she would have been knocking at the ever-ready-to-open door of Mrs. Brown, and once passing that threshold, woe, woe, woe, had been written upon every page of her life. Once having passed that door, every other but its like had been closed against her for ever. For the sin of entering that door, in her young years, the world would never forgive her. No matter, that gaudily dressed and luxuriously fed tempters had beset her and led her in. Such tempters—such school teachers for city children are allowed to monopolise the Broadway sidewalks, and hold their infant evening schools, if not by authority of the common council, at least by permission and countenance of the chief of police and all his "stars." No Proserpine can walk this street at night alone, without meeting, or at least subjecting herself to, the sad fate of Proserpine of old.

Few of those we meet in our late walks, are Proserpines or Vestas; although they may be goddesses of fire.

Seek not to lift the veil, you will find Pandora there; Blame not the girl who got her teachings in such a street, if, in her deep adversity she was tempted—tempted to leave that mother and brother, and slip away in the crowd, to go where she knew she would find a home. Where else should she go? She knew of none. No one of all that crowd offered to take her home with him. She had no hope. She was a fit subject for despair, and despair is the father of temptation. What a blessed thing is hope, charity, and a will to do good; when it flows from one young girl to another!

But who is it says, "come with us?" The voice seemed familiar, and yet not familiar to Sally's ear. If the person had been clothed in such a garb of poverty as she herself had always worn, she would have known her, although it was three years since they had met. She was not; she wore a neat tidy calico frock, and clean white sun-bonnet, hastily put on, and altogether looked so neat, so smart, so comfortable, as though she had a home which she meant to take them to, when she said, "come with us," that the tempter's spell was broken. Sally would not have gone with Julia Antrim, for all her gold and silks, good suppers and other enjoyments. The words were few and common-place. How often the mother and children had heard them before—"come with us." But they never sounded as they did this night. There is something in the tone, as well as words. There is a magnetic power in kindness. Kind words are always winning, whether from friend or stranger. These came from strangers. Not altogether so; the man had been one of the drunken companions of Bill Eaton; had helped to make him such, and now he was going to pay part of the damage to his family. The girl, in her father's drunken days, had been one of Sally's street companions; they had begged, and stole, and peddled hot corn and pea-nuts together. But Sally knew her not. How could she? Then she was, ragged and dirty, far worse than Sally; her parents were far poorer, and lived in a worse room, one of the worst in Centre street, and both of them were great drunkards, and she was, so everybody said, "the worse child that ever run unhung."

How could she know the well behaved, nice looking young lady, walking by her side. But she did know that she spoke kind words in a sweet tone, and her heart was touched, and she went on with a light step. That blanket wrapped a happier heart that night, than ever fluttered under the silk dress of her former playmate, Julia Antrim.

They went on; the old man gave his arm to the widow and led the little boy; the daughter walked with Sally. They enter the *front* door of a good house—when did either ever enter the front door before—up one flight of clean stairs, and there is their home, a room, and two bed-rooms, and kitchen; small to be sure, but a most comfortable home, for the old man and his daughter. He was a carpenter, and made from a dollar and a half to two dollars a day; she was a stock-maker, and could earn from three to five dollars a week, enough to pay nearly all expenses. "Three years ago," said he, "I was the most hopeless drunkard that ever tumbled into a Centre street cellar. And my wife——but no matter—

she is in heaven now. All that girl's work. She reformed us; she made me a sober man, and, God willing, I shall never fill a drunkard's grave."

"Oh, if she could only reform my husband, how I would bless her."

"It is too late."

"No, no; it is never too late; while there is life there is hope."

"Yes, true; but—"

"But what? what is it? what do you know?"

"Why, you see, ma'am, I was in the crowd last night when the accident happened. It was me that first picked him up; and so, you see, I went up with him. It was me that told you that you couldn't go, 'cause I knew how 'twas with the children, and how you hadn't much to do with at home; for I had been sort o' watching Bill, and he had promised to go with me this very night to sign the pledge; and so, you see, I went up with him, and they dressed his wounds, and I knew he wouldn't get over it, his blood was so bad, and it was so warm; but he might have lived a while, and so when they got things fixed, I thought I would come down and tell you about it; but just as I got down to the gate, a fellow came running after me to go back—it was a'most morning then—and so back I went. They said he had got crazy while I was in the room with another old friend, and when—when I—I—"

"Yes, I see; he is dead."

"Yes; he is dead. When I came back he was about gone, but he was just as rational as I am now. 'Oh, Jim,' said he,

'Jim Reagan, if I had only taken the pledge when you did, I should have been a man now. But I am glad I am going. My folks will be a great deal better off without me.'"

"Oh, no, no, no! he was my husband—their father—he might have reformed."

"'Tell them,' said he, 'that I am dying, and that for the first time in ten years I feel as though I had my senses. If I could see them and know they forgave me all the wrongs I have inflicted upon them! Do you think my wife could forgive—'"

"Yes, yes; everything, everything."

"So I told him, and that seemed to quiet him. And then I begged him to forgive me for what I had done towards making him a drunkard. 'Oh,' says he, 'I can forgive everybody—even those who used to sell it to us, who used to take the bread out of our children's mouths for liquor, but I never can forgive those who made the law, or licensed them to murder us. I forgive everybody else that ever injured me, and I die in peace. Tell my wife I die loving her. God bless her and my poor children, what will become of them? Good bye, Jim; go and see my wife, and tell her good bye, and that I die as I wish I had lived; but it is too late, too late. God bless my wife!'

"I could not speak, I turned my eyes away a minute, looked again, and poor Bill Eaton was gone—gone to Heaven, I am sure, if sincere repentance would take him there. Well, you see, I could not do anything more for poor Bill, for he was gone where we must all go pretty soon, and so I come down and waked up Maggie."

There was a start—a sudden wakening up to consciousness on the part of Sally, she had recognised the name.

"And says I, Maggie, daughter, come get up, and go with me to see a poor widow and children in distress. Oh, I wish you could have seen how she bounded out of bed—we sleep in beds, good clean beds, now, and how quick she dressed herself, and how neat, and cheerful, and pretty she looked, and how sweetly she said, 'now, father, I am ready, who is it?' and when I told her, how her heart bounded with joy, and then she told me she knew Sally, but had not seen her for a long time, and so, arm in arm, we went out, and you know the rest. Poor Bill!"

"Oh, that I could have seen him—could have heard him speak soberly and affectionately once more—I think I could have given him up without a murmur."

"No. You would not have been willing to give him up to die, just as he had begun to live. Be content, you must not murmur. Who knows but all this overwhelming affliction will work together for your good, and your children's good."

"Yes, mother, I am sure it will for mine. It has already, for I will be like Maggie; don't you remember Maggie?"

"No. I don't recollect but one Maggie—'Wild Maggie of the Five Points'—the most mischievous, ragged, dirty little beggar in all that dreadful neighborhood; and her father, the most filthy drunkard I ever saw. Why he was a great deal worse than——."

"Your husband. Speak it out, I am not ashamed to own it, now I have reformed."

"You—you, not you; this is not Maggie."

"Yes, mother, this is 'Wild Maggie,' and this is her father. This nice young lady, that said so sweetly, 'Come with us,' this is 'Wild Maggie,' and this is—is—"

"Old Jim Reagan, the miserable old drunkard, that used to live in a miserable cellar, in Centre street, and finally got turned out of that, and this is Maggie, and this is our home."

And he looked around proudly upon the comforts of this home, and contrasted them with the miseries of that.

Now Margaret—Mag or Maggie, no longer—began to "fly around." Breakfast was to be got, and what was much more difficult, a full-sized woman, a half-grown girl, and a quarter-grown boy, were to be clothed. How was it to be done? One of her dresses, "with a tuck,"—tucks are fashionable in these days—was soon made to fit Sally. The father said, he would go out and get some clothes for Mrs. Eaton and little Willie, for, thank God, he was able to do it, for what he saved by soberness, not only enabled him to live and clothe himself, but to fulfil that best of all Christian injunctions, to be kind to the widows and fatherless, and he did not know of any that he was under more obligations to than the wife and children of Bill Eaton, and, God willing, he was going to clothe them, and then he was going to go with them to Mr. Pease, the man that had been the means of reclaiming him, and get them a home in the House of Industry, until they could find some other one, or a way to earn a living.

Apparently it was not willed that he should spend his scanty store to clothe the naked at this time; the will to do so was equally acceptable to the great Will, as though the deed were done, for just now there was a rap at the door, indicating an early visitor. Who could it be ? Margaret ran down to see. A boy from a second-hand clothing store, entered with a large bundle.

"I wants to know as how if the woman that was burnt out is here ?"

"Yes."

"And a little boy and gal ?"

"Yes."

"This is the place then. Are you the gal what was at the fire and said, 'come with us ?'"

"Yes, why do you ask that ?"

"'Cause the gentleman told me to ask, and when I was sure I was right, to give the gal these three gold pieces, one for each word, and the bundle of clothes and the letter to the woman. That's all. So here they are. I am sure I is right for you don't look as though you could tell a lie if you tried. Why what ails the gal ? I'll be blamed if I see anything to cry about. Why, hang me, what does it mean ? I feel just so I should cry too if I stayed in this house long. So good bye. I am sure it is all right ?"

And the door closed behind him, and he was gone. What could it mean ? Was she dreaming ? No ! There lay the bundle, there glistened the half eagles in her hand. It could not be a dream, yet it was a mystery. How could any one know so soon that her roof contained one so needy ? Who had heard those words, those three little words, every one of which had turned to gold? Yes, and will yet turn to fruit more precious.

How she wished she had asked the boy who it was, who had been so suddenly raised up, so mysteriously sent to visit the widow in her affliction. Perhaps the letter would tell. So she took it and the bundle up stairs and opened both. One contained full suits for the mother, daughter, and little boy, all black—the other was a letter to Mr. Pease.

"Can this be the work of man?" said Mrs. Eaton; "who knew, who could know, that I must wear the widow's weeds, so soon?"

"There is a spirit of intelligence which maketh known secret things. How could any one without such spiritual aid know that you was a widow, that you was destitute, that we had bid you come with us, that I was just going out to buy clothes, and here they come like manna in the wilderness to Israel's host. Who will deny spiritual influence and special interposition now?"

Who will believe it, when they are told how all this seeming mystery will melt away with the shades of the night which brought it into the minds of these simple people?

"But what is in the letter, my child, does that tell anything?"

"Nothing, father; it is addressed to the Rev. Mr. Pease, at the Five Points House of Industry, requesting him to give a home to a poor woman and two children, and says the writer will see him about it soon."

"Ah, that is just where I intended to take them, after the funeral."

"Yes, and see how nicely these clothes fit them, just as well as though made on purpose. How could anybody guess so well?"

"It is no guess work. There is something more than guess work about this."

So there was.

"Breakfast is ready, father."

"Then let us eat it in thankfulness and then."

And then!

CHAPTER II.*

LITTLE KATY.—A MIDNIGHT INTERVIEW.

What is said in this, will apply to everything similar.

"Here's your nice Hot Corn, smoking hot, smoking hot, just from the pot!" Hour after hour one evening, as I sat over the desk, this cry came up in a soft, plaintive voice, under my window, which told me of one of the ways of the poor to eke out means of subsistence in this over-burdened, ill-fed, and worse-lodged home of misery—of so many without means, who are constantly crowding into the dirtiest purlieus of this notoriously dirty city, where they are exposed to the daily chance of death from some sudden outbreaking epidemic like that now desolating the same kind of streets in New Orleans, and swallowing up its thousands of victims from the same class of poverty-stricken, uncomfortably-provided for human beings, who know not how, or have not the power, to flee to the healthy hills and green fields of the country. Here they live—barely live—in holes almost as hot as the hot corn, the cry of which rung in my ears from dark till midnight.

* This chapter was published under the simple title of "Hot Corn," among the "City Items" of the New York Daily Tribune, August 5, 1853. It is but slightly altered from the original text.

"Hot corn! hot corn! here's your nice hot corn," rose up in a faint, child like voice, which seemed to have been aroused by the sound of my step as I was about entering the Park, while the city clock told the hour when ghosts go forth upon their midnight rambles. I started, as though a spirit had given me a rap, for the sound seemed to come out of one of the iron posts which stand as sentinels over the main entrance, forbidding all vehicles to enter, unless the driver takes the trouble to pull up and tumble out of the way one of the aforesaid posts, which is not often done, because one of them, often, if not always, is out of its place, giving free ingress to the court-yard, or livery stable grounds of the City Hall, which, in consideration of the growth of a few miserable dusty brown trees and doubtful colored grass-patches, we call "the Park."

Looking over the post I discovered the owner of the hot corn cry, in the person of an emaciated little girl about twelve years old, whose dirty shawl was nearly the color of the rusty iron, and whose face, hands, and feet, naturally white and delicate, were grimmed with dirt until nearly of the same color. There were two white streaks running down from the soft blue eyes, that told of the hot scalding tears that were coursing their way over that naturally beautiful face.

"Some corn, sir," lisped the little sufferer, as she saw I had stopped to look at her, hardly daring to speak to one who did not address her in rough tones of command, such as "give me some corn, you little wolf's whelp," or a name still more opprobrious both to herself and mother. Seeing I had no look of contempt for her, she said, piteously, "please buy some corn, sir."

"No, my dear, I do not wish any; it is not very healthy in such warm weather as this, and especially so late at night."

"Oh dear, then, what shall I do?"

"Why, go home. It is past midnight, and such little girls as you ought not to be in the streets of this bad city at this time of night."

"I can't go home—and I am so tired and sleepy. Oh dear!"

"Cannot go home. Why not?"

"Oh, sir, my mother will whip me if I go home without selling all my corn. Oh, sir, do buy one ear, and then I shall have only two left, and I am sure she might let little Sis and me eat them, for I have not had anything to eat since morning, only one apple the man gave me, and part of one he threw away. I could have stole a turnip at the grocery when I went to get—to get something in the pitcher for mother, but I dared not. I did use to steal, but Mr. Pease says it is naughty to steal, and I don't want to be naughty, indeed I don't; and I don't want to be a bad girl, like Lizzy Smith, and she is only two years older than me, if she does dress fine; 'cause Mr. Pease says she will be just like old drunken Kate, one of these days. Oh dear! now there goes a man, and I did not cry hot corn, what shall I do?"

"Do! There, that is what you shall do," as I dashed the corn in the gutter. "Go home; tell your mother you have sold it all, and here is the money."

"Wont that be a lie, sir? Mr. Pease says we must not tell lies."

"No, my dear, that wont be a lie, because I have bought it and thrown it away, instead of eating it."

"But, sir, may I eat it then, if you don't want it?"

"No, it is not good for you; good bread is better, and here is a sixpence to buy a loaf, and here is another to buy some nice cakes for you. Now that is your money; don't give it to your mother, and don't stay out so late again. Go home earlier and tell your mother you cannot sell all your corn and you cannot keep awake, and if she is a good mother she won't whip you."

"Oh, sir, she is a good mother sometimes. But I am sure the grocery man at the corner is not a good man, or he would not sell my mother rum, when he knows—for Mr Pease told him so—that we poor children are starving." Oh, I wish all the men were good men like him, and then my mother would not drink that nasty liquor, and beat and starve us, 'cause there would be nobody to sell her any—and then we should have plenty to eat."

Away she ran down the street towards that reeking centre of filth, poverty and misery, the noted Five Points of New York.

As I plodded up Broadway, looking in here and there upon the palatial splendors of metropolitan "saloons"—I think that is the word for fashionable upper class grog-shops—I almost involuntarily cried, "hot corn," as I saw the hot spirit of that grain, under the various guises of "pure gin"—"old rum"—

"pale brandy"—"pure port"—"Heidsick"—or "Lager-bier"—poured down the throats of men—and ah! yes, of women, too, whose daughters may some day sit, at midnight, upon the cold curbstone, crying "Hot corn," to gain a penny for the purchase of a drink of the fiery dragon they are now inviting to a home in their bosoms, whose cry in after years will be, "Give, give, give," and still as unsatisfied as the horse-leech's daughters.

Again, as I passed on up that street, still busy and thronged at midnight, as a country village at mid-day intermission of church service, ever and anon, from some side-street, came up the cry of "Hot corn—hot corn!" and ever as I heard it, and ever as I shall, through all years to come, I thought of that little girl and her drunken mother, and the "bad man" at the corner grocery, and that her's was the best, the strongest Maine Law argument which had ever fallen upon my listening ear.

Again, as I turned the corner of Spring street, the glare and splendor of a thousand gas lights, and the glittering cut glass of that, for the first time lighted-up, bar-room of the Prescott House—so lauded by the press for its magnificence—dashes our eyes and blinds our senses, till we are almost ready to agree, that first class hotels must have such Five Point denizen-making appurtenances, as this glittering room, shamelessly, invitingly open to the street; when that watch-word cry, like the pibroch's startling peal, came up from the near vicinity, wailing like a lost spirit on the midnight air—"Hot corn, hot

"HOT CORN! HERE'S YOUR NICE HOT CORN!"—*Page* 45.

corn!—here's your nice hot corn—smoking hot—hot—hot corn."

"Yes, yes!" I hear you cry—"it is a watchword—a glorious watchward, that bids us do or die—until the smoking hot, fiery furnace-like gates of hell, like this one now yawning before us, shall cease to be licensed by a Christian people, or send delicate little girls at midnight through the streets, crying 'Hot corn,' to support a drunken mother, whose first glass was taken in a 'fashionable saloon,' or first-class liquor-selling hotel."

"Hot corn," then, be the watchword of all who would rather see the grain fed to the drunkard's wife and children, than into the insatiable hot maw of the whiskey still.

Let your resolutions grow hot and strong, every time you hear this midnight city cry, that you will devote, if nothing more,

"Three grains of corn, mother,
Only three grains of corn,"

towards the salvation of the thousand equally pitiable objects as the little girl whose wailing cry has been the inciting cause of this present dish of "Hot Corn—smoking hot!"

CHAPTER III.

WILD MAGGIE.

"A woman sometimes scorns what best contents her."

It is human nature to scorn many things which would content us—which do content us after we once taste them.

One of the reasons why the vicious scorn those who would make them better; why they scorn to change their present wretched life, or miserable habitations, is because they know not what would best content them.

When that missionary first located his mission to the poorest of New York city poor, the drunkards, thieves, and prostitutes of the Five Points, he was scorned by those he came to save. He and his mission were hated with all the bitter hate which the evil mind oft feels for the good, made still more bitter by the sectarian venom of ignorant Catholics towards the hated heretic Protestants. Every annoyance that low cunning could invent was thrown in his way.

Feeling the inefficiency of the system so long and so uselessly practiced, of giving Bibles or tracts to such people, to be sold or pawned for a tenth part of their value, he began a new system. This was to give employment to the idle, to teach all, who would learn, how to work, how to earn their own living, and that industry would bring more content than drunkenness and its concomitant vices. Though stolen fruit may be sweet, the bread of toil is sweeter, and he would teach them how to gain it.

One of the first efforts made was work for the needle; because that was the most easily started, can be carried on with less capital, and, on the other hand, produces the least capital—or rather poorest pay to those who labor. Yet it is better than idleness, and he soon found willing hands to work, after he opened his shop, and invited all who would conform to the rules, and were willing to earn their bread, rather than beg or steal it, to come and get work—such as coarse shirts and pants—work that they could do, many of them with skill and great rapidity, but such as they could not get trusted with at any common establishment—the very name of the place where they lived being sufficient to discredit them—so that security, which they could not give, for the return of the garments, closed the door against their very will to work.

Another discouraging thing against the very poor who did occasionally get "slop shop work," arose from some gross, cruel, wicked, downright robbery, perpetrated upon "sewing women" by some incarnate fiend in the clothing trade. The difficulty to get work, the miserably poor pay offered to those who

"Stitch, stitch, stitch,
Band and gusset and seam,
Seam and gusset and band,
With eyes and lamp both burning dim,
With none to lend a helping hand,"

is enough to sink stouter hearts than those which beat in misery's bosom.

Sunk in misery, poverty, crime, filth, degradation, want; neglected by all the world; hated by those who should love; trodden down by those who should, if they did a Christian duty, lift up; living in habitations such as——but no matter, you shall go with me, by and by, to see where they live—how could they lift themselves up, how could they be industrious and improve their condition, how could they accept bibles and tracts, with any promise of good?

So thought the missionary; and so he set himself about giving them the means to labor, with a hope and sure promise of reward.

Some of those who sent him there to preach salvation to the heathen of the Five Points differed with him—differ still—thinking that a Christian minister degrades himself when he goes into a "slop shop" to give out needle-work to misery's household—or attempts to teach industry to idle, vicious children, or reform degraded women, by teaching them the ways of living without sin, without selling their bodies to buy bread, or in their despair, to exchange the last loaf for rum.

So he opened a shop—now enlarged into a "House of Industry"—and soon found his reward. But he was annoyed, hated, persecuted, beaten—but God and a good will conquered.

Among other petty, vexatious trifles—it is trifles that annoy—a little girl, in rags and filth, with a mat of soft "bonny brown hair," no doubt well colonized, bare-headed and bare-footed, in cold or heat, used to come every day to the door, ringing her shrill musical voice through the open way, through the crack or key-hole, if it was shut, calling him all sorts of opprobrious names, mixed with all sorts of sentences of Catholic hatred to Protestantism, that showed that she was herself a missionary from adults of evil minds. Then she would call over the names of the inmates, with all their catalogue of crimes, giving little scraps of their history, and their hateful nick-names—singing some of the songs they used to sing in their drunken debauches at Pete Williams's; and such a voice as she had would have won her worshippers in high life, an she had been with them and of them. And her features and blue eyes were as beautiful as her voice was strong and sweet; and there she would tell him, and the crowd of idlers who came to listen, and laugh, and shout at her cunning tricks and evident annoyances, for what purpose he wanted all them old ——'s; and so it went on, day after day. All attempts to get rid of her were of no avail. Scolding, threatening, were alike unheeded. "Catch me first," was her answer. Then he followed her to her home, to expostulate with her parents. Vain effort!

Up Anthony street to Centre; come with me, reader, let us look at that home!

There is a row of dens all along upon the east side of that street, full of those whom hope has forsaken, and misery has in her household. Above ground, below ground, in cellar or garret, back room or front, black and white, see how they swarm at door and window, in hall and stairway, and out upon the sidewalk, all day in idleness, all night in mischief, crime, and sin.

Elbow your way along among the standing, and step over the prostrate drunken or sleeping women and children along the side-walk. Stop here—here is a sort of hole-in-the-ground entrance to a long, dark, narrow alley, let us enter. "No, no, not there," you will exclaim. "Surely human beings cannot live there?"

Yes, they do. That girl has just gone down there, and we will follow.

"Better not go there," says a young urchin in the crowd; "a man was stabbed down there last night."

Encouraging; but we enter, and grope along about a hundred feet, and a door opens on the right, the girl we have followed darts out, up like a cat, over a high fence, on to a roof, up that, into a garret window, with a wild laugh and ringing words, "You didn't do it this time, you old Protestant thief, did you? You want to catch me, to send me to 'the Island.' I know you, you old missionary villain you. I heard Father Phelan tell what you want to do with the poor folks at the Points; you want to turn them out of house and home, and build up your grand houses, and make them all go to hear you preach your lies; you do, you old heretic, but you didn't catch me. I'll plague you again to-morrow."

We entered her home—the home that the missionary was trying to turn her out of. Can it be possible that human nature can cling to such a home, and refuse to be turned out, or occupy a better one.

The room is one of a "row," along the narrow dark corridor we entered, half sunken below the ground, with another just such another row overhead, each ten or twelve feet square, with a door and one little window upon this narrow alley which is the only yard; at the end of which there is a contagion-breeding temple of Cloacina, common to all.

In "the house" that we enter, a man lies helplessly drunk upon a dirty rug on the floor; a woman, too much overcome to rise, sits propped up in one corner. There is altogether, perhaps, fifty cents worth of furniture and clothing in the room.

And this is the loved home of one of the smartest, brightest, most intelligent little girls in this God-forsaken neighborhood.

The missionary made known his errand and was told that he might do anything he pleased with the girl, if he would catch her and tame her.

"For," said her mother, "what do we want with her at home —*at home!*—She is never here, only to sleep."

Only to sleep! Where did she sleep? On the damp, bare floor, of course, where else could she sleep in that home?

The next morning various devices were contrived to catch her, to force her into a better home. All failed.

When did force ever succeed with one of her sex?

If the serpent had *bid* our first mother to eat the apple, she would have thrown it down the villain's throat, splitting his forked tongue in its passage.

Finally it was arranged that a boy, noted as "a runner,"

should stand behind the door, and when she came with her jibes, sometimes provoking mirth, and sometimes ire, he should jump out and catch her.

"Catch me if you can!" and away went she, away went he, under this cart and over that. Now he will have her—his hand is outstretched to seize his chase—vain hope—she drops suddenly in his path, and he goes headlong down a cellar. When he came up there was a great shout, and a great many dirty bare-footed girls about, but that one was nowhere in sight. So back he goes, enters the door; and a wild laugh follows him close upon his heels.

"You did'nt catch me this time, did you? Don't you want another race? Ha, ha, ha."

And away she went, singing:

"Up, up, and away with the rising sun,
The chase is now before ye;
Up, up and away with hound and gun,
The chase is now before ye."

It was a chase that cunning must catch, strength could not win. Everybody said she never could be caught and tamed. She had run wild all her young years. She was not by nature vicious, but she was most incorrigibly mischievous. She was, so everybody said, and he ought to know, beyond the hope of redemption. Yet everybody was mistaken. Reader, you already know this girl, for this is "Wild Maggie, of the Five Points." This is the kind, sweet, tender-hearted Margaret, you have read of in a former chapter, ministering to the wants of that poor widow and destitute children, living in comfort, with neatness and industry, and her father, in a happy home; and that father the poor, miserable, wretched, besotted drunkard, whom we found in that wretched hole, in that dark alley in Centre street.

What a change!

It was a change for good. It was a deed of mercy to redeem such a child as this from a course of life that has but one phase—one worse than useless object—one wretched termination.

What magic power had wrought this change?

Words of kindness, charity, hope, teachings of the happiness attendant on virtue, religion, industry; by these the worst can be redeemed.

How?

"Finding every effort unavailing," said the missionary, "I changed my tactics. I was busy one morning in the workshop, laying out work, when I cast my eye towards the open door, and there saw Wild Maggie, waiting for a word upon which she might retort. Without seeming to notice her, I said, loud enough for her to hear, 'Oh, how I wish I had some one to help me lay out this work.' There was a look of intelligence spreading over her face, which seemed to say as plainly as looks could say, 'I could do that.'

"'Will you?' I said; she started as though I was mentally replying to her passing thoughts.

"She did not say, 'Yes,' but she thought it. I had touched a chord.

" 'Maggie,' said I, with all the tone and looks of kindness I could command, 'Maggie, my girl, come in; you can help me; I know you are smart, come, I will give you sixpence if you will help me a little while.' She stepped into the door, looked behind it suspiciously, and started back. She remembered the trap. 'No, I won't. You want to catch me and send me to the Island. I know you, you old Protestant. Old Kate told me yesterday, that you had sent off Liz. Smith, Nance Hastings, and hump-backed Lize, and a lot of girls.'

" 'So I have, but not to the Island. They have all got good places where they are contented and happy. But I don't send anybody away that don't want to go. I won't send you away, nor won't keep you if you don't want to stay.'

" 'Will you let me come out again, if I come in, when I am a mind to?'

" 'Yes, certainly, my dear child.'

"My dear child!" Where has she ever heard those words? In former days, before her father and mother had sunk so low, as they now are, when she used to go to school, to church, and sabbath-school, and wear clothes, such as she was not ashamed of. Want of clothing will sink the highest to the lowest state of rags, and dirt, and misery.

" 'Will you swear, that you will let me come out, and you won't beat me. Limping Bill and one-eyed Luce, his woman, says, you licked little Sappy till she died.'

" 'They are great liars.'

" 'So they say you are. That you preach nothing but lies.'

" 'Well, I won't lie to you, Maggie, and I won t whip you, but I won't swear. Did you ever know any good man swear?'

"She thought a moment, and replied, 'Well, I don't know—I know them that swear the most will lie. Will you let the door stand open? If you will I will come in?'

" 'Yes,' and in she came.

" 'Now, what do you want I should do?'

" 'There, do you look at me. I am laying out shirts for the women to sew. That pile, there, that is the body; this, the sleeves; that, the collar; these, the wristbands; these, the gussets; here are six buttons, and here is the thread to make it, and then it will be a shirt when made. Now we roll it up and tie a string around it; now it is ready to give out. Now, you can do that just as well as I can, and you don't know how much it will help me.'

" 'Yes, I can, and I can beat you.'

So she could. She was just as quick at work as she was at play and mischief, and the piles disappeared under her nimble fingers much more rapidly than they did under his, and so he told her. Who had ever praised her work before, though all had "her deviltry?"

The spirit of reformation had already commenced its glorious work.

"When that job was finished, she turned her sweet blue eyes upon me, with an expression which said as plain as eyes can speak, 'I am sorry that job is done. I like that, can't you give me another?'

" There was no other which she could do just then, but she said, 'What shall I do now?'

" Well, Maggie, I have no more work for you to-day, but here is your sixpence, I promised you, and here are some cakes; come again to-morrow, you can help me every day. I like your help."

She did not want to go. She had tasted of a fruit which had opened her eyes, and she would fain clothe herself in fig leaves, so they hid the deformity of dirt, and rags, and sin. Wild as the fawn, as easily as the fawn subdued. At the approach of man, that timid animal bounds into the thickest brake and hides away; but once in the hands of man, it turns and follows him to his home, licking his hand as though it were with its own dam. So was Wild Maggie tamed.

" What shall I do now?"

What should she do? A score of little girls were huddling around the door, for the news was out that Maggie, Wild Maggie, had been caught and caged, and they wanted to see " what would come of it."

" A thought struck me," said the missionary. " I asked her if she could read. Yes, and write. Had she been to school? Yes. Then you shall play school. You shall have these benches, and you shall call in those children, and you shall be the teacher, and so you may play school."

Was there ever a happier thought engendered. Maggie was delighted, the children came rushing in, ready for " a play never before enacted in this theatre."

For an hour or more she plied her task diligently, and

it was astonishing with what effect. How she reduced her unruly materials to order. How she made them say, yes, ma'am, and no, ma'am, to their school mistress. How she made them sit and "look like somebody." Taught this one his A B Cs, and that one to spell B-a-k-e-r. How she told this one to wash his face, next time he came to school, and that one if she had any better clothes, to wear them. Poor Maggie, she never thought of the poverty of her own.

"Now," said she, "every one of you sit still; not a word of noise, and no running out while I am gone, or I shall punish you worse than shutting you up in a dark closet. Mr. Pease, will you look to my school a moment?"

Away she bounded. Oh, what a step! Step! it was more like flying. A moment, hardly time for a few pleasant words to her school, and she bounds in again, with a little paper parcel in her hand. What could it mean? It means that,

> Many a flower in wilds unseen,
> The sweetest fragrance grows;
> From many a deep and hidden spring,
> The coolest water flows.

She first inquires, "have they all been good?" "Yes, all." Then she unwraps her parcel. How they look and wonder, "what is it?"

What is it? Simply this.

She has been out and spent her sixpence to do unto others just as she had been done unto. Did ever cakes taste sweeter? Did ever benevolence better enjoy herself than

Maggie did, while thus distributing her rewards? What a lesson of self-sacrifice! The first sixpence—the whole treasure of this world's goods, spent to promote the happiness of others. This was a hint. It were a dull intellect that could not improve it. The children were further fed, and bid to come again to-morrow. "And this," said he, "was the beginning of our ragged beggar children school, that has proved such a blessing to this neighborhood.

"Maggie," said I, taking her by the hand and looking her in the eye. "Maggie, you have helped me a great deal to-day, will you come again to-morrow?"

The string was touched, and tears flowed. When had tears, except tears of anger, filled those eyes before? What had touched that string? Kind words!

"If you will let me stay, I wont go away. I can learn to sew. I can make these shirts."

"Yes, yes; and if you are here, these children will come, and we will have school every day."

And so Wild Maggie was Wild Maggie no more. She was tamed. Her life had taken on a new phase. To the questions, what would her father say? what would her mother say? she replied, "What do they care? what have they ever cared? Though they were not always so bad as they now are."

No, they were not always so bad as they now are. None of his class were always so bad as they now are. Once her father was James Reagan, a respectable man, a good carpenter, and had a good home. Now where was he. Sunk, step by step, from hotel to saloon, from saloon to bar-room, from bar-room to corner grocery, from grocery to cellar rum hole, from a good house to a filthy, underground den in Centre street. He has but one more step to take—one more underground hole to occupy.

But such as he may reform. He did. You have seen that. Will you ask, how? You shall know.

Maggie became one of the household. She was washed, and fed, and clothed; and how she worked, and learnt everything, and how she listened at the temperance meetings to what "the pledge" had done, and how she wished her mother would come and try—try to leave off drinking, and become "the good mother she was when I was a little girl." For her father she had no hope. For her mother, she determined to persevere. When she was sober she would talk, and cry, and promise, but the demon rum would overcome her, and then she would curse her daughter, and call her all the vile names that the insane devil in her could invent.

And so it went on; Maggie still determined, still trying. The right time came at last. One night, Maggie was not at the meeting. By and by, there was a little stir at the door. What is the matter? A little girl is pulling a woman, almost by force, into the room. It is Maggie and her mother. She has got her old ragged dress off, and looks quite neat in one that Maggie has made for her. But she hides her face. She is ashamed to look those in the face she would have once looked down upon. A woman is speaking—women can speak upon temperance—just such a woman as herself—is it not herself—is she awake, or does she sleep and dream? If awake, she hears her own story. The story of a woman with a drunken husband. And she traces his fall from affluence down to beggary; then her fall, down, down, down, to a cellar in Farlow's Court; there her husband dies; there upon a pile of straw and rags upon the floor, in drunken unconsciousness, she gives birth to a child—a living child by the side of its dead father.

"What a night—what a scene, but you have not seen the worst of it. The very heavens, as though angry at such awful use of the gifts of reason, and the abuse of appetite, sent their forked messengers of fire to the earth—less dangerous than the fire that man bottles up for his own damnation; and the water came down in torrents, pouring into that cave where the dead, and living, and new born were lying together, and overflowed the floor, and when I felt its chill," said she, "I awaked out of my drunken sleep, and felt around me, to see, no, I could not see, all was pitch darkness. My child cried, and then—then a whole army of rats, driven in by the rain, driven by the water from the floor, came creeping on to me. Oh! how their slimy bodies felt as they crept over my face. Then I tried to awaken my husband, but he would not wake, and in my frenzy I struck and bit him—bit a dead man—for his was the sleep of eternity. Then I summoned almost superhuman strength, and creeped up the stairs and out into the court. I looked up; the storm was gone; there was a smile in heaven—it was the smile of that murdered babe; for when I had begged a light, and went back again to that dreadful,

dreadful habitation—why are human beings permitted to live in such awful holes—has nobody any care for human life—what did I see? Mothers, mothers—mothers that sleep on soft couches—hear me, hear me—hear of the bitter fruits the rum trade bears—the rats had devoured the life blood of that child. What next I know not. I know that I have never drank since—never will again—by signing this pledge I was saved—all may be saved."

"All? all? Can I—can I be restored as you have been—can I shake off this demon that has dragged me down so low that my own mother would not know me; or knowing, would spurn me? Can I be saved?"

It was Maggie's mother.

"Yes, you, you, I was a thousand times worse. Look at me now."

"Yes, mother, you. Come." And she took her by the hand and led her up to the table, put a pen in her hand—dropt upon her knees—looked up to her mother imploringly—up to heaven prayerfully—her lips quivered—the tears rolled down her cheeks—"Now, mother, now."

'Tis done. She wrote her name in a fair hand—Mary Reagan—'Tis done.

'Tis done!—'tis done!—wild Maggie cries;
'Tis done!—'tis done!—the mother sighs;
'Tis done!—'tis done!—in chorus join,
To bear aloft the news along.
'Tis done!—'tis done! a voice replies,
Stand forth, be strong, and you shall rise.

And so she did. She never fell. She came to live in the house with Maggie. "I cannot go back," she said, "to live with your father, if I would stand fast; and I cannot think, after hearing that woman's story, last night, of ever drinking again. I know that woman; I knew her when she was a girl, one of the proudest and prettiest. My husband has spent many a dollar with hers in the bar-room. Oh yes, I knew her well. I did not know her last night; but when she told me who she was—that she was Elsie Wendall—then I knew her. Oh! I could tell you such a story—but not now. No! no, I cannot live with your father again, for I never will drink any more—never—never!"

"But what, if father will take the pledge?"

"Oh! then I should be a happy woman again. But there is no hope."

"Yes, there is hope. I shall watch him; and, mother, I *will* save him."

It was a great promise—a great undertaking for a young girl to promise with an "I will." When did "I will" in woman's mouth ever fail?

That will was the strength of her life. It was for that she now lived and labored. Now she had hope—now 'twas lost—now revived again. Now he worked a month—sober for a whole month—then down he went if he happened to go into one of his old haunts, or meet with some of his old companions, who said, "come, Jim, let's take one drink—only one—one won't do any hurt"—but two follow the one. Then Maggie would look him up, get him sober again, and get him to work.

God bless that child! God did bless her, for she stuck to him, until he finally consented to come once, just once to the temperance meeting—but he would not sign the pledge—he never would sign away his liberties—no—he was a free man. Well only come, come and listen—come and see mother. That touched him. He loved mother—Yes he would come. The evening came. Maggie watched every shadow that darkened the door. Finally the last one seemed to have entered, but Jim Reagan was not among them. Maggie could not give it up. She slipped out into the street, it was well she did. She was just in time. A knot of men were talking together, of the tyranny of temperance men, wanting to make slaves of the people, getting them to sign away their rights—rights their fathers fought and bled for."

Yes, and so had they—at the nose.

They had just carried the point, and started to follow Cale Jones over to his grocery, who was going to stand treat all round. One lingered a moment—looked back—as though he had promised to go that way—but appetite was too strong for conscience, and he turned towards the rum-hole. Just then a gentle hand is laid upon his arm, and a sweet voice says:

"Father, come with me, come and see mother—don't go with those men."

Woman conquered.

When Cale Jones counted noses, to see which he should charge with the treat he had promised "to stand," he found Jim Reagan was not in the crowd.

"Why, damn the fellow, he has given us the slip after all

our trouble. I thought we had made a sure thing of it. I tell you what it is, boys, we must manage somehow to stop this business, or trade is ruined. If people are not to be allowed to drink anything but water, there'll be many an honest man out of business. Times is hard enough now, what'll they be then?"

Just then Tom Nolan, the mason—it used to be Drunken Tom Nolan—was telling what they would be, at the temperance meeting.

It was a propitious time for Maggie. She led her father in, he hung back a little, and tried to get into a dark corner near the door. That she would not allow; some of Satan's imps might drag him away from the very threshold of salvation. She led him along, he was sober now, and looked sad, perhaps, ashamed.

"James, you here? Oh!"

It was his wife. He knew her voice, it was that of other days. He stared at her; could it be her, so neat, and clean, and well dressed, and speaking so fondly to him—to him—for she had refused to see him ever since she took the pledge. Now, she came forward, took him by the hand, ragged and dirty as he was—she knew what would clean him—led him to a seat and sat down by his side. Maggie sat on the other. For a minute the speaker could not go on. There was a choking in his throat, strong man as he was, and there were many tears in the eyes that looked upon that father, mother, and daughter, that night.

"Jim Reagan," said the speaker, "I am glad to see you here. You are an old acquaintance of mine."

Jim Reagan looked at him with astonishment. Could that well dressed laboring man, clean shaved and clean shirted, be Tom Nolan?

"I don't wonder that you look inquiringly at me, as much as to say, 'is that you?' Yes, it is me, Tom Nolan, the mason, me who used to lay around the dirty rum holes with you, begging, lying, stealing, to get a drink. Do you think that now I would pick up old cigar stumps and quids of tobacco, to fill my pipe? Do you think I would wear a hat, as I have done, that my poor beggared boy picked out of the street? Look at that. Does that look like the old battered thing I used to wear? Do these clothes look like the dirty rags I wore when you and I slept in Cale Jones's coal-box? Do I look like the drunken Tom Nolan that kept a family of starving beggars, with two other families, in one room, ten by twelve feet square; and that a garret room, without fireplace, without glass in its one window; with the roof so low that I could only stand up straight in one corner; and that mean room in the vilest locality on earth, in a house—ah! whole row of houses, tenanted by just such miserable, rum-beggared human beings—buildings owned by a human monster—houses for the poor which are enough to sicken the vilest of beasts; such as no good man would let for tenements, even when he could get tenants as degraded as I was—tenements that any Christian grand jury would indict, and any court, which desired to protect the lives of the people, would compel the owners to pull down, as the worst, with one exception, of all city nuisances.

"How did I live there? How did my wife and children ever live there, in that little miserable room, with seven others, just such wretches as ourselves? How do hundreds of such men, women, and children as we were, still live there? I was in that same room—the place my children used to call *home*—this evening. The entrance is in Cow Bay. If you would like to see it, saturate your handkerchief with camphor, so that you can endure the horrid stench, and enter. Grope your way through the long, dark, narrow passage—turn to your right, up the dark and dangerous stairway; be careful where you place your foot around the lower step, or in the corners of the broad stairs, for it is more than shoe-mouth deep of steaming filth. Be careful too, or you may meet some one—perhaps a man, perhaps a woman—as nature divides the sexes; as the rum seller combines them, both beasts, who in their drunken frenzy may thrust you, for the very hatred of your better clothes, or the fear that you have come to rescue them from their crazy loved dens of death, down, headlong down, those filthy stairs. Up, up, winding up, five stories high, now you are under the black smoky roof; turn to the left—take care and not upset that seething pot of butcher's offal soup, that is cooking upon a little furnace at the head of the stairs—open that door—go in, if you can get in. Look; here is a negro and his wife sitting upon the floor—where else could they sit, for there is no chair—eating their supper off of the bottom of a pail. A broken brown earthen jug holds water—perhaps not all water. Another negro and his wife occupy another corner; a third sits in the window monopolising all the air astir. In another corner, what do we see?

A negro man, and a stout, hearty, rather good looking, young white woman."

"Not sleeping together?"

"No, not exactly that—there is no bed in the room—no chair—no table—no nothing—but rags, and dirt, and vermin, and degraded, rum degraded, human beings—men and women with just such souls as animate the highest and proudest in the land."

"Who is this man?"

"Dat am Ring-nosed Bill."

"Is that his wife?"

"Well, I don't know that. He calls her his woman."

"And she lives with him as his wife—you all live here together in this room?"

"Well, we is got nowhere else to live. Poor folks can't lib as rich ones do—hab to pay rent—pretty hard to do that alone."

"How much rent for this room?"

"Seventy-five cents a week, ebry time in advance."

"Who is this man?"

"They calls me Snaky Jo. 'Spose may be my name is Jo Snaky. Don't know rightly."

"What do you do for a living?"

"Well, mighty hard to tell dat, dat am fact, massa. Picks

up a job now and then. Mighty hard times though—give poor man a lift, massa."

"Is that man and woman drunk."

"Well, 'spose am, little tossicated."

"A little intoxicated! They are dead drunk, lying perfectly unconscious, in each other's *emesis*, upon the bare floor. The atmosphere of this room is enough to breed contagion, and sicken the whole neighborhood, and would, but that the whole neighborhood is equally bad. Let us hasten down to the open air of the court—it is but little better—all pollution—all that breathe it, polluted. Yet, in that gate of death I once lived. Look at me, James, you knew me then. Look at me now, you don't know me. You knew me a beast—you may know me a man—you may know yourself one. Sign this paper—there is a power of magic in it—and you shall go home with me, and see where I live now, and I will clothe you and help to sustain you in your sober life, just as Thomas Elting did me, and with heaven's blessing, we will make a man of you."

"Too late! too late! not enough of the old frame left to rebuild."

"It is never too late. Look at the piles of old brick, and tiles, and boards, and joist, and rafters, and doors, and glass, of the pulled down houses. Are they wasted? I am a mason, you a carpenter; if we cannot put them back and build up the same old-fashioned edifice, we can make a good, snug, comfortable house. Come, sign the contract, and let us set right about the job."

"Father, come, father!"

He turned and spoke a few low words to his wife, to which she replied:

"Yes, I will. Keep the pledge one month and I will go and live with you, die with you."

"Then try it, father, come." And she led him forward, just as she had done her mother. You have seen, shall see, how heaven blessed her for filial piety.

"I used to write. 'Tis a long time since I did. Maggie, my hand trembles. Help me—guide the pen. I cannot see clearly."

No wonder. There was a tear in each eye. There were other tears when Maggie took him again by the hand, and again said:

"Come, father, let us pray;" and then all kneeled down together, and then Mr. Nolan took him by the arm, and said, "Come, James, let us go home."

Not yet. He had one more act to perform. He shook his wife's hand, and said, "Good bye. I shall keep it." Then he looked wishfully at Maggie, as though he wanted something, yet dare not ask it, for fear he should be repulsed. Still the yearning of nature was upon him. It was a long time since he had felt it as he now felt, but he was beginning to be a new man. Maggie was his only child, his once loved, much caressed child. Would she ever cling those arms around his neck again. She had shown herself this night one of the blessed of this earth. She had done, or induced him to do, what no other soul on earth could have done, and

4

how his heart did yearn to clasp her in his arms. He stoppe half way to the door, and looked upon her with tearful, loving, thankful eyes. It needs no wires, no magnet, no human contrivance, to convey the magnetism of the heart. She felt its power, as it sprung from the lightning flash of loving eyes, and quick as that flash, she made one bound, one word, "Father!" and her arms were around his neck, her lips to his, and here let us shift the scene.

CHAPTER IV.

THE TEMPTATION.—THE FALL.

Eve was tempted of Satan, and fell.
So have been her children.

About two months after the events of the last chapter, a few of the new friends of James Reagan joined together, procured a comfortable room in Mulberry street, and put in the necessary articles of furniture, and his wife, faithful to her promise, came to live with him. There was a great contrast between this and the home where we visited him in Centre street. Nolan and Elting stuck to him, and he stuck to the pledge. Margaret watched him, visited him, went with him and her mother to church and temperance meetings, and, finally, became satisfied and happy that her father had made a complete reformation, and that he had outlived all danger of relapse; so she accepted a good offer to go into the country, and live in a farmer's house, where she would learn housework. It was her fortune, but his misfortune, thus to be separated. She was his ever-watchful guardian angel. His wife was affectionately kind, and they lived together, as of old, happily. And so, as of Adam and Eve in paradise, they might have lived, if there had been no serpents in New York. They beset him—waylaid him—tempted him—but no art could induce him to enter their sulphurous dens. Cale Jones swore that he would get him back; that he would have him among his old cronies again, or die in the attempt.

"Them ere cold water chaps aren't a going to crow over me that ere way, no how. I tell you what it is, boys, you must contrive some way to get Jim in here some night; he has got money now, and if he won't drink himself, he shall stand treat any how. We've treated him many a time."

"Dat am de fac," says Ring-nosed Bill.

"Shut your clapper, you drunken nigger, you; who axt you to put in your oar. If you want to do anything, just get Jim Reagan, by hook or crook, in here once more."

"And you will give him what you did Pedlar Jake."

"Shut pan, or I'll chuck your ivory into your bread-basket. What's in your wool, Snakey?"

"Dis nigger knows how to fix him. Make him come his self."

"Let her rip, Snakey; how'll you do it?"

"Jis go to work at right end foremost. 'Spose you the debble stick him forked tongue right out all at once to frighten Fader Adam? No, sir-ee; he creep round mighty sly, and wiggle him tail at Mudder Eve, and den she come it over de old man. Dat am the way. Aren't you got no gumption?"

"I understand. Who shall the Eve be, Snakey?"

"Smoky Sal. She is a pet of his. He got her in."

"I know it. She is in that old missionary's claws. How are you going to get her out?"

"Dat easy 'nuff, so you work him right. Gib us a drink, Cale. I isn't going to grab for you for nothing."

"I'll give you a gallon if you bring him in. How 'll you do it?'

"Do you think this nigger am a fool, sure? 'Spose I gwine to tell you, and lose the gallon. Take notice, Ring-nose, it's a fair trade. So jis you git ready to-morrow night for business, case he'll be down then."

The next night the trap was set. Snakey went to One-eyed Angeline, and promised her a share in the gallon, if she would contrive a plan to get Smoky Sal out of the House of Industry, and get her over to Cale Jones's, and get her drunk.

These two had long been sisters in sin. One had reformed, or was trying to reform, for Reagan had got her into the House, and seemed very anxious for her, having, as he said, been the cause of her downfall. The other hated her for her reformation, and would drag her back, down, down, to the wretched life she had escaped from.

So she sent word to Sally that she was sick and almost dying, and begged her to come and see her. How could she refuse? So she went, and found her with her head tied up, and in dreadful pain. Directly in came Snakey Jo, with the first installment of the gallon. It was to bathe her head. Can an old inebriate put liquor upon the outside of the head without putting it in? Sally could not. She smelt—she tasted—she drank—was drunk—and then Angeline took her down to Cale Jones's grocery, and into his back room, and then that black imp of a worse than slave's master, watched for Reagan as he started for home, and with an air of honesty that might deceive the wariest old fox into a trap, he told him how " Angeline had coaxed Sally into the grocery, and he had been watching an hour"—that was the only truth he spoke—he watched for another victim—" and she hadn't come out yet, and he was afraid she was in trouble; and now, Mister Reagan, I is so glad I is fell in wid you, accidental like, case I didn't know as you was in the Points, case you can get her out, and get her back home."

With a natural impulse to do good, he determined, imprudently, to be sure, to do what he had not done since he signed the pledge—to enter a rum-hole. There he found the two women as the negro had told him. Sally was completely overcome, and lying in one corner of "the back room." Back it was, quite out of sight or hearing of the street, where many a victim had been robbed at a game of cards, or by more direct means. It was in this room that Pedlar Jake got his quietus.

"I had been in the room often before," said Reagan. "I knew the way, and I paid no heed to the hypocritically angry words I was greeted with as I entered, and told to clear out and mind my own business. I pushed my way through the crowd of loafers, and entered the door of death. That old witch, Angeline, took care to get out of my way as I went in. I sat down upon the bed and tried to rouse up the victim of this infernal plot, little thinking that I was the greatest one of the two. The room was very close and foul, and as I had been unused, lately, to breathe such air, it made me sick. 'Tom,' said I"—let me stop and moralize a little upon this name. I would never call a child, Tom. There is something fatal in the word. I have known more drunken Toms than of all other names. It is a low-bred name. Bill, Jim, Joe, Sam, Ike, are all bad, but none equal to Tom. "Two of my drunkenest companions," said Reagan, "afterwards, my best friends, were Toms—now Thomas Elting and Thomas Nolan." Parents, don't nickname your children, it is a step down that may carry them to the bottom of the ladder.

Give your children good names; names they will not be ashamed of in after life, and never cut them short. Never call, William, Bill; or, Catherine, Kate; or, Mary, that most beautiful of all names, a name I love, Moll; it will, perhaps, be the direct cause of their ruin as they grow up. Who would think of speaking a foul word to Miss Mary Dudley? Who would speak with respect to Moll Dud? Parents, think of it.

Now, here was another Tom. A bright, active boy—Tom Top, whose proper name was, Thomas Topham. What if he had been called Charles? why, his nickname would have been an elongation to Charley, a name that everybody loves. At any rate, he would not have been, drunken Tom—a poor, neglected orphan boy, who, for want of some one to guide and keep him in the path of virtue, had strayed into the very worst of all paths of vice. From a home, where he received a fair education, and had a good mother, but a father who learned him to drink, and who thought it cunning to call him, Tom Top, he was come down to be a mere hanger-on around Cale Jones's grocery.

"God never works without an object," is an axiom of those

who look every day to him for counsel. We shall see in time how the villain was defeated in his object of bringing Reagan into this place, and making use of Tom for an instrument of his ruin.

"'Tom,' said I, 'bring me a glass of water.' He did so, I tasted it and set it down a moment for the ice to melt. When I took it up again, I swallowed the whole tumbler full at a gulph. In a moment my throat, my stomach, my brain were on fire. I had drank half-a-pint of white whiskey. Those wicked wretches had hired Tom to substitute one glass for the other. What transpired for three days after, I know not."

The next morning, before sunrise, his wife came down to the Points in an agony of fear. "Was Reagan there?" was her hopeful inquiry. Hope sunk and almost carried her with it when told that he left there before ten to go home. "Then he is lost, lost, lost!"

All that day he was searched for up and down, high and low, but nobody had seen him. How the villains lied, for they were all the time gloating over their victory—double victory—two stray sheep won back—back to the wolf's den. All that day the pack were carousing upon the money robbed from Reagan.

"What a glorious haul, boys," says Cale Jones, "we must have Tom Elting and Nolan, next, and then hurrah, boys, we'll break up old Pease and drive him out of the Points yet."

How could human nature become so infernally depraved, as to rejoice over and glorify such deeds of darkness?

By Rum. The very parent of total depravity.

At night, after their day's work, Elting and Nolan came down and joined the search, looking into every hole that was most likely to have been used for his tomb, worse than tomb, for it was the burial-place of his soul. They did not look in Cale Jones's back room, for he " took his Bible oath that Jim Reagan had never entered his door in a three month."

Finally, after the pack had spent every cent of his money, and pawned every article of his clothing, they were ready to get rid of his company. But they were not quite satisfied with the misery they had made for his wife, and so they plotted a scheme so wicked that the most incarnate one of all the hosts of the infernal regions would blush to own the deed.

They knew that Sally had been a source of disturbance, a cause of jealousy to his wife in by-gone years, and so they laid their plan. Madalina, a little beggar girl, an Italian rag-picker's daughter, was promised a sixpence to go, as she would not be suspected, to tell Mrs. Reagan, that Tom knew where her husband was.

It was a faint hope, but drowning men catch at straws.

Tom was hunted up. He was easily found, for he had his instructions, " to bring the old woman along." Did they hope in her frenzy of despair and jealousy that she too would fall? Yes they did.

Could human ingenuity contrive anything more harrowing to the mind of a wife, searching for her absent husband, than an introduction into a room where he was in bed with another woman, folding her, in his drunken insanity, in his arms, protesting how he loved her, loved her better than he did—better than—his grog?

The monsters missed their aim. Mrs. Reagan spoke kindly to him as though in her own bed; begged him to get up and go home with her. No he would not. She might go back to her old missionary paramour. She might go to —— no matter where, he was drunk. But he could not get up, for the villains had stripped him of every stitch of clothing; they had not even left him a shirt. So she went away, sorrowing.

"Tom," said she, "come, go home with me, that is a good boy, I feel so faint and weak." Tom was a good boy; who had ever said it though? One, one he remembered, and these words came like hers and nestled down in his heart. They will live there and drive out evil ones.

Tom went home with her, giving her his arm and telling her to lean upon it. Tom was not the best of guides, he made several missteps that day, for tears dimmed his eyes, but he made one good step, it was up the ladder of reform.

"Mrs. Reagan," said he, "let me stay here to-day, I have got no home, and I don't feel as though I wanted to go back to Cale Jones's."

No. He did not want to go back there. He had heard the sound of his dead mother's voice, saying, good boy. Nobody would say, good boy, if he went back there. Conscience too was doing her work; conscience told him what he had done to a woman who now said, "good boy."

So he stayed—he was a good boy—she was sick and he waited upon her all day. At night he was going to get Mr.

Elting and Nolan to go with him and bring Reagan home. That would be his reward. He has his hand upon the door to go out, but waits a moment to see who comes. He opens it to a hurried footstep, and in bounds Wild Maggie, her face radiant with health, strength, and the lovely bloom of country life.

"Where's father? Mother sick? What's the matter?"

Her mother draws the clothes over her face. She would not have her daughter see her weep.

"Tom, my boy, tell me; come, Tom, that is a good boy—the truth, nothing but the truth—I must know it."

Good boy, again, and his heart overflowed. He could stand kicks, and cuffs, and curses, without a tear, but he could not hold out against, "good boy."

"Maggie, I will not lie to *you*, I could not; but I can't tell you the truth."

"Why?"

"I am 'fraid you won't call me good boy again."

"Yes, I will. I don't believe you are a bad one."

"And you won't hate me?"

"No, no; she cannot hate you, for you have been good to her mother, to-day."

"Mother! Oh! I know all about it. You need not tell me. Only, where is he? I will go and bring him home."

"Did Heaven ever give a mother such another child?"

Yes, many such. Many a flower would send its blossomed sweets to many a heart, but for blighting frosts in its young years.

"What sent you home, Maggie?"

"I don't know, mother; I felt as though I was wanted. Something told me so. I dreamed so for three nights, and so I came."

She was soon told everything. Tom made a full confession; and still she did not hate him. She told him, how he could help her. He should go with her; she was going to bring her father home. She gave him a little bundle of clothes to carry; and away they went. She stopped on her way down, at the police office, made her complaint, and took an officer along with her, who arrested Cale Jones and the two women; the rest of the gang were prowling for prey somewhere else. The women were sent to the Island, next day, for they had no friends. The plotter of villainy had. The Alderman of the Sixth Ward, was his friend; political friend; him he sent for; and after being an hour in custody, he was discharged; and this was the end of his punishment.

Reagan, since his wife's visit in the morning, had steadily refused to drink any more, and had become in a measure sober. It was a sad meeting with his daughter. At first, he refused to see or speak to her. He was ashamed. Nature overcame him at last, and he got up and pulled off the dirty suit his robbers had put on him, preparatory to kicking him into the street, and put on the clean ones, which Maggie and Tom had brought him; and then they took him, each by an arm, and went home. It was a sad home; it never will be a happy one again. Then she went to work and got him some supper, spending of her own little store to buy some tea, and such things as he could eat.

"Now," says she, "I have got another thing to do to-night, for I must go back again in the morning. Tom, I am going to provide you with a home. You must go to the House of Industry, reform, and make a man of yourself."

Reader, do not forget. This ministering angel, is Wild Maggie.

Most willingly he went with her, and was most kindly received by the Superintendent. There we will leave him awhile. We shall see him again perhaps.

Maggie went back to her country home. Her father remained sick for some days, and then went to work, but his spirit was broken, he grew more and more uneasy, and finally, in a fit of despondency, met with one of his old cronies, and back he went, down, down, to his former degradation. Had he gone back and renewed his pledge, after his first fall, when he was dragged down, he might have been saved; but he would not; he said, he had proved himself incapable of ever being a man again, and so he sunk in despair. Week after week his clothes, his furniture, his wife's clothes, even her daughter's gift-Bible, went for rum. Nothing was left, but starvation. Yes, there was one thing left for her—one thing that that wife had never before received from her husband.

A blow, a black-eye, and a kick. It was one drop too much in her cup of affliction, and she parted with him for ever, and came back to her old home, the House of Industry.

Tom welcomed her with a smile; he was door-keeper now.

"'It is better to be door-keeper,'" said he, "'in the house—you know the rest. I will call Mr. P. I am sure, he will give you a home, he said as much yesterday. I shall write to Maggie now, and let her know all about it."

"You are very kind, Tom, to say that."

"Well, wasn't she kind to me? Where should I have been all this time, if it had not been for her? I think, we will get the old man in again, yet."

"No, no, he is passed everything, now. He never was so bad before, never struck me a blow before. A blow from him! Oh! it is dreadful. I never can forgive that."

"Don't say that. 'Forgive us our trespasses as we forgive those who trespass against us.'"

"True, my boy, you have taught me a lesson. I will forgive, but I don't think he will ever get over this bout; he is very violent."

"The most violent fires are soonest burnt out."

Tom had faith, she had none, she was a sad victim of despair—a despairing wife. But time will heal the deepest wounds. She went to work, grew cheerful, and contented there to spend the remainder of her life, which she said, would not be long. Of that she seemed to have a presentiment, and made all preparation which it becomes a reasonable mortal to make for such a prospective journey. She seemed to have but one wish.

"Oh! if I could see my husband as he was a few months

ago, I should be willing to die then. But I cannot bear to die now with the thought upon my mind, that he would never shed a tear at my grave."

His time was coming. Tom was a philosopher. "Didn't I tell you," says he, "that the fire would soon burn out. He was here last night, walking up and down the pavement for hours, looking down into the kitchen when you were at work."

"Perhaps he wanted to strike me again."

"No, he was as sober as a judge."

"Oh, dear! then may be he was hungry, poor man."

"So I thought, and went and bought him a loaf of bread. When I gave it to him, he burst into tears, and walked away to a cart and sat down to eat it. He was hungry, and for fear he would be dry, and go to that cursed hole—"

"Don't swear, Tom."

"I can't help it; it is one, and why not call it so? I did not want him to go there, and so I went and got him a cup of water, and carried to him, and then I thought if everybody knew what a blessed thing it is to give these poor old drunkards bread and water instead of rum, how much happiness they might make in the world. And then I talked to him about taking the pledge again, but he said, 'no, Tom, I took it once, I don't want to break it again.' 'No,' said I, 'you did not break it, it was me that did it, I was the guilty one.' And then I told him all about it. He never knew before. The rascals there told him, that he and Sally came there together and called for whiskey, and then got drunk and went to bed together, and he believed it; his mind was so confused that he forgot all about the past, and he never knew till now that they had lied to him so shockingly. 'You don't know,' says he, 'Tom, what a load you have lifted off of my conscience.' Then I asked him where he was going to sleep that night?

"'Where? where should I? In the cart or under it. Anywhere I can find a hole. Me that have had a house of my own, and built a score of houses for others to sleep in, have not slept in one these two months. Perhaps never shall again.'

"'Yes you will,' says I; 'you will sleep in that one to-night.'

"'What! under the same roof with my wife once more; I don't know as I could stand it; it is more happiness than I deserve.'

"'No, it is not; and if you will go away in the morning, and stay away all day, and come back at night as sober as you are now, I will ask the Superintendent to take you in for good.'

"'I will, I will! I will go away and sweep the streets to-morrow; they will give me another loaf of bread, and that is more than I have had for a whole week.'

"So you see, he will come again to-night, and then it is temperance meeting, and we will get him in. Depend upon it, if he ever takes the pledge again he will never break it."

True to his word, Reagan came the next night sober.

"See," said he, "Tom, I have got a quarter of a dollar, and have not spent it for liquor. If some of the harpies knew I had it, how they would be after me."

He hesitated long about going into the meeting. He was afraid his wife would be there, and he could not bear to meet her. She was equally afraid to meet him. Finally, one of the assistants went out and talked with him.

"Do you think," he replied, "that I could ever be a man again? I am afraid there is not enough of me left to make one. Manhood is all gone. I feel as though I had made a beast of myself so long, that I must always be a beast. But if you think there is enough left of the old wreck—"

"Enough? Yes; come along."

This was a new voice, just come up on the other side. He looked around; it was Nolan.

"Nolan, my old friend—you were a friend to me; and I will try if Mr. Pease will agree to shut me up and keep me out of the way of these alligators. Look at them. Don't they lie about just like alligators in the mud and swamps, ready to snap up every poor dog that comes within reach of their tails or jaws?"

Well, he took the pledge, and in due time we will see how he kept it.

While I give my readers a little respite from the contemplation of such characters as have been introduced in the preceding chapters, I propose to introduce a little episode in the life of two of those which they have seen engaged in the noble work of reclaiming and sustaining a poor inebriate in his efforts to become a sober man. That they had reason to believe in the possibility of such reclamation, the reader will understand after reading the historical facts of the next chapter.

CHAPTER V.

THE TWO PENNY MARRIAGE.

"And ye twain shall be one flesh."

"What God hath joined together, let no man put asunder."

No, not even rum; yet it often does. We have just read of one of the many thousand sad instances that have occurred in this world, of rum separating those who had taken upon them that holy ordinance which makes them as one flesh, one heart, one mind; and, unless such have one mind both to be drunk together, how can they live with one another? How can they live in rum's pollution in the holy bonds of matrimony? There is nothing holy about such a sinful life.

Do away with the cause—abolish intoxicating liquor from society, and you will not only rivet those holy bonds with golden rivets, but you will shut up nine-tenths of the brothels and gaming houses in this city. Without rum they could not live over the first quarter's rent day. With it their profits are enormous—its effects awful.

I could point you to a house in this city, with its twenty-five painted harlots, where the sales of wine in one year have been thirteen thousand bottles, costing $15,000, and selling for $39,000. And why not a profit, since men and women will get drunk in a palace, the mere repairs or additions to which, in one season, cost the almost incredible sum of $70,000?

Who furnished the money? Who made the inmates what they are? Those who *made the wine;* not those who furnished the grape juice, for it is probable that the whole did not contain a thousand bottles full of that liquor.

What caused the inmates to be what they are? Rum!

Who made them harlots? Not those who marry, or are given in marriage.

Marriage is one of the best preventives of licentiousness, but it is not often perhaps that it produces so positive a reformation as in the following cases.

"I have married," said Mr. Pease to me one day, "some very curious couples. That of Elting was very remarkable."

He was sitting one evening, trying to post up his books, amid continued interruptions, such as, "Little Lucy's eyes are worse to-night, sir."

"Let me see. She must go into the hospital. Send the sore-eye nurse to me. Take this little girl to your room—keep her eyes well washed with cold water, and use that ointment. Report to me to-morrow. Go."

"That is a fine-looking woman."

"Yes, and an excellent nurse. She lived last year in one of those Centre street cellars. She came here with both eyes nearly out of her head; gouged by a drunken husband. We put her into the sore eye hospital, and soon found she would make a good nurse for the afflicted children."

"Mr. Pease, is it the powder once and the pills every hour, or is it t'other way,"

"Exactly. The other way. You have hit it. The powde" is Dover's Powder, to allay fever. The pills are cathartic. Go."

"Cathartic. I never heard of that pill-maker before. Wonder if he will make as many as Brandreth has," says this interrupter as she goes away.

"Susan Apsley says you promised her she might go out this evening."

"Did she come in all right when she was out before?"

"All right, sir."

"Let her go."

"Please, sir, may I go with her?"

"Who is this."

"Juliana, sir. I want to go and see my cousin Madalina, sir."

"Oh, yes, I remember. You are the little Italian tambourine girl. Yes, you may go. See if you can get that pretty cousin of yours to come and live here."

"She would like to, sir, but her mother won't let her."

"Very well. Go."

And he resumed his work. "7 and 5 are 12, and 8 are 20; two 1's are 2—"

"Yes, but two ones want to be made one."

"How is that—what do you want?"

Reader, will you just turn to the illustration of the couple that now presented themselves as candidates for matrimony.

The delineator and engraver have made one of the most perfect daguerreian pictures ever got up from description.

"What do you want of me?"

"We want to be married, sir."

"Want to be married—what for?"

"Why, you see, we don't think it is right for us to be living together this way any longer, and we have been talking over the matter to-day, and you see——"

"Yes, yes, I see you have been talking over the matter over the bottle, and have come to a sort of drunken conclusion to get married. When you get sober, you will both repent it, probably."

"No, sir, we are not very drunk now, not so drunk but what we can think, and we don't think we are doing right—we are not doing as we were brought up to do by pious parents. We have been reading about the good things you have done for just such poor outcasts as we are, and we want you to try and do something for us."

"Read! can you read? Do you read the Bible?"

"Well, not much lately, but we read the newspapers, and sometimes we read something good in them. How can we read the Bible when we are drunk?"

"Do you think getting married will keep you from getting drunk?"

"Yes, for we are going to take the pledge too, and we shall keep it, depend upon that."

"Suppose you take the pledge and try that first, and if you

can keep it till you can wash some of the dirt away, and get some clothes on, then I will marry you."

"No; that won't do. I shall get to thinking what a poor, dirty, miserable wretch I am, and how I am living with this woman, who is not a bad woman by nature; and then I will drink, and then she will drink—oh, cursed rum!—and what is to prevent us? But if we were married, my wife, yes, Mr. Pease, my wife, would say, 'Thomas'—she would not say, 'Tom, you dirty brute,'—'don't be tempted;' and who knows but we might be somebody yet—somebody that our own mothers would not be ashamed of?"

Here the woman, who had been silent and rather moody, burst into a violent flood of tears, crying, "Mother, mother, I know not whether she is alive or not, and dare not inquire; but if we were married and reformed, I would make her happy once more."

"I could no longer resist the appeal," said Mr. P., "and determined to give them a trial. I have married a good many poor, wretched-looking couples, but none that looked quite so much so as this. The man was hatless and shoeless, without coat or vest, with long hair and beard grimed with dirt. He was by trade a bricklayer, one of the best in the city. The woman wore the last remains of a silk bonnet, and something that might pass for shoes, and an old, very old dress, once a rich merino, apparently without any under garments."

"Your name is Thomas—Thomas what?"

"Elting, sir. Thomas Elting, a good, true name and true man; that is, shall be, if you marry us."

"Well, well. I am going to marry you."

"Are you? There, Mag, I told you so."

"Don't call me Mag. If I am going to be married, it shall be by my right name, the one my mother gave me."

"Not Mag? Well, I never knew that."

"Now, Thomas, hold your tongue, you talk too much. What is your name?"

"Matilda. Must I tell you the other? Yes, I will, and I never will disgrace it. I don't think, I should ever have been as bad if I had kept it. That bad woman who first tempted me to ruin, made me take a false name. They always do that, sir, and so she said I must take another name, I did not know what for then; and so they called me Mag, and that is the name he knows me by, and I never would have told him my right name, only that we are going to get married, and reform."

Could they do it—could beings sunk so low, reform? We shall see.

"It is a bad thing, sir, for a girl to give up her name unless for that of a good husband. Matilda Morgan. Nobody that is good knows me by any other name in this bad city."

Yes, it is a bad thing for a girl to give up her own name for a fictitious one. I could tell a touching story of an instance of a poor sewing woman, who went to one of these name-changing houses to work, not to sin, who was coaxed to be called Lucy, instead of her own sweet name of Athalia, and how she was accidentally discovered and rescued from the very jaws of ruin by her own uncle. But not now, I must

THE TWO PENNY MARRIAGE COUPLE.—*Page* 95.

go on with the marriage. The bride and bridegroom are waiting, and the reader for a share of the feast.

"Now I am going to join you two in wedlock; it cannot make you worse, it may better. Look me in the face. Now, Matilda and Thomas, take each other by the right hand, look at me, while I unite you in the holy bonds of marriage by God's ordinance. Do you think you are sufficiently sober to comprehend its solemnity?"

"Yes, sir."

"Marriage being one of God's holy ordinances, cannot be kept in sin, misery, filth, and drunkenness. Thomas, will you take Matilda to be your lawful, true, only, wedded wife?"

"Yes, sir."

"You promise that you will live with her, in sickness as well as health, and nourish, protect, and comfort her as your true and faithful wife; that you will be to her a true and faithful husband; that you will not get drunk, and will clothe yourself and keep clean?"

"So I will."

"Never mind answering until I get through. You promise to abstain totally from every kind of drink that intoxicates, and treat this woman kindly, affectionately, and love her as a husband should love his wedded wife. Now, all of this will you, here before me as the servant of the Most High,—here, in the sight of God, in heaven, most faithfully promise, if I give you this woman to be your wedded wife?"

"Yes, I will."

"And you, Matilda, on your part, will you promise the same, and be a true wife to this man?"

"I will try, sir."

"But do you promise all this faithfully?"

"Yes, sir, I will."

It was a woman's "I will," spoken right out with a good, hearty emphasis, that told, as it always tells, the faith and truth of woman, when she says, "I will."

"Then I pronounce you man and wife."

"Now, Thomas," says the new wife, after I had made out the certificate and given it to her, with an injunction to keep it safely—"now pay Mr. Pease, and let us go home and break the bottle." Thomas felt first in the right pocket, then the left, then back to the right, then he examined the watch fob.

It is probable that the former owner of this principal article of his wardrobe, owned a watch. It is more likely that the present owner had been often in the hands of the watch, than that he had often had a watch in his hands. He was evidently searching for lost treasures.

"Why, where is it?" says she. "You had two dollars this morning."

"Yes, I know it; but I have only got two cents this evening. There, Mr. Pease, take them. It is all I have got in the world—what more can I give?"

Sure enough; what could he do more? He took them and prayed over them, that in parting with the last penny, this couple might have parted with a vice—a wicked, foolish practice, which had reduced them to such a degree of poverty and wretchedness, that the monster power of rum could hardly send its victims lower.

So, by a few words, I hope, words of power to do good, Thomas and Matilda, long known as, drunken Tom and Mag, were transformed into Mr. and Mrs. Elting, and having grown somewhat more sober while in the house, seemed to fully understand their new position, and all the obligations they had taken upon themselves.

"For a few days," said Mr. P., "I thought occasionally of this two-penny marriage, and then it became absorbed with a thousand other scenes of wretchedness which I have witnessed since I have lived in this centre of city misery. Time wore on, and I married many other couples; often those who came in their carriage and left a golden marriage fee—a delicate way of giving to the needy—but among all, I had never performed the rite for a couple quite so low as that of this two-penny fee, and I resolved I never would again. At length, however, I had a call from a full match to them, which I refused."

"Why do you come to me to be married, my friend?" said I to the man. "You are both too poor to live separate; and, besides, you are both terrible drunkards, I know you are."

"That is just what we want to get married for, and take the pledge."

"Take that first."

"No; we must take all together—nothing else will save us."

"Will that?"

"It did one of my friends."

"Well, then, go and bring that friend here; let me see and hear how much it saved him, and then I will make up my mind what to do. If I can do you any good, I want to do it."

"My friend is at work—he has got a good job and several hands working for him, and is making money, and won't quit till night. Shall I come this evening?"

"Yes, I will stay at home and wait for you."

He little expected to see him again, but about eight o'clock the servant said that man and his girl, with a *gentleman* and *lady*, were waiting in the reception room. He told him to ask the lady and gentleman to walk up to the parlor and sit a moment, while he sent the candidates for marriage away, being determined never to unite another drunken couple, not dreaming that there was any sympathy between the parties. But they would not come up; they wanted to see that couple married. So he went down, and found the squalidly wretched pair, that had been there in the morning, in conversation, and apparently very friendly and intimate, with the lady and gentleman. He had the appearance of a well dressed laboring man, for he wore a fine black coat, silk vest, gold watch-chain, clean white shirt and cravat, polished calf-skin boots; and his wife was just as neat and tidily dressed as anybody's wife, and her face beamed with intelligence, and the way in which she clung to the arm of her husband, as she seemed to shrink out of sight, told that she was a loving as well as a pretty wife.

"This couple," said the gentleman, "have come to be married."

"Yes, I know it," said Mr. P., "and I have refused. Look at them; do they look like fit subjects for such a holy ordinance? God never intended those, whom he created in his own image, should live in matrimony like this man and woman. I cannot marry them."

"Cannot! Why not? You married us when we were worse off—more dirty—worse clothed, and more intoxicated."

"The woman shrunk back a little more out of sight. I saw she trembled violently, and put her clean cambric handkerchief up to her eyes."

"What could it mean? Married them when worse off? Who were they?"

"Have you forgotten us?" said the woman, taking my hands in hers, and dropping on her knees; "have you forgotten drunken Tom and Mag? We have never forgotten you, but pray for you every day!"

"If you have forgotten them, you have not forgotten the two-penny marriage. No wonder you did not know us. I told Matilda she need not be afraid, or ashamed, if you did know her. But I knew you would not. How could you? We were in rags and dirt then. Look at us now. All your work, sir. All the blessing of the pledge and that marriage, and that good advice you gave us. Look at this suit of clothes, and her dress—all Matilda's work, every stitch of it. Come and look at our house, as neat as she is. Everything in it to make a comfortable home; and, oh! sir, there is a cradle in our bedroom. Five hundred dollars already in bank, and I shall add as much more next week when I finish my job. So much for one year of a sober life, and a faithful, honest, good wife. Now, this man is as good a workman as I am, only he is bound down with the galling fetters of drunkenness, and living with a woman as I did, only worse, for they have two children. What will they be, if they chance to live, and grow up to womanhood in Cow Bay? Now he has made up his mind to try to be a man again—he is a beast now—he thinks that he can reform just as well as me; but he thinks he must take the pledge of the same man, and have his first effort sanctified with the same blessing, and then, with a good resolution, and Matilda and me to watch over them, I do believe they will succeed."

So they did. So may others, by the same means.

They were married, solemnly, impressively, solemnly married; and pledged to total abstinence in the most earnest manner; and promised most faithfully, not only to keep the pledge, but to do unto others, as Elting had done unto them. Both promises you have seen that they have kept well.

As they were parting, Elting slipped something into Nolan's hand, and told him to pay the marriage fee.

"I thought," said the missionary, "of the two pennies, and expected nothing more, and therefore was not disappointed when he handed me the two reddish-looking coins. I thought, well, they are bright, new looking cents, at any rate, and I hope their lives will be like them. I was in hopes that it might have been a couple of dollars this time, but I said nothing, and we parted with a mutual God bless you. When I went up stairs, I tossed the coin into my wife's lap, with the remark, "two pennies again, my dear."

"Two pennies! Why, husband, they are eagles—real golden eagles. What a deal of good they will do. What blessings have followed that act."

And what blessings did follow the last one; will always follow the pledge faithfully kept; will always follow a well formed, faithfully kept union, even if it is a "two-penny marriage."

CHAPTER VI.

THE HOME OF LITTLE KATY.

"There is a special Providence in the fall of a sparrow."

"He, that of the greatest works is finisher,
Oft does them by the weakest minister."

I HAVE still another little episode in this life drama—a scene in one of the acts, which we may as well put upon the stage at this point of the story, though it is quite unconnected with those that immediately precede it; yet you will find a character here, in whom you have, perhaps, taken some interest. It is the termination of the story of the Hot Corn girl, whom you read about in chapter second, whose portrait you have already looked at in the frontispiece of this volume.

You have read in the story of Little Katy, what a world of cheap happiness can be bought with a shilling. No one of the thousand silver coins wasted that night in hotel, saloon, bar-room, grocery, or rum hole, gave the waster half the pleasure that that shilling gave to three individuals—he that gave and those who received. No ice-cream, cake, jelly, or health-destroying candy, tasted half so sweet as the bread purchased with that sixpence.

No man ever made so small an investment, that paid so well, both in a pecuniary point of view and large increase of human happiness, for it has been the means of waking up benevolence, not dead but sleeping, to look about and inquire, what shall I do to remove this misery-producing curse from among us? Thousands have read the story of Little Katy, and thousands of little hearts have been touched. Many hands have been opened—more will be. These little stories, detail ing some of the sufferings which crime and misery bring upon the poor of this city, will be, as some of them already have been, read with tearful eyes. You have read the story of a poor neglected child of a drunken mother—not always so—wasting her young life away with no object but to live, with no thought of death. It is a sad tale, and it is not yet finished. The next night after the interview with that neglected, ill-used little girl, the same plaintive cry of "Hot corn, hot corn!—here's your nice hot corn!" came up through our open window, on the midnight air, while the rain came dripping down from the overcharged clouds, in just sufficient quantities to wet the thin single garment of the owner of that sweet young voice, without giving her an acceptable excuse for leaving her post before her hard task was completed.

At length the voice grew faint, and then ceased altogether, and then I knew that exhausted nature slept—that a tender house-plant was exposed to the chilling influence of a night rain—that an innocent girl had the curb-stone for a bed and an iron post for a pillow—that by and by she would awaken, not invigorated with refreshing slumber, but poisoned with the sleep-inhaled miasma of the filth-reeking gutter at her feet, which may be breathed with impunity awake, but like the malaria of our southern coast, is death to the sleeper.* Not soothed by a dreamy consciousness of hearing a mother's voice tuning a soft lullaby of

"Hush, my child, lie still and slumber;"

but starting like a sentinel upon a savage frontier post, with alarm at having slept; shivering with night air and fear, and, finally, compelled to go home, trembling like a culprit, to hear the harsh words of a mother—yes, a mother—but oh! what a mother—cursing her for not performing an impossibility, because exhausted nature slept—because her child had not made a profit which would have enabled her more freely to indulge in the soul and body-destroying vice of drunkenness, to which she had fallen from an estate, when "my carriage" was one of the "household words" which used to greet the young ears of that poor little death-stricken, neglected, street sufferer.

* On many of the Rice and Sea Island plantations in South Carolina and Georgia, in fact upon almost all the coast lands of these States, the malaria is so deadly in its effects upon the sleeper, that every effort is made to keep awake by those who are accidentally exposed for a single night to its influence. Many of the most beautiful residences in the vicinity of Charleston, are uninhabited by white persons in summer. The negroes are not at all, or only slightly affected. The overseers often have a little cabin in the most convenient pine woods, to which they retire before nightfall.

No doubt, though to a less deadly degree, the malaria arises from the filth in our dirty streets, killing its thousands of little children every year.

It was past midnight when she awoke, and found herself, with a desperate effort, just able to reach the bottom of the rickety stairs which led to her *home*. We shall not go up now. In a little while, reader, you shall see where live the city poor.

You shall go with me at midnight to the *Home of little Katy*. You shall see where she lies upon her straw pallet in a miserable garret; yet she was born in as rich a chamber as you or you, who tread upon soft Turkey carpets when you go to your downy couches.

Wait a little.

Tired—worn with the daily toil—for such is the work of an editor who caters for the appetites of his morning readers—I was not present the next night to note the absence of that cry from its accustomed spot; but the next and next, and still on, I listened in vain—that voice was not there. True, the same hot-corn cry came floating upon the evening breeze across the park, or wormed its way from some cracked-fiddle voice down the street, up and around the corner, or out of some dark alley, with a broken English accent, that sounded almost as much like "lager bier" as it did like the commodity the immigrant, struggling to eke out his precarious existence, wished to sell. All over this great poverty-burdened, and wicked waste, extravagant city, at this season, that cry goes up, nightly proclaiming one of the habits of this late-supper eating people.

Yes, I missed that cry. "Hot Corn" was no longer like the

music of a stringed instrument to a weary man, for the treble-string was broken, and, for me the harmony spoiled.

Who shall say there is not music in those two little words? "Hot Corn" shall yet be trilled from boudoir and parlor, as fairy fingers run over the piano keys. Hot Corn! Hot Corn! shall yet be the chorus of the minstrel's song, and hot tears shall flow at the remembrance of "Little Katy." But that one song had ceased. That voice came not upon my listening ear.

What was that voice to me? It was but one in a thousand, just as miserable, which may be daily heard where human misery has its abode. That voice, as some others have, did not haunt me, but its absence, in spite of all reasoning, made me feel uneasy. I do not believe in spiritual manifestations half as strongly as some of the costermongers of the fruits of other men's brains, who eke out their existence by retailing petty scandal to long-eared listeners, would have them believe; yet I do believe there is a spirit in man, not yet made manifest, which makes us yearn after coexisting spirits in this sphere and in this life, and that there is no need of going beyond it, after strange idols.

I shall not stop to inquire whether it was a spirit of "the first, third or sixth sphere," that prompted me, as I left my desk one evening, to go down among the abodes of the poor, with a feeling of certainty that I should see or hear something of the lost voice, or what spirit led me on; perhaps it was the spirit of curiosity; no matter, it led, and I followed, in the road

I had seen that little one go before—it was my only cue—I knew no name—had no number, nor knew any one that knew her whom I was going to find. Yes, I knew that good Missionary; and she had told me of the good words which he had spoken; but would he know her from the hundred just like her? Perhaps. It will cost nothing to inquire. I went down Centre street with a light heart; I turned into Cross street with a step buoyed with hope; I stood at the corner of Little-Water street, and looked around inquiringly of the spirit, and mentally said, "which way now?" The answer was a far-off scream of despair. I stood still with an open ear, for the sound of prayer, followed by a sweet hymn of praise to God, went up from the site of the Old Brewery, in which I joined, thankful that that was no longer the abode of all the worst crimes ever concentrated under one roof. Hark! a step approaches. My unseen guide whispered, "ask him." It were a curious question to ask a stranger, in such a strange place, particularly one like him, haggard with over much care, toil, or mental labor. Prematurely old, his days shortened by overwork in his young years, as his furrowed face and almost frenzied eye hurriedly indicate, as we see the flash of the lamp upon his dark visage, as he approaches with that peculiar American step which impels the body forward at railroad speed. Shall I get out of his way before he walks over me? What if he is a crazy man? No; the spirit was right—no false raps here. It is that good missionary. That man who has done more to reform that den of crime, the Five Points of New-York, than all the Municipal Authorities of this Police-hunting, and Prisonpunishing city, where misfortune is deemed a crime, or the unfortunate driven to it, by the way they are treated with harsh words, damp cells—death cells— and cold prison-bars, instead of being reformed, or strengthened in their resolution to reform, by kind words; means to earn food, rather than forced to steal it; by schools and infant-teaching, rather than old offenders-punishing.

"Sir," said Mr. Pease, "what brings you here at this time of night, for I know there is an object; can I aid you?"

"Perhaps, I don't know—a foolish whim—a little child—one of the miserable, with a drunken mother."

"Come with me, then. There are many such. I am just going to visit one, who will die before morning—a sweet little girl, born in better days, and dying now—but you shall see, and then we will talk about the one you would seek to save."

We were soon treading a narrow alley, where pestilence walketh in darkness; and crime, wretched poverty, and filthy misery, go hand in hand to destruction.

"Behold," said my friend, "the fruits of our city excise. Here is the profit of money spent for license to kill the body and damn the soul." Proven by the awful curses and loud blows of a drunken husband upon a wife, once an ornament of society, and exemplary member of a Christian church, that came up out of one of the low cellars, which human beings call by the holy name of home!

The fetid odor of this filthy lane had been made more fetid by the late and almost scalding hot rains, until it seemed to us that such an air was only fit for a charnel house. With the thermometer at 83, at midnight, how could men live in such a place, below the surface of the earth? Has rum rendered them proof against the effect of carbonic acid gas?

We groped our way along to the foot of an outside staircase, where our conductor paused for a moment, calling my attention to the spot. "Here," said Mr. Pease, "the little sufferer we are going to see, fainted a few nights ago, and lay all night exposed to the rain, where she was found and beaten in the morning by her miserable mother, just then coming home from a night of debauch and licentiousness, with a man who would be ashamed to visit her in her habitation, or have 'the world' know that he consorted with a street wanderer."

"Beat her! for what?"

"Because she had not sold all her corn, which she had been sent out with the evening before. Poor thing, she had fallen asleep, and some villain had robbed her of her little store, and, as it is with greater crimes, the wicked escaped and the innocent suffered."

I thought aloud:

"Great and unknown cause, hast thou brought me to her very door?"

My friend stared, but did not comprehend the expression. "Be careful," said he, "the stairs are very old, and slippery."

"Beat her?" said I, without regarding what he was saying.

"Yes, beat her, while she was in a fever of delirium, from which she has never rallied. She has never spoken rationally, since she was taken. Her constant prayer seems to be to see some particular person before she dies.

"'Oh, if I could see him once more—there—there—that is him—no, no, he did not speak that way to me—he did not curse and beat me.'

"Such is her conversation, and that induced her mother to send for me, but I was not the man. 'Will he come?' she says, every time I visit her; for, thinking to soothe and comfort her, I promised to bring him."

We had reached the top of the stairs, and stood a moment at the open door, where sin and misery dwelt, where sickness had come, and where death would soon enter.

"Will he come?"

A faint voice came up from a low bed in one corner, seen by the very dim light of a miserable lamp.

That voice. I could not be mistaken. I could not enter. Let me wait a moment in the open air, for there is a choking sensation coming over me.

"Come in," said my friend.

"Will he come?"

Two hands were stretched out imploringly towards the Missionary, as the sound of his voice was recognised.

"She is much weaker to-night," said her mother, in quite a lady-like manner, for the sense of her drunken wrong to her dying child had kept her sober, ever since she had been sick; "but she is quite delirious, and all the time talking about that man who spoke kindly to her one night in the Park, and gave her money to buy bread."

"Will he come?"

"Yes, yes; through the guidance of the good spirit that rules the world, and leads us by unseen paths, through dark places, for His own wise purposes, *he has come.*"

The little emaciated form started up in bed, and a pair of beautiful, soft blue eyes glanced around the room, peering through the semi-darkness, as if in search of something heard but unseen.

"Katy, darling," said the mother, "what is the matter?"

"Where is he, mother? He is here. I heard him speak."

"Yes, yes, sweet little innocent, he is here, kneeling by your bedside. There, lay down, you are very sick."

"Only once, just once, let me put my arms around your neck, and kiss you, just as I used to kiss papa. I had a papa once, when we lived in the big house—there, there. Oh, I did want to see you, to thank you for the bread and the cakes; I was very hungry, and it did taste so good—and little Sis, she waked up, and she eat and eat, and after a while she went to sleep with a piece in her hand, and I went to sleep; hav'n't I been asleep a good while? I thought I was asleep in the Park, and somebody stole all my corn, and my mother whipt me for it, but I could not help it. Oh dear, I feel sleepy now. I can't talk any more. I am very tired. I cannot see; the candle has gone out. I think I am going to die. I thank you; I wanted to thank you for the bread—I thought you would not come. Good bye—Sissy, good bye. Sissy—you will come—mother—don't—drink—any more—Mother—good b—."

"'Tis the last of earth," said the good man at our side—"let us pray."

Reader, Christian reader; little Katy is in her grave. Prayers for her are unavailing. There are in this city a thousand just such cases. Prayers for them are unavailing. Faith without works, works not reform. A faithful, prayerful resolution, to work out that reform which will save you from reading the recital of such scenes—such fruits of the rum trade as this before you, will work together for your own and others' good. Go forth and listen. If you hear a little voice crying *Hot Corn!* think of poor Katy, and of the hosts of innocents slain by that remorseless tyrant—rum. Go forth and seek a better spirit to rule over us. Cry aloud, "Will he come," and the answer will be, "Yes, yes, he is here."

The commendation given to these stories, as they were published in the *Tribune*, was an inducement for me to "keep the cry of *Hot Corn* before the people," for I saw that they appreciated my labors; and I set about collecting other materials, and writing out notes made during many a night-watch among the habitations of men, yet the abodes of misery, with which this city abounds.

Many an anxious mind, after conning the preceding chapters, has yearned after further knowledge touching the things therein hinted at. Many have asked to know more of "Sissy," and Little Katy's mother. It is a laudable curiosity; it shall be gratified in due time. I have other stories—other scenes where you may stop a moment and drop a tear, and then we will walk on with our Life Scenes. First we will finish that of Maggie's mother.

CHAPTER VII.

MAGGIE'S MOTHER.

Let go thy hold—the glass has run out its sands—the wheel goes down hill. There is a time to mourn.

REAGAN took the pledge, and took up his residence at that house of the destitute. At first, he did not ask to live with his wife. He said, he was not worthy of her. He begged Tom to write to Maggie: "I know it will make her happy to learn that I am here." So it did. The rose had another rival now. Her cheeks blossomed afresh. Reagan worked busily—he did up a great many little jobs of joiner-work; and when there was nothing more to do at that, he said, let me go into the bake-shop, shoe-shop, anywhere. I will sit down with those women and use the needle, rather than be idle, or venture out where tempters will beset me. So he went on for some time, till he grew stronger and gained more confidence—his wife strengthened him by her counsel, and then he ventured out to work where he could earn good wages. It was curious to see him go quite out of his way, around a whole square, perhaps, to avoid going by one of his old haunts.

"I have suffered so much," said he to me one day, "from the temptation of these places, where the liquor is placed in our sight on purpose to allure and whet our depraved appetites, that it is no wonder that the poor inebriate loses his balance and falls into the abyss. If there was no liquor in sight, there would be no danger of our falling back into old habits. I never should think of going to look after it. The danger is when it is thrust right under my nose. Oh, that these rum shops might be shut up, or at least, kept out of sight!"

This was the earnest prayer of one who knew the demon power of temptation which one, who is trying to reform, has constantly to combat with.

Those who sell liquor know the advantage to them of this temptation. So they fix up the street corners with all the enticing attractions of artistic skill. The cool ice water; the free lunch; the ever-burning light for the smoker's convenience; the arm-chair and easy lounge, and cool room in summer, or well heated one in winter; the ever open, always free resting-place for the tired walker, or ennui-tormented genteel loafer, are only a few of the inducements to just "step in a moment;" and then the old appetite is aroused by the sight and smell of liquor in the glistening array of cut glass, and by the influence of a score of old companions standing before the bar—they will stand before another bar hereafter—or sitting at the little white marble tables, sipping or sucking "sherry cobblers" and "mint juleps" through a glass "straw."

Woe to the tired walker who has been tempted into one of these invitingly open rooms. If he has the power to resist his own inclination to drink, he may not have enough to resist the persuasion of half a dozen of his acquaintances, or the force of crazed brains and strong hands, by which he is dragged up and held, while they merit the curse denounced upon those who "put the cup to their neighbor's lips." Perhaps he will be taunted with meanness for coming in to drink water and rest himself, "and not patronise the house."

From this, those of us who desire to see those places of temptation shut up, may take the hint.

Let reading rooms be opened, free to all who choose to come in and read the papers, drink ice water, and enjoy their rest in the shade, or partake of the comforts of a warm room, for a five cent fee. A coffee and tea room, strictly so, may be attached. How much better than drinking such liquor as those who visit all our public places must do, or be set down as mean. "Let them stay at home," is a common answer to those who say they fell by the temptations of such places.

"Suppose," said Jim Reagan to me one day, "that we have no home. That was my case when I was a young man. I lived in a common boarding-house; in my little uncomfortable room I would not stay; where else had I to go but the public bar room, and there I learned to drink; I was a good fellow then; a genteel young man, and married a genteel young girl; I did not go down all at once—it was step by step, slow but sure—to Cale Jones's grocery and the Centre street cellar."

True, thought I, as I entered the front door of the first hotel in this great metropolis, the largest in America, and looked through the splendid marble hall, two hundred feet long, lighted by glittering chandeliers, into the immense drinking saloon of that fashionable place of resort; and I said to myself, "some of these fine forms of men, clothed in fine linen and rich broad cloth, may some day fall as low as thee, poor Jim Reagan. You began your course in just such a genteel drinking room."

"Yes," says he, "and the first drink I ever took in one, for I was brought up a temperance boy, I was dragged up by the strength of two companions, and held while the bar-keeper baptised me, as he called it, by pouring the liquor down my throat, over my head, and saturating my clothes till the smell made me sick, and then they gave me more to settle it. 'A hair of the same dog,' said they, 'will cure the bite.' Bite it was. No mad dog's bite ever caused more sin and sorrow than that bite did me. We cry, 'mad dog,' and kill the poor brute; the worse than brute we 'license' to live."

Thus he would sit and talk by the hour. "If I can only keep out of the way of the tempters," said he, "I never shall drink again."

He was now accumulating money; he always came home to sleep, "for," says he, "I feel, as sure as I enter this door, that I am safe."

It was determined, as soon as Maggie came again, that they would go to keeping house. "If that blessed child was only with me," said the father, as the tears rolled down his furrowed cheeks, "I should feel as though I had a shield through which none of these traffickers in human souls could reach me. My wife is like an aged counsellor, there is wisdom in her every word, but she cannot go out through the streets, leaning upon my arm, still full of manly strength, like Maggie, while I lean upon her still greater strength—the strength and might of a strong mind."

"Here is a letter from our dear child," said Mrs. Reagan to her husband, one evening as he came in from work. "Sit down and read it aloud, for some how, my old eyes get dim every time I try; I cannot imagine what is the matter with them."

I can. They were full of tears. Strange, that we shed bitter and sweet water from the same fountain.

Reagan put on his spectacles, took the letter, looked at the first words, took them off, wiped the glasses, looked again, repeated the operation, laid both letter and spectacles upon the table, got up and walked the room back and forth, then he tried to speak—to utter the first words of that letter; if he could get over that he could go on, but he could not, they stuck in his throat. At length he got them up—"Dear father and mother, I am coming home to kiss you both." Simple words! Common every-day words. But they were strong words, for they had overcome the strength of a strong man, and he fell upon his wife's neck and wept like a child.

"Such words to me—me who have kicked, and cuffed, and froze, and starved, and abused that child for years. Oh, God, preserve my life to make her ample amends for my wrongs and her love! Oh, God, preserve her life to make us both happy, and drop a tear at our grave!"

Prayer calms the spirit. Realization and acknowledgment of sin soothes the soul.

Reagan could now read the letter without difficulty. His spectacles did not need wiping again. It was dated,

"Near KATONA, Westchester County, New York.

"DEAR FATHER AND MOTHER:

"I am coming home to kiss you both. I don't know but I shall kiss Tom, for he has written me all about it—I know it all—I know how you was brought in, and how you took the pledge, and how you have kept it, and how industrious you have been, and how you have saved your money, and how you want to go to housekeeping again, and all about it—I know it all. Tom writes me every week. He is a good boy. Well, in two months I am coming down. You need not look for me before, and then, if you want me, I will come and live with you."

"If we want her! Did you ever hear the like? But, then, what is she to do? She is a big girl now, and must not be idle. I wish she had a trade. Every child ought to have a trade."

"Well, well, wife, let us have the balance of the letter."

"Yes, yes, go on; you need not mind what I say. Go on."

"Let me see; where was I? 'Come and live with you,' that's it."

"And now I must tell you such a piece of news—good news. Oh, it was a good thing I came up here. I have got a trade—a trade that will support us all when you get so you cannot work."

"Heaven bless the girl, what is it?"

"Do wait, wife, and you shall hear."

"It is a nice, genteel trade, too. Now we will take a house, and father will work at his trade, and mother will do the house-work, and I will work at my trade, and we shall live so happy."

"So we shall. But, dear me, why don't she tell what it is?"

"So she will if you let me alone. A girl must have her own way to tell it; probably she will do that in a postscript."

"Well, read on. I am so impatient."

"Perhaps you would like to know what my trade is?"

"Why to be sure we should. Why don't she tell?"

"So I will tell you. I am a stock-maker—those things the gentlemen wear round their necks. And it is very curious how I learned the trade. A lady from New York—oh, she is a lady!—came up here on a visit, and for work she brought along some stocks to make. She lives in New York. I believe she keeps a few boarders, and makes stocks. She is a widow lady, quite young, and very pretty, only she is in bad health; she has no family, only her uncle, who is an old bachelor—a nice old gentleman, who has adopted her as his daughter, and is going to give her all he has when he dies. She has no father and mother, as I have, and no brothers and sisters; nobody to love but the old uncle—he does love her, so do I. I did not at first. I was afraid of her.

I thought she was some grand city lady; and she used to sit and sew in her room, only when her uncle—Papa she calls him, and he calls her daughter—'Athalia, daughter,' so sweet; is it not a sweet name? Her name is Athalia Morgan—"

"Morgan, Morgan—Athalia Morgan. I will warrant it is she. Don't you remember, wife, that old Morgan, the great shipping merchant? his son married a sewing girl; and his sister married George Wendall."

"Oh, oh, how singular! It was she that was talking when Maggie took me into the temperance meeting that night, telling how her husband died. And now Maggie has met with another of the family. And her husband must be dead too."

"Yes, he died just as miserable a death as Wendall. Let us read on and see what of his wife. I hope he did not drag her down with him as I did mine."

"James, James, you are not to speak of anything that is past."

"Well, well," and he brushed away another tear and read on:

"After she had been here a few days, our folks told her about me, and how I used to run the streets, and how I got into the House of Industry, and how they got me from there, and what a good girl I had been—yes, they did—and then Mrs. Morgan, she began to talk to me so kindly; and then I told her everything about myself, and some about you, and she told me a great many things about herself. Oh, it would be such a story to put in a book. And then she grew as fond of me as I was of her. And every day when I had my work done, and every evening, I used to be up in her room, and she showed me all about her work, and I used to help her, and now she declares that I can make just as good a stock as she can, and almost as fast. She can make eight in a day; when I help her, odd times and evenings, she can make twelve. Last week she made, with what I did, seventy-two, and put them all in a box. How nice they do look! That is seventy-two York shillings—nine dollars! And she says when I come home to live, she will recommend me—I must have a good recommend to get work—when I can get just as much such work as I can do. Oh, but she is a good woman! I guess you would cry though as much as I have, to hear her story. I will tell it you some day. Mrs. Morgan is going down to-morrow. I wish I was. But I cannot. In two months my time is up; then you will see me. Now, good night. Say 'good by' to Tom for me. Kiss mother, father, and ever love your

"MAGGIE."

"Oh, James, something tells me that if she don't come before that, I never shall see her. But you will be happy with her. You will live a long life, I hope, for her to bless and comfort you in your old age. You are not so old and so broken down as I am."

"All my fault, all my fault. If I had treated you as a rational man should treat a wife, you would not be so broken down now."

"You must not look back. Look ahead and aloft. Think what a treasure of a daughter you have got. How I should like to see her once more before I go to my rest, and give her my blessing; and oh! how I should like to see that blessed woman, that Mrs. Morgan. I want to bring her and Elsie together, and make peace on earth as there will be in heaven, where I hope to meet them both. They will soon follow. This life, at best, is short. Mine will be, I am sure."

"Don't have such gloomy forebodings, wife; it seems to me that you were never in better health."

"I know it, and never more happy."

This was on Thursday evening. On Saturday evening everybody was astonished to see Maggie come bounding in, with a step as light and quick as a playful lamb.

"Where's mother? Is she well? Has anything happened? Where is father? Is everything all right with him?" were the questions she asked, in such rapid succession that nobody could answer any one of them.

"Where is Tom? Is he well? Where is Mr. Pease and Mrs. Pease? Are they well? Is mother in the kitchen?"

"Yes, yes, yes, yes, to the whole string."

Away she went, three stairs at a time, and then she almost overwhelmed her mother with kisses and questions; and up she went to the third story, and there was father in his room, reading the Bible. When had she ever seen that before? The last time she saw him, he was so dreadfully intoxicated that he did not know his own child, that was lifting him out of the gutter. Now he was sober, well clothed, cheerful, and happy. As she opened the door he read:

"Who hath woe? who hath sorrow? who hath contentions? who hath babbling? who hath wounds without cause? who hath redness of eyes?

"They that tarry long at the wine; they that go to seek mixed wine.

"Look not thou upon the wine when it is red; when it giveth his color in the cup; when it moveth itself aright.

"At the last it biteth like a serpent and stingeth like an adder.

"Thine eyes shall behold strange women, and—"

And he looked up, as his ear caught a little rustle of a woman's clothes, and his eyes beheld a strange woman—a beautiful, neatly-dressed young woman, with laughing, bright eyes and rosy cheeks, and such a saucy little straw hat, so tastily trimmed—Mrs. Morgan did that—and altogether such a lady-like girl, that he did not recognise her, and he turned his eyes again to the book and repeated:

"Thine eyes shall behold strange women—"

"Father!"

The book dropped from his knees to the floor, as he sprang towards her.

"Am I so strange, father, that you did not know me?"

"Indeed, my daughter, I was afraid to speak; I did not know but a strange woman had been sent to punish me, to 'sting me like an adder.' Oh, Maggie, you don't know how I feel that I deserve it. And yet you are so good. You are a strange woman. It is strange, passing strange, to think that my daughter, my little neglected, dirty, ragged, mischievous—"

"Wild Maggie, father."

"Yes, she had run wild; should be the lovely—you do look lovely, Maggie—girl now in my arms. Oh, Maggie! Maggie! this is all your work."

"No, no, father; you must give the good Missionary his share of the credit; and the good people all over the country who have sent him money and clothes to feed and clothe the naked, and reform the drunkard. What should we have been to-day, if he had not come to live in the Five Points, father?"

"I should have been in my grave; a poor, miserable drunkard's grave; it is awful to think where else I should have been."

"Well, well, father, you are happy now,"

"Yes, I am, and so is mother, and we shall be more so when we get a home of our own, and all live together. Why, Maggie, why, who did dress you up so neat?"

"Oh, my new friend I wrote you about, Mrs. Morgan—you got my letter—yes—well, I do wish you could see her, she is such a good woman."

So they talked on, and then the old lady came up, and then Maggie told how they had arranged it all. On Monday, father was to see if he could find a couple of nice rooms, and Maggie was going to see Mrs. Morgan, for Mrs. Morgan's old uncle had told Maggie, that whenever she wanted to go to keeping house, to come to him, she did not know what for, but she was sure it was something good, for he was a good man, but he never let anybody know what he did for poor folks, he did love to do things in his own way. And Mrs. Morgan was going to write up to the people where she lived, and if father and mother wanted her, they would let her come before her time was up.

"Your father will want you."

"Will you, too? Do not you want me, mother?"

"I do not know, Maggie, I can hardly tell. Who can tell what a day may bring forth. I am glad to see you; I have been praying all day, that the good Spirit would direct your steps hither to-day."

"Did you pray that last night?"

"Yes."

"And this morning?"

"Yes."

"I thought so—I felt it, all night, all the morning, just as though a little stream of fire was running through me, all over; now in my head, now in my heart, now in my very fingers' ends; now I started at a whisper in my ear, that sounded just like mother, saying, 'Oh, Maggie! Oh, that she would come! Oh, that I could see her once more!' and then I felt as though I must come. I was afraid something was going to happen. But now I find you all well, I see what a foolish girl I have been."

"No, Maggie, not foolish, not foolish; something tells me that you have only obeyed the dictates of a good heart, guided by an invisible power. But we will not talk about it any more now. I have arranged a place for you to sleep to-night, for the house is very full, and we can scarcely find beds for those we have, and there are applications for more poor children every day. Do you remember that pretty little Italian beggar girl, Madalina, that you used to go out with sometimes? She is going to sleep in that little room, and you may sleep with her."

"Oh, mother, she is so dirty!"

"She used to be, she is not so now. She was so when she ran the streets, just like another little girl."

"Oh, mother, I know who you mean, but I did not know that she had been improved."

The next day, the father and mother and daughter were sitting side by side in the chapel, and it was the remark of more than one, "Oh, what a change!" "Is it possible that that is old drunken Reagan and his wife, that used to live in that Centre street cellar, and that that is 'Wild Maggie?' What a change! Why she is real pretty, and so bright, and so affectionate—see how she looks out the hymn for her mother; and now they all kneel together. Well well, that is better than all drunk together."

After morning service, Mrs. Reagan went into the kitchen to assist about dinner.

"I cannot tell how it is," said she, "but I feel as though this was the last meal I shall ever eat with my husband and Maggie; perhaps I shall not eat this."

She never did.

Half an hour after that, the house was in wild commotion.

"Where is Mr. Reagan?—where is Maggie?—call the doctor!—oh, dear!—oh, dear! Mrs. Reagan is in a fit."

It was a fit which all must have sooner or later. Her forebodings, from whatever cause they came, had given her prescience of her death.

The husband and daughter were soon kneeling over her where she had fallen upon the floor, vainly trying to revive animation. The physician vainly essayed his skill.

"It is too late. My mother is in heaven."

"It is certain she is in the hands of God, and she died with a blessing on her lips for her child," said one of the women who were present when she fell.

"What did she say, Angeline?"

"Sally, how was it? you heard it best."

This is drunken Sal and old Angeline, whom you have seen before. They, too, are inmates; sober, industrious ones, of the House of Industry.

"She said, 'Oh, God, forgive me all my sins! And my husband, forgive him, oh, Lord! as I do. Margaret, oh, God! I thank thee for sending her to see me once more—God bless as I do my dear Maggie. I die in peace, I die—dying—hap—Oh!' and she fell forward; I caught her in my arms, and laid her down gently, but she never breathed again."

"Oh, mother, mother, are you dead, dead, dead! Will you never, never speak to your Maggie again? Oh! it is so hard to part with you now, just as we were going to be so happy, and all live together."

"Yes," said Angeline, "and that reminds me to tell you that she said just before she died, but I thought she was talking wild like, that if she did not see you again, that I must tell you not to go back to Westchester, but you must be sure to stay with your father, he would be so lonesome when she was gone."

The poor husband was lonesome; he already felt it. Then he felt what blessings he had left. He had good health and strength, and a most affectionate good child to comfort him in his old age. And then he poured out such a prayer, as all ought to hear who lack courage to go on in the glorious work of lifting up the fallen, and giving strength to the feeble, and forgiveness to the erring. The day closed in sadness, yet there were some who witnessed the sad scene who felt that "it is good to be afflicted."

The next day after these events I was in Greenwood Cemetery, that lovely resting-place for the dead. It is a landmark in this progressive age, that shows the good fruits of an improved state of society. If any of the readers of these Life Scenes, are curious to know what becomes of the falling leaves of this great forest of human beings, let them go over the Brooklyn South ferry, and follow some of the score of mourning trains that go every day to put away some dead trunk, or lopped limb, or twig, leaf, or flower, perhaps nothing but a bud, which they will plant in earth to blossom in heaven; and they will see where a portion of the fallen go to decay. It is a place for a day, not of gloom, but sweet meditations, such as does the soul good.

I was meditating over a late made grave. It was by the side of one almost old enough to be forgotten, and yet the number of years since it was made were very few, and very, very short. There was a rose bush growing at the head, but I saw through the green leaves the name of "Morgan, Æt. 62." I was not curious to know what Morgan, for my thoughts were far away. I did wonder, it is natural to do so, if that was Mrs. Morgan by his side, and if they had always lain so quiet, without words of contention, or "Caudle Lectures." My doubts were soon to be solved, for now came a cart and a couple of stone setters. How quick, and how carelessly they work; now the hole is dug, now they lift the little stone out of the cart, now they set it upright, now they fill in the dirt around it, now they give a few stamps with heavy boots just over the head of the sleeper—he hears them not—now the stone is planted, now they jump into the cart, slash the whip, and curse the poor old horse for his laziness, and rattle away with a whistle and merry glee. Now we can read the name on the new stone. Ah, it is not his wife—it is "Walter Morgan, Æt. 27." His son—perhaps, an only son —how soon he has come after his father. It is a common name, or I might moralize farther upon what I know of that name. I am interrupted, and walk off a little way and turn to look again. A fine, benevolent looking gentleman—faces do look benevolent—is getting out of a carriage. He is about the age of the elder Morgan. His brother, perhaps. Now, he lifts out a rose bush, in bloom, in its little world, all its own, in an earthen pot. Ah, ha! that is to be planted at the new stone just put in its place. Now he lifts out a lovelier flower. It is a young widow. Fancy is at work now; it says, "Is she pretty?" We are too far off to discern features, but we can think. We do think that a widow who comes to plant a flower at her husband's grave, is a flower of a woman, let her face be what it may.

So I sat down with pencil in hand, writing, "Musings at the Tomb." I had just written, "Benevolent old gent and beautiful young widow," and was going to add, rose bush planted at husband's grave, and all that sort of thing, when somebody slapped me on the back—that knocks out the sentimental—with a clear hearty expression of, "my old friend."

"Why, Lovetree, is this you? Athalia—Mrs. Morgan, I should say."

"No; always call me by the name you first knew me by."

"Then I should call you Lucy."

"No, no, not that, not that."

"Forgive me, but I did not intend to call up unpleasant reminiscences. Ah, what have we here? A little train of mourners, with a tenant for that open grave. See, that is the Missionary from the Five Points."

"And, oh, uncle, that is Maggie, our little Maggie from up the country. It must be her mother. Yes, it is, for she takes the arm of a man with a crape on his hat—it is her father. Her mother has her wish. He will drop a tear at her grave. See, he does; his handkerchief is at his eyes. Oh, it is a sad thing for a husband to follow the wife he has lived with forty years, to such an end as this. Poor Maggie, how she weeps. I must go and see her as soon as the ceremony is over. Suppose, uncle, that we take them in our carriage home with us, it will not be quite so melancholy as it will be to go back to the house of death."

"So we will, and then I will arrange the plan for them to go to housekeeping together. I have already got a place in view."

So they met, and so Athalia said, "Come with us."

And so they went. Maggie looked upon it as another remarkable interposition, or something, at any rate, that she could not account for, that Mrs. Morgan should have felt impelled to come over here to-day, of all other days, and that they should meet so singularly; "for," said she, "fifty different parties might be riding about among these hills, and dales, and groves, looking at this lonely poor grave, and at that twenty thousand dollar monument, and yet no one know that the other was so near. Well, it is a place where all must come. I hope we shall all meet our friends as happily as I have mine to-day."

So they went home with Mrs. Morgan, and three days after they went to a house of their own.

You have already seen how they were able afterwards to say to others, "Come with us," when a houseless widow and her two children stood in the street the night of the fire—the night that rum and its effects made Mrs. Eaton a widow.

Perhaps you would like to see the benevolent gentleman that clothed the naked after that fire? You have seen him. Turn back a leaf and look at him again as he lifts that rose-bush out of the carriage, to plant at that grave. You did not see him in the crowd at the fire, but he was there, and heard his protégé say, "Come with us." He was just going to say it, but he liked it better that Maggie had said it first. Then he said to himself—it was one of his odd freaks of benevolence—I will surprise the dear girl directly, and make her remember those golden words to her dying day.

You have seen him. It was Athalia's uncle.

Who is Athalia?

Turn over. Read.

CHAPTER VIII.

ATHALIA, THE SEWING GIRL.

"How full of briars is this working day world."

"With fingers weary and worn,
With eyelids heavy and red,
A woman sat in unwomanly rags,
Plying her needle and thread."

Athalia wore not unwomanly rags at the period when I shall commence her history. She was clad in the garb of a country girl, just arrived in the city, in the full expectation that fortune awaited her, just as soon as she could learn the trade of a dress-maker. Oh, how she worked, and laughed, and sung! She was the life of the shop. Sometimes she thought of home—home where mother was—and then she wept. But the sunshine of youth soon sends the clouds and dew drops that dim the eye away to forgetfulness.

Athalia was sixteen—sweet sixteen in face and mind. What a bright blue eye, what soft brown hair, what wit, and oh, what a voice in song! and such a heart, 'twas tuned for others' woes, and not her own.

Why comes this mountain flower from her country home?

Her father was a farmer—ah! *was*—would be still, only that he had swallowed his farm. The mortgage to the store at the cross roads, the damage paid in a law suit for a fight, and the cost of throwing his neighbor's horse down his well, had left him without a home for himself, and so his children went forth into the world to seek bread; the daughter, of course, by the needle, the sons at sea.

Athalia chose the city. How little she knew the danger. She would have shuddered to see a man sit carelessly down upon a powder keg with a pipe in his mouth. Not half so dangerous is that, as for a young country girl, with a beautiful face, to come here.

Oh, how she worked one whole year to learn her dress-maker's trade, without one cent of compensation. Such is the law. The law of custom with milliners' apprentices.

Then she went home. How joyfully her mother opened her arms; how sweet was that kiss—a loved mother's kiss. Did she love her father? How could she love a man who often cursed, and sometimes beat that mother? She went home to stay, to ply her new trade among her old neighbors. How could she love her father when he would not let her stay, and, like a drunken brute as he was, drove her back again to the city?

"You have learnt a city trade, and you have got city airs; nobody wants you here."

It was not so. Everybody wanted her there but her miserable father. Everybody else loved Athalia. They saw no city airs; all they saw was that a rough diamond had been polished. What is it worth without?

So she came back to the city with a heavy heart. What was she to do? She could go back to her old shop and work eighteen hours a day, for twenty-five cents, and scanty food; lodging, as she had done during her long year of apprenticeship, three in a narrow bed, in a room with just air and space enough for the decent accommodation of a cat, nothing more. What hope in such a life? What would she have at the end of the year? Just what she had at the beginning? No; for one year of youth would be gone.

She could not go back; there was no hope there. So, with another girl just as poor, but just as willing to work, she took a room, and took in work, or went out to do it. Then how she was exposed, how in danger. Libertines live in genteel families. Ah, and are pet sons of mothers who would give dollars to dissipated rakes, and grudge shillings to poor dress-makers. And if the poor girl should be caught in the snare of such a son, how the mother would rave and drive her away unpaid, because she had disgraced her "respectable boy."

Mrs. Morgan was one of Athalia's lady "patrons." Haughtily proud, yet not, like some of her class, positively dishonest, cruelly dishonest. She wanted the labor of the poor sewing girl, because she possessed great taste, and could dress her daughters better, and what was still more, though so little practised by the rich, cheaper, than she could get their dresses at a "regular establishment." That was just what the daughters most disliked. They knew that none of their acquaintances wore such neat-fitting dresses, but when the question was put, "Where did you get them made?" they could not answer, "Oh, we always get everything at Madame Chalambeau's fashionable establishment in Broadway."

They could not change their mother's policy, and so they determined to drive poor Athalia out of the house.

They had another object. Athalia was beautiful. Her face was such as we are apt to conceive that an angel must have. And everybody who came in the house while she was there, and saw her, said, "Oh, what a sweet face!"

This was gall and wormwood to the "young ladies," for their faces were just such as you would suppose were made out of those two ingredients, and they were true indications of their minds. So they hated the poor seamstress for double cause.

At first she came to the table with the family. But the girls could not help observing that she was the diamond, they the setting, to all eyes. She was better bred than they, with all their boarding-school education. Where had she got it? In a country school house, and her mother's kitchen.

Once, once only, after tea she was invited to sing. Who supposed that she could touch a piano note. She accepted the invitation, as all well-bred girls do, who know that they can sing, and Walter offered his arm to lead her to the piano.

Walter was the brother, the only "son and heir of our family." He had just returned from a lady-killing Niagara tour, and met Athalia for the first time at the tea table. It was the last time, the sisters said, that he should meet her there. She went home that evening; she had finished her job and received her poor pay. That was one of Mrs. Morgan's virtues; she paid the stipulated price to those who worked for her.

What daggers, scorpions' stings, and poisoned darts, poor Athalia and Walter would have felt, while he stood over her at the piano, if they could have felt the glances of scornful, angry eyes. How he was taken to task afterwards for paying attention to "a sewing girl," particularly for waiting upon her home.

How he justified himself. Just as though there was need of it. But aristocracy had stept down to the level of one who

"Plied her needle and thread,
 In poverty, hunger, and toil;"
Who sang with a voice of saddening song,
 Of the home on her own native soil.

Of the spring and the brook where it flow'd,
 Of the plums and the pears where they grew,
Of the meadows and hay lately mow'd,
 And the roses all dripping with dew.

And her heart it went journeying back,
 While her fingers plied needle and thread,
Till the morning came in at a crack,
 Where it found her still out of her bed.

Shall I ever work thus like a slave,
 With the scorn of the rich and the proud?
For they think that a seamstress must crave
 For the work that is making her shroud.

Walter justified, apologised, for he was bound in the iron fetters, "polite custom."

"I found," says he, "when I came home, a beautiful, well-dressed, well-behaved girl, to all appearance a young lady, at your tea table."

"Well, she shall never come there again. I always told mother that she might know better than to bring her to the table; and the pert minx, if she knew her place, would never try to stick herself into genteel company. So much for having a dress-maker in the house."

"Elsie, Elsie, I am ashamed of you."

"I think you had better be ashamed of yourself, mother."

"I found her," resumed Walter, "at your table, and I took the only vacant seat, by her side. I did not find her pert, but on the contrary, I must say it, better behaved, better spoken, than my sister Elsie, when speaking of or to her mother."

"You had better insult me, by your comparison, Sir Walter."

"No; I do not intend that. But I was only explaining why I paid attention to the lady."

"The lady—lady! That to a sewing girl who goes out to work by day's work. Did you learn that at college or at Saratoga?"

"I have learned to call every female lady, who looks, acts, and talks like one. I hope my sister Elsie will not unlearn me. I found the lady at your table. I found her polite and diffident. She is not a forward minx. I walked with her to the parlor."

"Yes, and she should have known better than to go there. Why did she not go back to her work?"

"Elsie, she had done her work, and was waiting for your father to come home, so I could get some money to pay her; for I should be ashamed to keep her out of her money, or oblige her to call again. You had spent all the change I had in the house in your afternoon shopping. It was me that asked her to stay. It was me that asked her into the parlor. It was me, your mother, that asked her to sing one of those plaintive, sweet songs, I had heard her sing to the children while at work. It was you that urged her. What for? That she might fail. Elsie, Elsie, there is envy in your heart."

"And she did sing. Was ever anything sweeter? I can repeat every word, for every note went down into my soul, and printed itself like the magnetic telegraph. Listen:

"Oh, I was born where waters leaping,
  Cascade down the green, green hill;
Oh, I was born where lambkins bleating,
  Leap along the clear, clear rill.
Oh, I was born where lightning flashes,
  'Luminate the green, green trees;
Oh, I was born where the wild wind dashes,
  Raging o'er the deep, deep seas.

"Oh, now I live amid confusion,
  Commerce wears an ugly frown;
Oh, who would give that sweet seclusion,
  For all the pleasures of the town?
Oh, how I love my native mountain,
  Hills and glens and all their flocks,
Oh, how I love that sweet sweet fountain,
  Every tree, and all the rocks."

"Smitten—smitten—my brother Walter smitten with my dress-maker! Faugh! I wonder if he went home with her, for he went out at the same time?"

Yes, he did go home with her. It was her first false step. But ye that stand fast, do not censure this first step of her fall. She was young and handsome; so was he. Theirs were such hearts as nature sports with. Both were touched. He went home with her. They got into a stage at Seventeenth street to ride to Broome, for there was the home of the sewing girl. At Broome street he forgot to pull the check string. She did not notice it till the crowd of cars, carriages, and swarms of human beings, which fill up that great wide thoroughfare, Canal street, awakened her, from her reverie of wild thoughts, to the fact that they were already too far down. Before he could stop her she had pulled the string, and the driver held up and looked down through his little peep hole at his passengers, ready for his sixpenny fare, which he will contrive to make seven cents, if he makes change for you.

Walter acknowledged that he did not mean to stop the stage; he wanted Athalia to go to Taylor's, and take an ice cream with him. But she was inexorable. He plead, she said, no; she said it sweetly, and, finally, they compromised by her agreeing to go to-morrow evening.

The second false step!

Then he walked home with her. She said, good night, at the door, he said, "Oh, let me see you up these dim stairs."

"Oh, no, I am used to them, I can find my room in the

dark. If Jeannette is at home, she will hear a little signal upon the wall, and open the door, then it will be light."

"Give it then."

She did; Jeannette was not at home.

"Oh, let me go up, and just look in, and see where angels live."

Oh, flattery! thy power is great. Why should she refuse, since he was to come again, she had promised that? So she said, "come up, then," and away she tripped into the darkness, her step so light that he could not tell where it fell. Directly there was a little scratch, a flash, a blue flame, very small, and then a full white light, and a match, and then a lamp was burning.

"Come up. Take care of the narrow, crooked steps, they are not like your broad easy stair-case."

She had made another false step. Did far off visions of fancy revel in her brain, that she might some day go up that broad stair-case, arm in arm with that handsome young man? What if they did? you too have dreamed more unlikely day dreams.

"Come up, can you see?"

Yes, he could see,

"By the lamp dimly burning,"

just up there above him, one of the houris he had often read of, often dreamed of, never before seen. He went up, to her little heaven of a room. How could she sing that,

"Commerce wears an ugly frown,"

while everything looked so smiling in her mart? How could she long for the sweet seclusion of her country home, with such a bijou of a hermit's cell here? He stood amazed. He spoke not, but he thought. Did she divine his thoughts?—she answered them—how did she know them? The magnetic telegraph of the soul was at work.

"Yes, sir, we are obliged to keep our room neat, because ladies come here to get work done, and they would not give us their custom if we lived in a plain room."

Plain room! What would his sisters say to a plainly furnished room, if that was not one?

"True, it is plainer than theirs—I mean—but you did not speak—I thought you spoke—yes it is plain compared with rooms that ladies occupy. We pay enough though for the furniture to have good."

"Do you hire it then?"

"Yes, we neither of us had money enough to furnish a room, only a few things, and pay the rent in advance. So we hired a furniture man to put in the things, and we pay him for the use of them."

"How much?"

"Five dollars a month."

"Five dollars! Why there is not over a hundred dollars worth."

"No, sir; that is just what it was counted at. They are all second-hand articles. There is the bedstead; we furnished the bed and bedding; my mother gave me that; Jeannette has no mother; and the table, and the other little pine table, the bureau, the wash-stand, the six chairs, the rocker, and the sofa; we made those ottomans, and the curtains; and in that pantry ——. Oh, I declare how I am running on."

"Pray, tell me, Miss ——, I really have not learned your name yet."

"Athalia. I am sure you heard your mother call me that."

"Yes, but I was going to call you by your sirname."

"Lovetree, sir. Athalia Lovetree."

"Oh, that is a very sweet, pretty name."

"Yes, sir, so much so that I think I shall always keep it."

"So all the young ladies say. But it hardly ever proves true with one who owns so pretty a name, and a face prettier still."

More flattery. She did not hear it. No. She felt it though.

"Well, I am very sure I never shall change my first name. I never shall be called by any other than Athalia."

She thought so then; I wonder if she ever thought of it in after years?

"But you have not told me what is in that pantry."

"Oh, no matter; that is where we keep all our dishes and cooking utensils. We have a stove in winter; in summer, a little charcoal furnace behind the fire-board."

"And is your room warm in winter?"

"Why yes, sir, if we have plenty of work."

"Does work keep you warm?"

"Oh, no; but work gives us money to buy coal. There

was a time last winter, when we were out of work, that ——"

"You had no fire?"

"Yes, sir, but only a few days, we had to make up the month's rent, eight dollars for the room, and five for the furniture."

Walter put his hand in his pocket. What for? He felt how easy it would be to take out a hundred dollars, and tell her, to go and pay for that furniture, and not pay rent for it any longer. Then he thought how ridiculous, to be so affected by the woes and wants of a sewing girl. How his proud sisters would laugh at him. Pride conquered a heart prone to a good action.

"And so you went without fire, to pay that usurious old miser who owns this furniture, sixty per cent per annum, for the use of it. Sixty, yes, more than a hundred upon what it would sell for at auction. And what did you do for food in the meantime?"

Well, we did not need much, and should not have suffered any, if Mrs. Jenkins had paid me for my work. Oh, if she only knew how much we did need it. Jeannette was sick, and what little money I had, I spent for her; I had almost ten dollars due me for work, and could not get one. It is wicked to keep poor girls out of their money; indeed it is, when they are sick and suffering for it."

"And you suffered, while Mrs. Jenkins, with her thirteen servants, and coach and horses owed you for work?"

"Well, we did not suffer much, except I had to pawn my

black silk dress, the very one too that I needed most when it was cold, and had to do without fire when Jeannette was sick, and should, by all means, have had one. She is a sweet, good girl; I wish she was at home."

"Wish again, and you will see her."

Both started as though caught in something they were ashamed of. Why should they be? True he had approached very close to Athalia, as she stood watering her flowers and feeding her bird—both windows were full of flowers, and over each a canary bird; and he was watching all her operations with as much interest as though they were all his own.

"Poor things," she said, "they look neglected."

She loved flowers. So did he. He loved their owner, but he had not said so yet. He hardly knew it; he would not let any one know it; hence he started when Jeannette spoke, for he thought she must have seen it. He blushed and turned round, and then she blushed; there was a trio of blushes. What for? Jeannette did not think it was a stranger. She thought it was Charley Vail. Charley was a sort of beau, yet not a beau. He was Jeannette's cousin; and though he did not love her exactly, he liked her, and I guess that she liked him; Athalia thought more than liked him. Charley would have loved Athalia if she had given him the least encouragement, but she would not, for she hoped he would love his cousin and marry her. He was a good fellow, always ready to do anything on earth for "the girls"—in short he was Charley.

Jeannette blushed. She had reason to, for, thinking it

was cousin Charley—who else could it be, there in their room alone with Athalia, in the evening—she tripped up behind him and gave him a good hearty slap on the back. He turned around, she almost felt him hugging and kissing her, but he did not. She looked again, the light now shone in his face, and there she stood before a stranger. Is it any wonder she blushed? is it any wonder he blushed? is it any wonder they all blushed? She played with her bonnet strings; he twirled his hat; Athalia could not play with any thing. She had the lamp in one hand, and the bird cage in the other. But she could laugh, and she burst out in such clear, musical tones, as she said, "Why, Jeannette, did you think it was Charley?"

That explained the whole. He understood the blow now. Did he also understand what Charley would have done, if it had been him that got the blow. Perhaps he thought, for he said,

"You have struck me, miss. I never take a blow without giving one back. There."

Did he strike her? What! strike a woman! Shame! Oh, no; but he caught her in his arms, before she could be aware of the movement, and such a kiss! such a good, hearty kiss as he gave her. Ah, well! who would not? She was a nice, sweet girl, not quite so pretty as Athalia, but one that a colder heart than his might relish in just such a case. She pouted a little, and talked about great liberty in a stranger; but who took the first liberty? True; but "that was a mistake."

"Then count the other a mistake too."

"No, that was done on purpose."

"So it was, and I should like to do it again, but I will not, so rudely. Pray forgive me."

What had she to forgive? what to be angry about. How could she hold out against that, "I should like to do it again?"

After all, she was not half so angry as Athalia. And what was she angry about? That he had kissed Jeannette instead of her? Take care, little heart, jealousy is creeping in among thy pulsations. Take care, big heart, for just now Charley enters the scene, and before he has observed that a stranger is in the room, he has kissed Athalia.

Mischief has broke loose to-night. What is in the men? What is in Walter Morgan, that a kiss given to that girl, for the first time seen that night, should send a pang to his heart? How it goes throbbing through every nerve, and pricks into the very core of sensation. Take care, big heart and little heart, nature is at her sports, and she always makes pleasures sweet by contrast with pain.

Finally, all are reconciled. How they do laugh over the queer mistakes. Jeannette would have sooner struck a bear than him, yet he did not bite her. Charley would have sooner kissed that same bear, and risked the hug, than have kissed Athalia before a stranger, for he is a good boy, a little mischievous, but would never do a thing to hurt the feelings of another, particularly a woman.

How they did sit, and talk, and laugh, and enjoy happiness, such as Walter had never found in rose-wood furnished parlors.

What would his proud sisters say, if they knew how "low he had sunk himself, to keep company with sewing girls?" But he would not tell them. Take care, young man, you are breaking in upon the conventionalities of life. You must stick to your *caste*, in America as well as India. You may lay your heart at the feet of anything that is old and ugly, even as your sisters, so that she is *ton* and of the *ton*—the upper *ton*. But offer to love one who lives, barely lives, by her needle, and see how your own flesh and blood will hate you.

So passed the evening away. Then Walter would go. But he wanted to hear Athalia sing once more. No. She had no piano. His hand was in his pocket again. How he would like to send her one to-morrow, but he dared not say so. He did look around the room, to see where he could set it. There was no room. She could not sing any more to-night. Ask Jeannette. She sings a beautiful little song while we are at work. No, she could not. She was afraid to sing before strangers. But Charley asked her, in his blandest manner, and then she would sing one verse if he would go right home. How anxious she was to get rid of him. So she sung:

"Why bitter life with useless tears,
With mourning unavailing?
Why bitter hope with ceaseless fears,
Of shoals where we are sailing?
With lively song and music peals,
Make life just like the ocean,
When flapping sails a zephyr steals,

To toss us with its motion,
Motion, motion, motion.
To toss us with its motion."

"There now, I hope you are satisfied. If not you may go, for I shall not sing another word to-night. I don't know how I came to do that."

No, they were not satisfied. Who ever knew a man that was? Who ever got one favor of a woman, that did not ask for two more? So they both asked both the girls to go to the theatre to-morrow night, and both promised.

More false steps. How many will it take to reach the end?

Walter went home, never more happy. You have seen how he was taken to task. He had defied the laws of caste.

It did not require stronger Argus eyes than his two sisters possessed to see how deeply he was enamored with Athalia. How they did wish they knew whether she had dared to look up to him, as he had down to her. How should they find out. It does not take mischief-makers long to contrive their plot. If one woman wants to ruin another one, there is one always ready to assist her in her wicked design. No doubt he was the father of millinery, for he caused the first apron to be made, and he has assisted largely in all the designs of female apparel from that day to this. Sometimes his fashion is very fig-leafish, barely hiding a portion of the body, while the limbs, head, neck, shoulders, and other "excitements," are left exposed to Adam's rude gaze. Then he contrives his fashion of so much cloth, that those who follow it may lose their souls in its attainment, and those who make them may feel, as they

> "Work, work, work,
> Till the stars shine through the roof,"
> That they are weaving a web with sin for the woof,
> "Till the brain begins to swim,
> Till the eyes grow heavy and dim,
> Sewing at once, with a double thread,
> A dress for the living and dead."

Mischief is always busy. It must be so with an envious wicked woman.

The Morgans changed their tactics, and adopted those more wicked than I could invent.

They soon found that they wanted more dresses, and what was very remarkable, they did not want to go to the French dress-maker. What could be the reason? They had watched their brother; they had seen him go to Athalia's; they had seen him in the theatre with her; they had met them walking, arm in arm, in Broadway, "the shameless hussey;" and once they had entered Thompson's, and walked upstairs to take ice cream, "actually over our heads." Walter Morgan, the richest merchant's son, in New York, gallanting a seamstress—their own dress-maker. And every day some of their acquaintance were asking them, "Who is that beautiful girl I saw with Walter?" Of course they did not know; how could they tell that he had taken up with "such a thing?" In vain they talk to him, he was mum, or if he spoke of her, it was with the highest respect. Would he marry her? Ah, there was the rub.

"It is a pity," said Elsie, "that he would not ruin her, and that would be the end of it."

Did a spirit furnish that cue, or was it a wicked woman's own conceit? At any rate, it was a cue upon which they acted. Athalia was sent for, and the young ladies never were so affable before. Every opportunity was contrived for Walter to accomplish the purpose of a villain. Their schemes had the exact contrary effect desired. He had made such advances at first as "men about town" do make, and had met with such a decided repulse, not an angry one, but a virtuous one, that he never would try again.

"I expected it," said she to his proposals, "I am used to it—I am almost every day exposed to such tempting offers, to escape a life of poverty—I have ceased to look upon them as insulting—nature, and fashion, and the state of society, are such in this city, that a girl with an unfortunate face like mine, must fall, unless she is possessed of such fortitude as but few young girls are naturally gifted with. You may ask me that question every day; every day you may, if you feel like wounding the feelings of a poor girl, repeat your question, and every day you will get the same answer."

"Athalia, forgive me. Oh, forgive me; I never will repeat the question again; whether you forgive me or not, you need have no fear of that.

What a failure then had his sisters made. They did just what they did not intend to do; they led Walter to think, that his family would approve a match with one so virtuous, so beautiful, so lovely, even if she was a sewing girl, and he began to build castles in the air upon this foundation. They were very sandy, and a storm was approaching that would soon beat upon the frail walls, and like all such fabrics, down they will tumble.

CHAPTER IX.

ATHALIA, THE SEWING GIRL.

"One sorrow never comes but brings an heir,
That may succeed as its inheritor."

"Proper deformity seems not in the fiend
So horrid, as in woman."

MARRIAGE, death, bankruptcy, poverty, sin, and, finally, "plucked like a brand from the burning," are the contents, the introduction, and peroration, of this chapter. If you are satisfied at a glance, you can pass on, the filling up, is but the shading of the sketch. But if you are curious to know who marries, who dies, and who does worse—read.

"It is but a step from the palace to the tomb," yet the road sometimes seems a long and dreary one, leading through strange, dark places.

I have come to the conclusion, that lovers of romance, and those who cater for them, writing tales of fiction, have mistaken their vocation. Let them gather up and detail a few of the incidents of real Life Scenes as they occur, and there will be no occasion for fiction. So let us on with our narration of events.

Mr. Morgan was a merchant, wealthy as Crœsus, perhaps more so; and he had more need to be, for he lived "up town," in "up town" style. The simple interest upon the cost of his house and furniture was seven thousand dollars a year, and his annual expenses double that sum.

Of course his daughters had never taken a stitch in their lives. They had been to school, where nothing useful is taught; and learned what is called music, and could waltz to perfection. Walter, had been to college. What had he learnt? To drink a bottle of wine every day after dinner, and "fill up," with mint juleps, sherry coblers, and brandy smashes, the intermediate time. Not one useful thing had either of them been taught, not one lesson in the art of self-support; all was self-indulgence. They laughed, or would have laughed at the idea, if any one had dared to mention it, that the time would ever come, that they would have occasion to lift a hand to procure their own bread.

It is a bad school—it has many scholars.

Mr. Morgan came home one day in unusual glee; he was naturally a stern man. He had heard of the very successful voyage of the Matilda—named after his daughter—to China, where she would load with teas and silks for a home voyage. She was insured in a very rich London office. Some of his cautious friends advised him to "hedge," by insuring also in other offices; he had never met with a single loss in his life; he had often been his own insurer, and took about half the value of the Matilda now on his own insurance book, which showed a great many thousand dollars in his favor.

"Yes," said a Paul Pry, of my acquaintance, "more thousands than he is now worth, if his debts were paid."

Who believed it? Not the banks, which loaned him any amount he desired. Not the wife, and son, and daughters, for that stern husband and father never told them of his business.

"That is my business," was the cut-off valve which always shut down upon every question as certain as that of the steam engine at the point where it must change the motion.

After dinner and the second bottle, the family were startled by the sudden announcement he made for to-morrow.

"We start for Lake George to-morrow morning; come, get ready."

"Why, father, what has started you all of a sudden?"

"That's my business."

"Well, we cannot get ready, no way in the world."

"Pshaw! I could get a ship ready before ten o'clock."

"But we cannot get new hats."

"Plenty of time. Start right out."

"To-night? Buy a hat in the evening, who ever heard of such a thing? What would Mrs. Grundy say?"

"Ask her, she is going with us; or rather, we are going with them. Grundy is in shoal water, and wants to get out of sight a few days; and I want he should, for I am on his paper heavy."

"Oh, it is absolutely impossible for us to go to our milliner to-night."

"Go in the morning, then. Time enough."

"What? before ten o'clock. How vulgar you are, father."

"Very well; if you cannot get up new flying gibs, go to sea with the old ones."

"Well, I suppose we might send for Madam Pantanosi to call in the morning; but, dear me, there are our dresses all in the work-room, not one of them done. You don't expect Athalia is going to finish them to-night, do you?"

"Have you no others?"

"What if we have? the Grundys know that we have new ones making, and of course, will expect to see them. You don't expect your daughters, I hope, to wear old dresses, on a tour to the Lakes?"

"Why not? That is the place to wear them."

"You may talk, father, but it is out of the question."

"Well, settle it your own way. I go to-morrow, and if you are going with me, you had better be getting ready; besides, let me tell you, young Wendall is going up too. We are going to have some great sport, fishing."

That decided Elsie. If George Wendall and the Grundys were going, she must go, for he and Minnie Grundy needed watching. She would go, if she wore the old hat, and a dress that had been worn twice before.

"Where is that seamstress? she must work all night, and get my dress done any way."

"Elsie, daughter, she cannot do that, her eyes are very weak. You had better take her along with us, the poor girl; give her a little country air, and let her finish your dresses there."

"Yes, yes, that's it, wife, let her go along. She appears to be a right, tight little craft. A sail will do her good. What a pity she did not hail from the right port."

"You have very curious notions, father."

"That is my business."

"Well, for my part," says Matilda, "I think she can go just as well as not; our maid and she can have a room together, and nobody need to know that we have brought a seamstress along with us; if they did, they would think it very vulgar. Of course, she won't come to the table with us, at the hotel."

"No, indeed; I guess she will not; though, I suppose, we shall have a private table; shall we not, father?"

"That is my business."

But as it was settled that she was to go, it was, finally, thought necessary to tell her so, and she was sent for, and told of the arrangement.

How could she go? How start so sudden? How leave Jeannette? She could not go. Yet she would like to. Perhaps she never would have another opportunity. She would go down and see Jeannette, and if she could go, she would come up very early. Away she ran upstairs for her little straw hat and black mantilla. Walter had been a "silent member" of the party. What wild thoughts ran through his brain, when he found that Athalia was to be one of the party. Did he dream of the shady walk, the moonlit lake, and egg-shell boat, with only two in it, floating upon the glassy surface of the water? Did he think that he should climb the rocks with her, and wander through the ruins of old Ticonderoga? Yes, he did dream; youth do dream. Did she dream, while she stood before the glass, tying her bonnet strings? What of? Of the hook that he would bait and put in her hands, and the fish that would be caught. Fish! It is not fish alone that young girls catch, when young men bait hooks for them, in wild woods, and lonely glens, where mountain streams murmur soft music.

As she came down upon the steps, Walter was waiting there. What for? For a poor sewing girl. He wanted, he said, that she should stop with him and pick out a hat and some little articles, a toilet box, and sundry conveniences or necessaries, to one on a journey, for his sister Matilda.

Oh yes, she would do that, with pleasure, if he wished it. He did wish it. The selections were made with great taste and without regard to expense. The hat was a little treasure.

What was that sigh for? Can a woman—a young girl—just on the eve, too, of a journey to a watering place, see such a hat shut up in its paper case, without a sigh? It is more than human nature ever could do. Athalia is human, and that hat is just such a one as she would like herself. She is too poor. So she sighed and went home.

"Shall I send it?"

"Let it be until I return, and then I will give directions."

It is no matter what Walter said to her on the way home, but she had determined to go with the Morgans, to Lake George, and so she told him.

"Good night then, I must go home and get ready, you know what the word is with father—'that is my business.'"

He had a little other business. He went back to the store, and gave the necessary orders about the purchase.

"Would the lady be kind enough to write a little note that he would dictate, and put it in the bonnet box?"

"Certainly, anything to oblige the gentleman. Was that his sister? His cousin perhaps? Well, she is very pretty, at any rate. Was that her name? What a sweet name."

What sweet words to Walter. How we do like to hear those we love spoken of in such words.

How Athalia busied herself getting her few things ready. What she lacked, Jeannette, the good soul, lent her. She never thought how lonely the room would be for the two or three weeks she would be away.

"I wish I had a few dollars to spare, Jeannette, I certainly would go and buy just such a hat as I picked out this evening for Matilda Morgan. It was very pretty. And Walter, he admired it too. He said it was so tasty, when I tried it on, to let him see how it looked."

Just then there was a rap at the door.

"Oh there comes cousin Charley."

No, it could not be Charley, it was a little rap. The door was opened, and there stood a little girl with a bandbox and bundle.—It is a shame to send such little girls out late in the evening with such heavy bundles.

"Does Miss Lovetree live here?"

"Yes."

"Then this is the place."

"Oh dear," says Jeannette, "more work. Who can this be from? Why, Athalia, what is the matter, you look amazed?"

"I am amazed. Is there no mistake in the direction?"

"No, it is Miss Athalia Lovetree. No. — Broome street, up-stairs."

"Oh! I cannot take it, indeed I cannot. Accept such a present from him? No, no, no."

He had thought of that. Jeannette by this time had the bandbox open. Did woman ever resist that temptation?

"Ah here is a note. This will explain the mystery."

"To Miss Lovetree :—

"As it is decided that you will go with us to Lake George, please accept a few things that you will need, which I have commissioned my son to buy.

"From your friend,

"Mrs. Morgan."

"Oh that is a different thing, if they come from her. And then for him to pretend all the time that they were for his sister. It is too bad. Oh, but it is a love of a hat though! is it not, Jeannette?"

Yes, it was; that was settled. First one tried it on, and then the other. Jeannette said it was a *bride's* hat. Athalia said she ought to be ashamed of herself to say so. Then all the other little bijouterie were overhauled, and looked at, and talked over, and praised, and then the note was read again, and the postscript; there was a postscript, there always is a postscript to a woman's letter. It was the postscript that gave it the air of genuineness. It read:

"P. S.—Don't say a word to me, or hint where the hat came from, for I don't want Mr. Morgan or the girls ever to know; nobody knows but Walter."

No, nobody knows but Walter. There was no fiction in that.

In the morning there was another rap—louder this time. It did not disturb any sleep though; there had been none in that room that night. It was John, come for the trunk and bandbox—two things that a modern lady never travels without. There was a wagon load of them left the Morgan and Grundy mansions that morning, and they and their owners all arrived, in due course of cars and locomotives, at Lake George.

Mr. Morgan and George Wendall fished, the girls flirted, Athalia sewed and sighed, and walked out evenings, slyly, with Walter Morgan.

More false steps. Sly walks in town are bad—in the country, dangerous. There are a great many precipices, down which such a couple may tumble.

George was a glorious fishing companion for the shipping merchant. He could row and drive, and get up all the fixings; and, after dinner, talk, and laugh, and drink, till both went to bed "glorious."

"Mr. Morgan, you drink one bottle too many."

"Pshaw. What if I do? that is my business."

It is sometimes the wife's business.

George was a boon companion, that was all. He had nothing, did nothing, lived somehow, dressed well—ill-natured folks said he did not pay his tailor.

Who ever thought that he would be Mr. Morgan's son-in-law? He did, and so had his daughter, Elsie, lately concluded, for the country air and scenery are provocatives to that end.

"Ask father."

"Enough said."

He did. He took care to ask him just at the right time.

"Why, George, my boy, good fellow to fish. Did not think you had your hook there. Got any bait? No. Well I have. Enough for both of us. I will bait your hook, boy. That is my business."

"Thank you, sir. When shall it be?"

George knew the art of fishing with a fresh bait, and never losing sight of the fish after he had tasted it, until he had him safe bagged.

"When shall it be? Now, now—right off to-night. Nothing like going to sea while the tide serves."

He was a prompt man always. It was no use to say no, after he had said yes, or, "that is my business;" so in half an hour after that, Elsie Morgan was Elsie Wendall.

Of course more wine was drank, after which a letter was brought to him, from his head clerk, marked, "Important—in haste." So Mrs. Morgan told him.

"That is my business; take it up to my room. Do you think I am going to read the stupid letters of old Precision at this time of the evening, and my daughter just married?"

At ten o'clock next morning, after the mail had gone, he read:

"Sir:—

"We have advices by telegraph from London, just as the steamer was leaving port, of the failure of the London insurance office, in which the Matilda is insured. She is now over-due, and not yet reported. Shall I insure her? Be sure to answer by first mail.

"JAMES PRECISION."

How the bell did ring; how he stamped, and swore, and wrote, and yet he could not send his letter till next morning.

"Why did not old Precision insure at once? Every dollar on earth would be swallowed up if that ship were lost."

Simply because he was Precision, and the merchant, who had directed him for forty years, had never given him leave to act, upon his own discretion, in an emergency like this.

"That is my business," was the unvarying answer.

Two days after, he had another letter from his precise clerk. He did not order it up to his room, to wait till next morning, for he was in a tearing passion when it was handed him; and he felt as though he would have opened it if the biggest rocks in that mountainous region had been piled upon it.

What had so disturbed the rich merchant? Those who have them not, are apt to fancy that riches and happiness are handmaids. What was the matter? His son, his only son, had just approached him, taking advantage, as Wendall had, of a propitious hour, when wine had done its work—he drank brandy since the news in that letter, and that fired, not soothed him—he approached him with a beautiful sweet girl upon his arm, to ask his consent to their marriage.

Mrs. Wendall screamed and fainted—that is, in appearance.

Matilda said,

"Why, Walter! to that girl—marry that thing—a dress-maker!"

Mrs. Morgan simply said, "Walter, you have disgraced yourself and the mother that bore you. And I never wish to see you again."

Athalia trembled and quailed before the storm of angry words and envenomed looks that surrounded her: How gladly would she have escaped. It was too late.

"Father, your consent."

"Never! You, my only son, marry a common sewing girl, never."

"It is too late. Here is my marriage certificate."

His father opened his mouth to curse him. What for? He had married a girl he loved—a girl, handsome, virtuous, industrious, but poor—a seamstress.

"A letter, sir;" said a servant.

"Give it me."

He tore it open and read;

"SIR:—

"Yours of the 12th inst. came too late. News reached the city an hour before that the Matilda was —— "

He did not say lost. He looked it. He looked at his son and his poor trembling little wife, as though he wished them both at the bottom of the sea, with the Matilda and her cargo—all his fortune! He felt all the envenomed bitterness that a violent natural temper can feel, when heated and inflamed by drunkenness; for he was drunk, fashionably drunk;

but not so much so but he could feel how irretrievably ruined he was, and that the failure to insure was occasioned by drunkenness, such drunkenness as the highest class of society indulge in, when they take an "extra bottle," after dinner, upon extraordinary occasions. He knew the fault was all his own. He had said, when urged to open the letter, an answer to which would have saved all, "that is my business."

It was a sad, sad business. That one more bottle had beggared himself, and all that were dependant upon him. He had just married one daughter to a man whose only qualification was "a good fellow," who could shoot, fish, smoke, drink, drive fast horses, cheat his tailor, and the poor widow boarding-house keeper, and, finally, take advantage of a besotted old rich merchant, when he had drunk just to the point of good-nature—when the indulger in strong drink feels like hugging everybody and "all the rest of mankind,"—to get his consent for him to marry his ugly daughter. It was a marriage of convenience, the obligations of which he intended to keep just as many other such obligations are kept in this city. All this ran through his mind upon the electric telegraph of the brain. Flash after flash it went through, and then came the heavy thunderbolt. He could have endured all the rest; he could not endure that his son should marry a sewing girl. Why? His father was a tailor, and he married a tailor's daughter, and he hated everything that could remind him of his own needle-and-thread origin. He hated her too, because she was so much more lovely than his own daughters.

For five minutes he sat with the letter in his hand, glaring at that, then at his wife and Matilda with a look of sorrow; then at Elsie and her half-drunken husband, with contempt; then his eye came back with a fixidity of hatred upon Walter and Athalia.

At length Walter ventured to break the awful silence.

"Father."

"Don't call me father again. I disown you, you poor milliner's apprentice. Beggar! Don't speak to me."

Walter paid no heed to the order, but said mildly, "is the Matilda lost."

"That is my business. Leave the room."

His sisters took up the cue.

"Yes, you had better go now. Go, and set up shop. You can carry home dresses for your wife."

He came to that afterwards. Then Elsie's husband put in a word of insult.

"I say, Walter, it strikes me, that is rather a costly topsail for a beggar's wife. I hope she gets her bonnets in an honest way. Who pays the milliners' bills?"

Walter raised his cane to strike the villain that could utter such a vile insinuation upon the character of a virtuous girl, and would have paid all his tailors' bills at one blow, but Athalia sprung upon his arm, and held it down. His father either thought, or pretended to think, that he raised his cane to strike him; probably not having heard the remark of Wendall, and thinking only of his own wrongs. He seized a bottle—a weapon that has knocked down its thousands—and sprang forward to strike down his son. His arm was already up, a horrid oath was struggling in his throat, his face turned black from the effects of suffocation, he reeled, the bottle fell to the floor with a crash, and he would have fallen down among the broken glass and spilt wine, but for Walter, who caught him in his arms, and bore him from the room towards his chamber. Athalia rushed out for a physician. It was too late!—Death had already said, "That is my business."

While these events were transpiring in the country, others of great import to the rich merchant's family were enacting in the city. Creditors are not slow when they see misfortune fall upon one, whom they were ready to bow to yesterday, to tread upon him to-day. Creditors and their ministers,—the judges, attorneys, sheriffs,—are all ready for a share of the pound of the broken merchant's flesh. Shylocks still live, and Antonios still fail.

That was a sad funeral cortége which accompanied the dead bankrupt back to the city. Sad, not so much from sorrow, as wounded pride and fallen greatness. It was sad to see the daughters of a dead father absolutely refuse to travel upon the same train, with an only brother's wife. He would not go without her, and so they went without him. It was night when they arrived. They had despatched John in advance, to set the house in order, and meet them at the depot with the carriage and a hearse. The latter was there, the former was not, and they had to submit to the indignity of a hired hack. At the house, all was dark. What could it mean?

"That villain, John, has got drunk again!" That was the fact. Who taught him? He was only following the long-studied precepts of his employer and lady, the young ladies, the young gentlemen, and all their fashionable associates, in their fondness for exhilarating drink. Why should he not get drunk?

They rung the bell angrily. It was a long time before it was answered. Then a heavy footstep came down stairs—not up from the servants' room—and approached the door, and opened the inner one, so that he could see through the blind who demanded admission. A sharp-faced, keen, black-eyed, weasel-looking man, with a chamber-lamp in his hand, and one of Mr. Morgan's dressing gowns upon his back, stood before the astonished family with the question trembling upon his lips, of "Vats you vant here?"

"Want? we want to come in, to be sure, why don't you open the door? Who are you? What are you doing here?"

"Vell, you can't come in. I is the sheriff's man, and he has put me keeper here, and he tells me not to let anybody in without his order. You must go to him. Vat you vakes me up for?"

And he closed the door in their faces, and they heard his heavy step reverberating through the long hall, and up the broad stair-case, as he went back to his lounge, "in my lady's chamber."

There were heavy hearts upon the outside of that door. The men had brought the coffin up, and set it down upon the steps. The hearse and hired hack had driven off. There lay the dead—he never would say, "This is my business," again —the wine-maker might say so. Both were silent. Neither would own his work. In the vaults of that house, three thousand dollars worth—no, *cost*—of wines were stored. Fifty thousand dollars worth of the richest rosewood and mahogany furniture, china, cut glass, and silver ware, stood idle, while its late possessor lay in his coffin upon the threshold, with his family standing around, vainly asking permission to rest the body of the dead owner one night, in its journey to the tomb. What should they do? Walter, if he had been there, could have directed what to do. He was not. Then he was cursed in thought, if not word, because he was not there.

"It is all his fault," said Elsie; "it was his abominable marriage that killed father."

Where was her husband? She looked around for him. He had slipped away "to get a drink." What a brute, she thought. So he was. That is what going to "get a drink" makes of a man.

"We must go to Mr. Grundy's," said the widow.

How? The hearse and hack were gone, and could not be got back in an hour. A passing cart was called, and the coffin of the millionaire placed upon it, and the family followed, to knock at the door of a neighbor's house, with the same results—to be answered by another sheriff's officer, but who, by chance, happening to be an American, and possessed of common sense enough to know that the dead would not steal, and those who attended upon him would not be likely to do so, he opened the door, lit the gas, called up one or two of the servants still left in the house, and did a few other things that natural humanity dictates upon such an occasion. An hour after, the Grundys themselves arrived, to find their home in the hands of a "keeper," who had let in the Morgans by courtesy, and now admitted them as mourning friends of the family.

Here, I draw the curtain. You have already seen the termination of a man who could leave his young wife and her dead father standing in the street, to go and "get a drink." It was him that died in the rat hole, in Cow Bay. It was Elsie that told how he died, how she gave birth to a child by the side of her dead husband, and how the rats sucked up the life blood of that child.

You have seen Matilda, before. Turn back to a picture, in Chapter V., and look at her upon her wedding-day. It is needless for me to go with you along the beaten path of her career, down, down, down, from ball-room to bar-room; from house of —— "a place to meet a friend"—to a house of —— "ladies' boarding-house"—to a house of common resort—the abode of wretchedness, woe, sin, degradation, disease, and "painted sepulchres"—from that to a low room, with "my man," and, finally, to fill the picture in the Two-penny Marriage.

Let the curtain fall—the dead rest in peace.

Watch the living.

CHAPTER X.

ATHALIA, THE SEWING GIRL.

"It is their husbands' fault, if wives do fall."

"The weakest goes to the wall."

WALTER came down on the train with the Grundys. They urged him to "abandon his folly, and go home with them." They little thought they had no home to go to themselves. He said, no; she was his wife, and he never would leave her. He thought so then. If he had left the bottle, he never would.

"Where shall we go, Athalia?"

"Come with me; I have a home."

So he went to her little room in Broome street. The door was fast, and the room dark. She rapped, and was soon answered by Jeannette's voice:

"Who is there?"

"It is me."

What a world of meaning is in those three little words. How the memory of many a wife will wander back into other days, when she heard a midnight rap, and putting her head out of the chamber window, where she had been "making a frock and rocking the cradle" all the early part of the night;

and how her heart palpitates at the answer to her half spoken, half whispered question, "Who is there?"

"It is me," comes up to her ready ear in the open window. Down goes the sash, for the wind might blow on "the baby;" they "have got a baby." In a minute, oh half that time, "me" sees the light through the key-hole, and hears a little step running down stairs. It stops an instant to set the lamp on the table. What for? She could hold it in one hand, while she unlocked the door with the other. Yes, but when the door is open she will have work for both hands—both arms will be around the neck of somebody.

"Heigho, for somebody!" I wish every loving heart had somebody; somebody to say, "It is me."

"Wait a minute."

A little light flashed through the key-hole, then the bolt went back with a click, then the door opened, a night-cap and white gown, a pair of blue eyes, and some pale red curls, were seen a moment, and then a very light scream, and Athalia and Walter were in the dark again. The door was closed in their faces. Was she, too, shut out from her home?

"Open the door, Jeannette. Never mind your night-gown."

"Oh, I cannot; indeed I cannot. That is not all. Charles is here."

Charles there, at that time of night, and she in her night-gown! What can it mean?

"Jeannette, what does it mean?"

"Now, don't go to being angry with me, Athalia." And

she opened the door a little way, and looked out. She had slipped on a wrapper, and slipped off the night-cap. What is there in a night-cap, or night-gown, that a lady should be ashamed to be seen in it?

"What does it mean, Jeannette?"

"Oh, now, don't go to being angry, Athalia, don't. Indeed I could not help it, I was so lonesome after you went away—only think of staying here all alone."

"Shame on you, Jeannette. And so because you were lonesome, you have taken cousin Charles to sleep with you."

"Yes; why not?"

"Why not! why, Jeannette?"

Why, Athalia, we are married. You don't think I would do it if we were not, do you?"

"Married! ha, ha, ha! Come in Walter, you can come in now. We are all married folks together. Ha, ha, ha!"

How her laugh did ring. She was anything but angry.

"Why, Athalia, you are only joking."

"No. I am in sober earnest."

How Jeannette did laugh, and hug, and kiss Athalia; and then she ran to the bed, and there was a "kiss in the dark."

"Come, Charley, get up and see the bride. Come, we are all married folks together."

"Oh, Jeannette, we must not carry on so with Walter now."

"Why not? Are we not all married? If we cannot carry on a little now, I don't know when we should."

"Yes, but—"

"What?"

"Walter's father is dead."

"Oh, dear! don't say that."

"I must; it is true. And Walter must stay here to-night; how shall we fix it?"

"Oh, that is very easy. There are two matrasses on the bedstead; we will lay one down here—the bolster will do for pillows—there are some nice clean sheets, and a spread. We will just take that side curtain and turn it round, and pin it to the window curtain, and then you see how easy it will be to have two beds and two bed-rooms. You and I will sleep on the floor, and Charles and Walter shall sleep on the bed."

No; that would never do. Charles and Walter would both sleep on the floor, and their wives should sleep where they always had, together on the bed.

That the girls would not listen to. They were their guests, and they must sleep on the bedstead—that was the state bed—the bed of honor—Walter had never slept on the floor in his life. Then the men put in their argument, and thus the question stood, until it seemed likely that both beds would remain unoccupied. Finally, it was settled by "compromise." Charley whispered Jeannette, and Jeannette answered aloud,

"Why not? So we will. Husbands and wives should sleep together. Always together. What business has a man sleeping with anybody else?"—with another woman she thought.

So it was settled how they should sleep. Then there was another contention where, that seemed likely to be as interminable as the first. Finally, Athalia settled it. She took Walter by the arm and said, "Come," leaving Jeannette and Charley with the light, "because they were married longer and were more used to it."

Walter was soon asleep. Athalia lay listening to a low conversation between Charles and Jeannette, in which she caught, now and then, a word. "The West—new country—log cabin—little farm—cows, and pigs, and chickens—and a baby"—she thought that—and she thought how happy they will be, and how much better off than here in the city. So she was not at all surprised when Jeannette told her, in the morning, what they had concluded to do. In three days they did it.

When I was in their little cabin, and heard from the lips of Jeannette several things that I should not have known otherwise, I found that they had realized all their hopes, for they had not built them high. And when she found that I knew Athalia, how she did hang upon my arm, and insist that I should stay all night, and sleep in the little bed-room where the rose-bush I had so much admired, everhung the window, and tell her the story, how she got along, and what became of her, and all about it.

Shall I begin at the beginning, or in the middle, or at the end?

"Oh, at the beginning, to be sure. Where is she now? Is she alive?"

That is it; you are a true woman. You tell me to begin at the beginning, and then the very first question you ask is about the end. I see you are impatient, and so I will gratify you. I will begin at the beginning of the end, and finish in the middle. Athalia, poor girl, she is—

"Oh, don't say that—not dead!"

No, no; she is alive and very well, and almost as pretty as ever. She is a widow, and lives in New York, and keeps a boarding house, and is making a comfortable living.

"A widow! why, where is her husband?"

Why, where should he be? if she is a widow, he must be either dead or in California; it is about all the same in New York.

"What did he die of?"

The same disease that kills nine-tenths of his class—rum!

"Oh, dear, and he such a fine young man. I would have married him myself, if it had not been for Charley. Well, I have one great blessing; if Charles is not so rich as Walter, he is as sober as a judge. Oh, I forgot to tell you that he is almost one; he is Justice of the Peace. But do tell me, did Walter leave her rich? The Morgans were very wealthy."

Ah, I see now; Athalia never told of their failure, and how all their wealth vanished like morning dew; that all those five dollar carpets, thousand dollar mirrors, and single chairs that cost more than all your neat furniture, were sold under the hammer to pay debts; and that Walter had not a cent in the world, and that he lived a long time upon the money which she earned, with,

"'Work, work, work.
From weary chime to chime,'

Through many a day and many a night,
'As prisoners work for crime;'

until she sighed and sung:

"'Oh, for only one short hour,
To feel as I used to feel,
Before I knew the woes of want,
And the walk that costs a meal.'"

"And did Walter do nothing?"

What could he do? He knew nothing—had never learned to do anything; besides that, how could he take to any occupation, when he had always been above work, and free from want. If his father had put him into his counting-room with old Precision, he might have been a good book-keeper, and could now have had employment upon a salary. As it was, he was a useless, worthless member of society. His father had been asked, if he did not think of putting Walter into some situation where he would learn to help himself, but his answer was, "that is my business;" and there ended the matter.

Finally, after some months of idleness, supported by his young wife's toil, a few friends concluded to advance him a thousand dollars, to go South, where, as he thought, he could make a fortune; and if he got away where nobody knew him, he could go into some sort of business. Athalia went with him. They landed at Savannah, put up at the best hotel, four dollars a day, and wine and cigars, upon an average, six more. It was easy to calculate just how long a thousand dollars would last at that business. Athalia pined in idleness; of course, a young "Northern merchant's" wife could not use her needle in a city where a lady, of any pretensions to fashion, would not help herself to a glass of water if the pitcher stood at her eldow. A slave, always ready at her bidding, must be called to wait upon "young missus."

It did not take Walter long to form new acquaintances; besides, he met with several of his old college chums, and so it was a day here and a night there, upon this plantation and that; of course, his pretty wife was always welcome, so long as nobody knew that she was a sewing girl. That secret leaked out at last, and then—

"What then?"

Then those who had courted and fawned around the rich merchant's wife, and thought she was the prettiest and best bred woman, and most intelligent, they had ever met with, and the most modest and most amiable—

"So she was. I never saw her equal."

Nor they either—but then she was a sewing girl, when he married her—perhaps never was married. That was finally annexed by envious, malicious, jealous rivals, who felt her superiority, and how much more she was admired by the gentlemen than they were.

All this came at last, by a true friend—a slave—to Athalia's ear. She had felt the chilling change, and, finally, obtained the secret from her yellow chambermaid. Her mind was instantly made up. That night she packed her trunk; Walter, as usual, was out "attending to business," such as young men often attend to at midnight in some private back room, sitting around a table, counting spots upon little bits of pasteboard.

The steamboat would leave the next morning for Charleston. She waited in vain for Walter, and then wrote a long letter, detailing all the facts and giving ample reasons for her course, and begging him to abandon his; to settle up what matters he had as soon as possible and follow her. Then she laid down for a short nap, with orders to Mary to wake her if Mr. Morgan came in, and if not, to call her in time for the boat at any rate, and then to give him the letter. It was an impulsive step, but that was her nature.

"So it was. She always thought and acted at the same moment; and almost always right."

In one week she was back in her old room, which she had let temporarily during her absence. In one week more she had an additional room and a few girls at work for her at dress-making. She issued her little card, sent it around to old customers, and got some new ones, and all the work that she could do.

In three months she had ceased to pay rent for furniture; she had bought and paid for it, and was making weekly deposits of little sums in the savings bank. Then her husband came back. Where his thousand dollars had gone you may judge, when I tell you that Athalia had to go and redeem his trunk, retained on board a brig for his passage. He could not go himself for it, he was sick; with what complaint you may easily judge; I shall not tell you, as he did not tell his wife, until she too was sick, and in her ignorance, neglected to call a physician, until so bad that she was laid up from work, and of course lost custom. How her little store melted under this accumulation of expense! Finally, they got agoing again, and she persuaded him to get into some kind of employment. What could he do? There was but one "genteel"—mark the word—business that he knew of. He became a bar keeper. He had one regular customer. It was Walter Morgan!

Down hill is an easy road. He took it.

Athalia soon found some of her best customers dropping off.

"What was the cause?"

There were two. In the first place Walter had been the means of getting a notorious courtezan to give her custom to his wife. He brought her there and introduced her as Mrs. Layton, formerly of South Carolina, now living with her nieces and daughter in this city. She used to come often, always in her carriage, with liveried servants.

Once Athalia rode home with her to fit a dress to "a sick young lady, that boarded with her." She found that Mrs. Layton lived in an elegant four story house, near a church and in a very respectable neighborhood in a fashionable street.

Her rooms were furnished with a degree of splendor almost equal to the Morgans. Little did she suspect the character of the house, particularly as her husband had introduced her there.

But there was another cause why she lost her best custo-tomers. In a fashionable soirée, to which Walter still found his way occasionally, when questioned by a score of his old acquaintances, with whom he used to flirt, and every one of whom were envious and jealous of Athalia, they rallied him most unmercifully upon his marriage with a sewing girl, and then the base cowardly wretch—rum makes such of gentlemen—declared upon his honor that he was not married. It was only a marriage of convenience.

"A mistress—a mistress—oh! that alters the case. And only to think we have been getting the shameless thing to make our common dresses. Well, I never will go near her again."

"Nor I. Nor I. Nor I."

"And that accounts for what I heard the other day, that she was seen riding home with that Madame Layton, who keeps a house of assignation in ——— street."

"How did she know that she kept such a house!"

It was Matilda Morgan, that said it. She had been there.

The train once lighted, which fires the dry prairie, how it sweeps on before the wind. It little regards who stand in the way. As little regards the slanderer, and as rapidly spreads the fire of a scandalous tongue, devouring its victims with a consuming fire.

Althalia was a victim. The man who should have been her shield, had himself thrown the first dart. It had been more envenomed by a pretended female friend, who had told her all that he said. She could have forgiven him everything else, she would not forgive him that. Things now looked dark. She was obliged to look for work among a class of customers where nothing but the direst necessity would have led her. Her husband had tended bar, until his employer found that he drank up all the profits. Now he was drinking up the hard earnings of his wife. Then he began to stay out nights. Where, she could only guess. One day she sent him to pay the rent. It was the last money she had. About a week after, the landlord called for it. He had not seen Walter, had not been paid, and was very sorry for her, but he must have the rent.

"Would he wait a few days? she hoped her husband would pay it."

There was a curl of derision upon his lip. What could it mean?

"Fact is, Mrs. Morgan, or Miss Lovetree, or whatever your name is, I let the premises to you, and look to you for the rent. I shall not run after such a miserable drunken ——— as Walter Morgan."

She did not drop dead under this heavy blow; she simply said, "you shall have your rent to-morrow."

"Very well then; and you may as well look for a new place too, in the course of the week."

"I intend to," was her calm reply.

When he was gone, she slipt on her bonnet and shawl, and thought she would take her watch and ear-rings, and a few little things, where her husband had twice taken them before, and whence she had redeemed them, after he had spent the money; for money he would have, and if she did not give it to him, he would steal her things and pawn them. He had done so now. All was gone, even her large Bible, the present of her dying mother. Her only alternative was to get a Jew to come and look at the furniture, and advance enough to pay the rent. On the way she thought she would take a dress home, and get the money for that. She knew it was going to a house of bad repute; she had been obliged to work for such, and on several occasions Walter had carried them home. It was a sort of perquisite with him to get the pay for such. She looked for the dress, that too was gone. There was another to go to the same house, which she could finish in about an hour. It was her only resource for the necessities of to-morrow. At nine o'clock she took it upon her arm and went out, and with trembling step, up to the door of a magnificent house, only one block from Broadway.

As the door opened for her, half-a-dozen "up town bloods," came out.

"I say," said one of them, before he was out of her hearing, "I say, Fred, that is Walt. Morgan's gal, let us go back and see the fun."

The voice was familiar, though the bloated countenance of the roué was not. She had heard it before. It was George Wendall.

"See the fun"—what could it mean? She felt like anything but fun. Is it fun for a man to see a woman's heart broken?

They went on, Fred remarking, "she is dev'lish pretty; curse me if I don't try my hand there. I will walk into her affections."

Such is the opinion of the roué—that the door of woman's affections is always open for every self-conceited puppy to walk in.

Her heart was in her throat. She choked it down, and went in and inquired for Miss Nannette, and was shown up to her room. A gentleman was there, whom Nannette introduced as Mr. Smith, from the South.

He might be from the South, but Athalia knew him to be a married man, with a sweet young wife and two children, in this city.

The dress was to be tried on, and Nannette began to strip off without a blush. Athalia did blush, and did object, and would not stay.

"Well, then, George, go down a few minutes to the parlor, that is a good soul, she is so fastidious."

No, he did not want to be seen there; he would go home.

"Well, then, give me some money to pay for making this dress. You gave me the stuff, you might as well go the whole figure."

He handed her a ten dollar bill; she handed it to Athalia, —the dress was only five—remarking:

"Give him the change; I won't take but a five out cf it this time."

Athalia had no change. She looked at him, to be certain of her man, and remarked:

"No; I will keep the whole, and credit him the balance, on account of seven dollars he has owed me these two months, for work for his wife."

He stammered something about mistake—not him—cursed blunder—and left the room.

The dress fitted beautifully, and Athalia felt the soothing influence of praise for her work, and would have left happier than she came, but just then her ear caught a voice in the next room. She listened. A woman replied:

"Yes, if you have brought any money. I have made up my mind that you shall not stay in this room another night without you give me more money."

"Oh, Josephine, I have got something better than money for you. Look here."

"Oh! you are a dear good fellow, after all. What a pretty watch, and what a dear little locket. That will do. Now you may stay all night, and to-morrow we will go down to Coney Island again, and have a good time. I'll pass for your wife, you know."

There was a door opening out of Nannette's room into a bath-room, and out of that, a window into the room where the voices came from.

It was but a thought; thoughts are quick, and so were her's, and the step that took her up on a chair, and her hand up to the curtain, which was the only thing preventing her from seeing who owned that voice.

She looked. What a sight for a wife! She saw, what she knew before, but would be doubly sure, that the voice was her husband's. She knew that—she knew that he was giving her watch, and the locket which contained the donor's likeness, that of a dear brother lost at sea—a treasure that she would not part with sooner than her own heart—to a woman to whom he had before given money—money that came, drop by drop, distilled from her heart's blood, through the alembic of her needle; and she would see—what woman would not—what wife could resist the opportunity of seeing?—she could not—what the woman looked like, who could displace her in her husband's affections. The first sight she caught was her Bible upon the table.

"What could she want of that?"

She was sometimes religious—a great many of them are, and read the Bible to find some text to justify their own course. They are also visited by clergymen, who prefer those of "a religious turn of mind." Then this Bible was elegantly bound, and very valuable. Then she saw her watch in the hands of a woman with ugly red hair, with dull, voluptuous eyes, thick lips, ugly teeth, a little snub nose, and a gaunt awkward figure, forming altogether one of the ugliest looking women, Athalia thought, that she had ever seen. The words burst involuntarily from her lips:

"Oh, how ugly!"

"She is uglier than she looks," said Nannette. "She has ruined more men than any other woman in the city. She has kicked that fool out half a dozen times because he did not give her more money. I should not wonder now, if he has stolen his wife's watch to give that wretch."

And this was the woman that Athalia had been toiling for her husband to pamper. Oh, how she did pray to die!

Nannette, when she learned the facts, was furious. She would have gone in and torn her heart out.

She said she never did have anything to do with a married man, if she knew it. George had lied to her, and never should see her but once again—once, to get her blessing.

Athalia was calm. She sat down a few minutes, to recover from this last stab in the heart, and then said she would look once more and then go home. She did look, and saw her husband locked in the arms of that red-headed fury. Then she went home; she did not go to bed; she worked all night putting her things in order. Next day, at ten o'clock, a red flag was fluttering at her window, and while Walter and his mistress were going down the Bay, her furniture was "going, going, gone," to the highest bidder.

At sundown she was homeless, friendless, worse than husbandless, alone, in the streets of New York!

CHAPTER XI.

LIFE AT THE FIVE POINTS.

MADALINA, THE RAG-PICKER'S DAUGHTER.

"Youth is bought more oft, than begged or borrowed."

Some wounds do never heal.

ALTHOUGH all my scenes are connected, and bear some relation one to the other, yet they are not continuous. Like the Panorama of Niagara, we must go back, cross over, look up, look down, first from this point of view, then from that, to see all the scenes of that wonder of wonders. So here, where a mighty torrent rushes on, sweeping a multitude down the great cascade, we have to look at scene after scene, before we can join them all together into one panoramic view. Our scenes, too, are as real and life-like as those. Sometimes a tree here, a flower there, then a little spray, then a cloud, or the natural color, a little heightened to give effect, and make the picture more vivid; but the rocks and rushing torrent, the real foundation of the picture, are all as nature made them. So it is with my present panoramic view of "Life Scenes in New York."

Again I shift the scene. Still you will find characters that you have met before, will meet again. It is a tale of sorrow, but a tale of truth.

A little girl was weeping there,
  Pearl drops of bitter tears,
And hope with her was sleeping where
  She spent her youthful years;
Her useless life was fleeing fast,
  Her only school the street;
The future, gloomy shadows cast,
  Where e'er she set her feet.

Her ev'ry day had one sad end,
  Her ev'ry night the same;
Or sick, or well, she had no friend,
  'Twere worthy of that name.
A mother gave this child her birth,
  Or else she had not been;
But Judas like that mother's worth –
  She sold her child to sin!

For gold she gave her child to sin,
  For gold her child betray'd;
What gold would you, dear mother, win,
  Your own to thus degrade?
What gold would you to others give,
  From sin such others save?
Though gold is good to those who live,
  'Tis useless in the grave.

Poor Madalina claims a tear,
  From those her story read

Pray stop and pay that tribute here,
It is her only meed.
Now con her story careful o'er,
Her life was one of grief,
She needs not now your pity more—
To others give relief.

I suppose there are some who will turn away in disgust from the double title of this chapter. What, they will say, can "Life at the Five Points" have in it that is interesting to me, who lounge on silk brocatelle, and look down upon beggar girls and rag-pickers—disgusting objects—through lace curtains that cost more, to every window, than would furnish a hundred families in that locality with better furniture than they now possess?

No doubt you will turn away in disgust at the very sight of the title of "The Rag-picker's Daughter." Yet you may find something in the character of "Madalina," which will make you love the name. I should not wonder, in some of my walks through the city in future years, to hear that pretty name spoken to some sweet child, yet to be born in rose-perfumed chamber.

Then pass not by my tale of one so lowly. See how sweet is a cup of cold water to the dying.

Read.

"Sir," said the door-keeper, to Mr. Pease, one night, "little Madalina, the beggar girl, is at the door, crying bitterly, and says she wants to see you."

"I suppose," said the tired missionary, "I answered hastily, perhaps petulantly, for I had been very much engaged all day. Tell her to go away, I cannot see her to-night; it is eleven o'clock, and I am very tired. She must come to-morrow."

The poor fellow turned upon his heel to go away, but as he did so, the glimpse of his hand and motion of the coat sleeve across his eyes, told a story.

"Tom," said Mr. P., "Tom, my dear boy, what is the matter?"

Tom did not turn round as he had been taught, and usually did, so as to look him full in the face when he answered; in fact he did not answer readily; there was a choking sensation in his utterance which prevented the words from coming forth distinctly.

Now, this boy had been but a short time in "the Home," and perhaps a more squalid, wretched, drunken boy, cannot be found in the purlieus of the Five Points, than he was when he was almost literally picked out of the gutter, as he had been once before he came here finally, in the way you have already seen. Once before, he had actually been dragged out of the filthiest hole in Anthony street, brought in, washed and dressed, before he came to, so as to be conscious of the change that had come over him. Then he was brought back again to his low degradation, by just such wretches and ways of the wicked as were brought to bear upon poor Reagan, and will be upon many others, while the destroyer is permitted to walk abroad like a pestilence at noon-day. Now this outcast, who had cared for nothing human, not even himself, stood vainly trying to choke down his grief for the sorrows of a little beggar girl.

Were the reminiscences of one, almost as low down in the scale of humanity, running through his mind—one who, after having been herself lifted up, had exerted an influence upon him to his salvation?

The tired missionary forgot his fatigue.

"Tom," said he, springing up, "I will go and see what is the matter. Who is this Madalina?"

"She is an Italian rag-picker's daughter, sir—they live in Cow Bay—I used to lodge with them sometimes. That is, the mother picks rags, and the father goes with the hand-organ and monkey."

"Ah, that is where the little tambourine girl came from that we have now in school There is a quarrel, I suppose, and the little girl has come for me."

Tom went down stairs, with a heart as light as his step, "which," said Mr. P., "I followed, I must acknowledge, rather heavily, for I did not quite relish the idea of being wakened out of a comfortable evening nap, to do police duty in Cow Bay, and I fear there might not have been quite as much suavity in my tone and manner towards the rag-picker's daughter, as we ought to use when speaking to those poor children, for I recollect the words were, 'What do you want?' instead of, 'What can I do for you, my child—come tell me, and don't cry any more.'"

"I don't want to be a beggar girl. I want to be like my cousin Juliana."

"Juliana—Juliana. I don't know her."

"It is the little tambourine girl, sir," said Tom.

"Oh, I see now. Juliana is your cousin, then. Come here Madalina; let me look at you, and I will talk about it. Did Juliana tell you to come here?"

"Yes, sir; she has told me a good many times, but they would not let me. I am afraid to stay there to-night, they are drinking and fighting so bad."

"I thought so; and you want me to go and stop them; is that it?"

"No, sir. I want to stay here."

"Oh, a poor little girl flying for fear from her own parents, because they are drinking and fighting so."

He drew her forward into the light, and looked upon as fine a set of features as he ever saw. Her hair, which, as a matter of course, was black almost as the raven's wing, and subsequently, when cleaned of dirt and its accompaniments, became almost as glossy, overshadowed a pair of the keenest, yet mildest, black eyes I ever met with. Her skin was dark, partly natural, and partly the effect of the sun upon its unwashed, unsheltered surface. Her teeth, oh! what a set of teeth! which, she afterward told me, she kept clean by a habit she had of eating charcoal. She was about twelve years old, slim form, rather tall, but delicate structure. Her dress consisted of a dirty cotton frock, reaching a little below the knees, and nothing else. Barefooted, bareheaded, almost naked, at the hour of midnight, of a cold March night, a little innocent child, wandering through the streets of New

York, vainly plying the words, "Please give me a penny, sir," to well-fed, comfortably-dressed men, whose feelings have grown callous by constantly hearing such words from such objects, to whom to give is not to relieve, but rather encourage to continue in the pursuit of such ill-gotten means of prolonging life, without any prospect of benefit to themselves or their fellow-creatures.

"Then you don't want to beg, Madalina! Why not?"

"Because people push me, and curse me, and to-day one man kicked me right here, sir." And she laid her hand upon her stomach, and a little groan of anguish and accusation against the unfeeling monster who had done the deed, went to the recording angel, and was set down in the black catalogue of rum-selling crimes, for a day of retribution yet to come.

"Kicked you! What for? Were you saucy?"

"No, sir; I am never saucy. My mother says if I am saucy, men won't give me anything. I must be very quiet, and not talk any, nor answer any questions."

"Then how came he to kick you?"

"I don't know, sir; I did not say a word, I only went into one of those nice rooms in Broadway, where they have such beautiful glass bottles and tumblers, and looking-glasses, and such a sight of all sorts of liquor, and where so many fine gentlemen go and sit, and talk, and laugh, and drink, and smoke; and I just went along and held out my hand to the gentlemen, when one of them told me to open my mouth, and shut my eyes, and hold out my hand, and he would give me a shilling. Now look what he did—he put his cigar all burning in my hand, and shut it up and held it there."

Horrible! she opened her hand, and showed three fingers and a palm all in a blister.

"Oh, sir, that is nothing to what another one did. He put a great nasty chaw of tobacco in my mouth, and then I could not help crying; then the man who sells the liquor, he ran out from behind the counter, and how he did swear, and caught me by the hair, and pulled me down on the floor, and kicked me so I could hardly get away. But he told me if I did not he would set the dogs on me and tear me to pieces."

"What did you go into such a place for?"

"I had been all day in the streets and only got three pennies, and I wanted to go home."

"Well, why did you not go?"

"My mother said if I did not get sixpence to-day she would whip me, and so I went to that place. I did not think such nice dressed gentlemen would do so. What if they should have to beg some day! My father used to dress as fine as they when he kept the *Café de l'Imperator*."

"And where have you been since they abused you so?"

"I crept up into a cart in Pearl street; I was so sick, after the tobacco and the kick, for it was very hard."

"Could you not get home?"

"No, sir. Besides, what if I could, and my mother had been drinking. She would kick me again, perhaps."

"What, then, are you going to do to-night? You cannot sleep in the street; it is too cold."

"Won't you let me sleep?"——

"With your cousin Juliana?"

"No, sir, not that; she is clean, and I—I wish I was. Won't you let me sleep on the floor?"

"You shall have a place to sleep to-night; and to-morrow, if your mother is willing, you shall come and live with your cousin Juliana, and be dressed as she is, and learn to sew; and when you get big enough"——

"Her mother will prostitute her, as she did her older sister to a miserable old pimp for ten dollars."

"Tom, Tom, what is that?"

"The truth, sir. Have I ever told you a lie since I have been in your house?"

"Well, well, Tom, take Madalina to the housekeeper, and give her somewhere to sleep to-night, and to-morrow morning you shall go to her mother and see what she will do."

"Lord, sir, I must go to-night. She will be off with her hook and basket, poking in the gutters after rags before the stars go to bed. These rag-pickers are early birds. I have known them travel four or five miles of a morning, to get to their own walk."

"Own walk. What is that?"

"All the city is divided up among them. Each must keep to his own walk. If one should trespass upon another, he would get a wet cloth over his mouth some night when he was asleep, and nobody would know or care how he died."

"The coroner's jury would inquire into the matter."

"Coroner! fiddlesticks! I beg your pardon, sir, but I did

not mean to answer you that way, though I did know that coroner's juries care the least of anybody how such fellows die. The verdict would be 'accidental death,' 'found dead,' 'died of visitation of Providence;' or, if the murderers got a chance, which they might do easy enough, to chuck the body in the dock, the verdict would be 'found drowned,' no matter if he had a hole in his head as big as my fist."

"They could not carry the body from this neighborhood to the river without being detected."

"Could'nt they. How did Ring-nosed Bill and Snakey Jo carry Pedlar Jake from Cale Jones's to Peck-slip and send him afloat?"

"What, dead?"

"Yes, sir, they put too much opium in his rum to get him to sleep, so they could rob him, and he did not wake up, and so they walked him off."

"Walked him off, how?"

"They stood him up and fastened one of their legs to his each side, so that when they stepped his feet travelled too, and so they went along, talking to him and cursing him for being so drunk, till they got to the dock."

"Where were the Police, do they never notice such things?"

"Lord, no sir, they steps round the corner when they sees a drunken man coming, particularly if he has one of his friends with him."

"And do you think, Tom, that the rag-pickers would murder a fellow-creature who trespassed, as they call it, upon their grounds, without compunction of conscience?"

"Conscience, sir, what do they know about conscience? The 'Padre' keeps their conscience."

"But the law, is there no law in this Christian City?"

"Law, pshaw! what has your book-law to do with rag-pickers' law?"

"True enough; or 'father confessors,' either."

The next morning Tom made his report. At first it was a positive refusal. "She can make sixpence a day, and pick up enough to eat."

"Well then she shall pay you sixpence a day. She can soon learn to sew and earn more than that. Juliana does it every day."

"But she shall not stay there nights. They will make a Protestant of her."

"That was not the sticking point," says Tom, "if she stays here, she cannot make a——of her there. The best I could do was to let her go home nights and come days. That is better than nothing. The poor little thing won't have to go begging, and be burned, and kicked, and vomited with filthy tobacco cuds, and then whipped if she don't bring home sixpence every night for her mother to buy rum with. If she cannot earn it here at first, I will, and we will get her away entirely, after a while."

Noble Tom! Glorious good boy! What a heart! How long is it since thou wert as one of them, kicked and cuffed, and groveling drunk in the gutter? Who thought then that thy rags and filth covered such a heart? Who knew of the virtuous lessons given thee by a pious mother; and how, after years of forgetfulness, sin, wretchedness, misery, that that good seed would vegetate and bring forth such sweet flowers and good fruit, as we are now tasting in these good deeds and kind words. What if nine of the fallen whom we lift up, fall back again? so that one stand, who shall refuse to lend a helping hand? Let us lift up the lowly and make the haughty humble. Why should they do evil?

Again the messenger went up to the Great Recorder, and a double deed of mercy was written down.

Wild Maggie, thy sins are forgiven. Look at thy work. This is the poor outcast boy of whom you said,

"Tom, I am going to provide you with a home. You must go to the House of Industry, reform, and make a man of yourself."

The work is more than half done.

Madalina, though still suffering from her brutal treatment, was a happy girl when she found that she was not to be driven out to beg in the streets.

But she could not understand why her mother wanted her to sleep at home. Tom could. "Too young! Pooh! before she is a year older, she will be lost." Too true! Before she had been in "the Home" six months, she had learned to read, write, and work, and had grown much in stature and fine looks. Then she would have been placed in some good family, but her mother would not consent. She still complained of her breast, and had frequent turns of vomiting. She always felt worse in the morning, "because," she said, "that was such a dreadful place to sleep."

Sometimes she did not come for a few days; her mother made her stay at home and sew. She had learned to work, and her services were worth more at that than begging.

One night she came in, in great haste, crying.

"What is the matter, Madalina?"

"My mother has had an offer for me."

"An offer for you. What is that?"

Tom looked daggers. "I told you so."

"What is it, my good girl. Tell me all about it."

"My mother bid me go out with her this evening, both of us dressed in our best. She said she had an offer for me, and was going to meet the man in Duane street.

"'What does the man want of me, mother?' said I.

"'Oh, he will make a fine lady of you, and you will live with him.'

"'But I don't want to live with him; I had rather live with Mr. Pease, at "the Home." I had rather live where Tom is, for Tom is good to me.'"

Young love's first happy dream!

"But we went on, and I held my head down, and felt very bad. By-and-by I heard my mother say, 'Here she is,' and I looked up a little, and saw two gentlemen—that is, they were clothed like gentlemen—and directly one spoke to the other.

"'I say, Jim, she will do; give the old woman the money, and let us take her up to Kate's.'

"Mercy on me, that voice! I felt that sore spot in my breast grow more and more painful. I looked up; *it was the man who kicked me;* the other was the man who put the tobacco in my mouth."

"What did you do?"

"I stood a little behind my mother while she held out her hand for the money, and when their eyes were turned I ran. I only heard them say, 'Why, damn her, she is gone.' Yes, I was gone, and here I am. Oh, I am so sick and so faint! do let me lay down, and don't let those men have me. Oh dear, the thought of it will kill me!"

So it did. A cruel blow had fallen upon a tender plant. The beggar girl might not have felt it. The little seamstress did. A taste of virtue, civilization, christianity, friendship, love, had given the food of sin and shame a hated taste. Sold by a mother to a libidinous brute—to a miserable rum-selling, —worse than rum-drinking—wretch, who wears gentlemanly garments, and kicks, burns, and gags little beggar girls. It was too much for human nature to bear, and it sunk under this last blow, worse than the first.

Madalina went to bed with a raging fever—a nervous prostration. All that kindness and skill could do, was done for the poor sufferer; but what could we do for the body, when the heart was sick?

Next morning her mother came and insisted that she should go home. They begged, pleaded, and promised in vain; go she must.

"Never mind," said Madalina, "it will be only for a little, little while. I shall be well—at least all will be well with me in a few days. I cannot endure this pain in my breast. *You will come and* see me. *Good bye.* Tom, you will?

It was an honest, manly tear that Tom turned away to hide. Poor fellow, he need not have been ashamed of it. Such is nature.

"She is worse, sir," said Tom, one morning, "and no wonder. I wish you would go and see her; she wants to see you once more. Such a place to be sick in! oh, dear! how did I ever sleep there? I wish you would go with me to-night, about ten o'clock, when they are all in. You will see life as it is."

"Very well, Tom, I will go. Call for me at ten, or when you are ready."

It was my fortune to drop in upon that very evening, and form one of the company to that abode of misery,—that home of the city poor,—so that I am able to describe it in my own language. The place where Madalina lived, is a well known Five Points locality, called "Cow Bay."

As you go up that great Broadway of wealth, fashion, luxury, and extravagance of this great city, from the Park and its marble halls of justice, you will pass another great marble front —it is the palace of trade, where the rich are clothed every day in fine linens, when they go "shopping at Stewart's." Further along are great marts, where velvet coverings for the floor are sold; for there are some who have never trod upon bare boards. You need not look down Duane street, unless you have a curiosity to see the spot where a miserable mother would sell the virtue of her child to a wretch whose trade is seduction. Don't look into that little old wooden shanty at the corner of Pearl street; it is a "family grocery." The little ragged girl you see coming out with a rusty tin coffee-pot, has not been there for milk for her sick mother—her father is in the hospital on the opposite side of the way—his arm was broken in a "family quarrel." You will pass the Broadway Theatre before you reach the next corner, with its surroundings of fashionable "saloons," into any of which you may go without fear of losing caste among genteel brandy-smashers and wine-bibbers. Perhaps you will be amused with a small play, such as burning, kicking, or vomiting a little beggar girl; for nice young men are fond of theatrical amusements. Do not go into that place of "fashionable resort," the theatre, if it is a hot evening, for it is worse ventilated than the black-hole of Calcutta, and if the fetid air does not breed a fever, it will breed a feverish thirst, which will tempt you to quench it in potations of poison. Probably that is why it was thus built.

A few steps beyond is Anthony street. Stop a moment here, and look up and down the great thoroughfare of New-York before you leave it. A hundred pedestrians pass you every minute; almost without an exception, every one of them richly dressed men and women, smiling in joy and happiness. Here is an exception, certainly. A woman in poverty's garb, with a bundle of broken boards and old timbers, from a demolished building, that would be a load for a pack-horse. She is followed by two little boys, with each a bundle, crushing their young years into early decrepitude. They have brought their heavy loads all the long way from Murray street. They turn down Anthony; look where they go. If they live in that street, it cannot be far, for there, in plain view, stands a large frame house, corner-wise towards you, right in the middle of the street. No, it only looks so, it is beyond the end of it. Yet look, note it well, the corner of that house so plain in view, pointing towards you, is one of the world-wide-known Five Points of New-York.

"What! not so near Broadway, right in plain sight of all who wear silks and broadcloth, and go up and down that street every day? Surely that is not the place where all those bad, miserable, poor outcasts live, that the newspapers talk so much about."

"The very spot, my dear lady."

"Really, this must be looked to. It is quite too bad to think that place is so near our fashionable street, and in sight too. I thought it was away off somewhere the *other* side of town. If I thought it would do any good, I would let Peter take a few dollars and some old clothes, and go down with them to-morrow."

"Try it, madam. Better go yourself. Let Peter drive you down; see for yourself what has been done and what is yet to do. Lend your hand to cure that eye-sore, which will pain you every time you pass, for you cannot shut it out of sight, now you know where it is; so near your daily walk or drive to Stewart's, or nightly visit to the theatre, or weekly visit to the church. Go to-morrow; don't put it off till next week."

In the meantime, reader, let us follow the woman and two boys with their heavy burden, on their homeward way to-night. We will go and see where they live.

So I followed down Anthony, past some very old rat-harbor houses, filled with human beings, almost as thick as those quadrupeds burrow in a rotten wharf; so on they go across Elm; now they stand a moment on the edge of Centre, for one of the little boys has taken hold of his mother's dress to pull her back—for she cannot look up with her load—with a sudden cry of, "Stop, old woman! Don't you see the car is coming? Why, you are as blind as a brick. That is black Jim a-driving, and he had just as soon drive over the likes of you as eat. Hang you for a fool, han't you got no sense, old stupid? There now, run like thunder, blast ye, for here comes another of the darned cars—run, I tell you!"

She did run with her great load, till she almost dropped under its overwhelming weight. Why should she thus labor—thus expend so much strength to so little purpose? She knew no other way to live. Nobody gave her remunerative labor for strong hands; nobody took those two stout boys, and set them to till the earth, or taught them how to create bread, and yet they must eat, and so they prowl about the pulled-down houses, snatching everything they can carry away—a sort of permitted petty larceny, that teaches those who practice it how to do bigger deeds; and those old timbers they split up into kindling wood and peddle through the streets.

Poor uncared for fellow creatures; working and stealing to escape starvation—living, for what?—running to escape being run over by an unfeeling driver who cared just as much for them as for so many dogs.

On they went, down Anthony street; and I followed, determined to see the *home* of this portion of the city poor. It was but one block further—only one little space beyond this great, wide, open, railroad street, whose thoughtless thousands daily go up and down from homes of wealth to wealth-producing ships and stores, little thinking of the amount of human misery within a stone's throw of the rails on which they glide swiftly along.

One block further, and the street opens into a little, half acre sort of triangular space, sometimes dignified with the name of "park," but why, those who know can only tell, for it has no fence, no grass, and but a dozen miserable trees; 'tis lumbered up with carts and piles of stones, and strings of drying clothes, and scores of unwashed specimens of young humanity, whose home is in the dirt, whether in the street or parents' domicil.

Here let us stop and look around. A very short street, only one block across the base of the "park," runs to the right from where we stand, past the "Five Points House of Industry," to Cross street. This is the most notorious little street in New York. Its name is Little Water street. It lead from the "Old Brewery" to "Cow Bay." Who that has lived long in this city, or read its history, particularly that portion of it written by Dickens, has not heard of the "Old Brewery?" It is not there now. That awful den of crime, poverty, and wretched drunken miserv has been pulled down, and in its place a substantial brick edifice, in which is a chapel and school-room, and home of another missionary, has been erected by the noble, generous efforts of the Ladies' Home Missionary Society, of the Methodist Church. The old tenants have been driven out or reformed. How different, too, are the present occupants of that large brick pile in Little Water street, from those who filled its numerous rooms before the missionary came there. Every room was a brothel or a den of thieves, or both combined. Now it is a house of prayer—a home for the homeless—a place of refuge for midnight wandering little beggar girls.

Before us lies the misnamed, neglected triangle, called a park. At the further end is the frame house that we see so plainly as we look down Anthony street from Broadway. At the left, as though it were a continuation of Little Water street, lies that notorious Five Points collection of dens of misery, Cow Bay. It is a *cul-de-sac*, perhaps thirty feet wide at the mouth, narrowing, with crooked, uneven lines, back to a point about a hundred feet from the entrance. Into this court I tracked the kindling-wood-splitters, and threaded my way among the throng of carts and piles of steaming garbage; elbowing my way along the narrow side-walk, and up a flight of broken, almost impassable steps, I reached the first floor hall of one of the houses, just in time to see that great load of wood and its bearer toiling up a narrow, dark, broken stairway, which I essayed to climb; but just then, from the room on the left, at the foot of the stairs, there came such a piercing, murder-telling, woman's shriek, that I started back, grasped my stout cane, determined to brave the worst for the rescue, made one step, pushed open the door, creaking with a horrid grating upon its rusty hinges, and stood in the presence of an Eve, before the fall, in point of clothing, but long, long after that in point of sin. As I entered the open door, she sprung towards it; her husband caught her by the hair, and drew her back, with no gentle hand or word.

"Let me go, let me go—help!—he wants to murder me; let me go—help, help, help!"

I did help, but it was help to the poor man, for she turned upon him with the fury of a tiger, scratching and tearing his face and clothes, and then settling with a grasp upon his throat, which produced the death-rattle of suffocation.

A strong silk handkerchief served the hand-cuff's place, and to bind hands and feet together; after which she lay quietly upon a little straw and rags, in one corner, the only articles of furniture in the room, except a bottle, broken cup, and something that looked as though it once had been female apparel.

"Is this your wife?"

"She was."

"What is she now?"

"The devil's fury. You saw what she is."

"Do you live with her?"

"I did for seven years."

"Did she drink then?"

"Sometimes—not so bad."

"Did you drink?"

"Well, none to hurt. I kept a coffee house."

"And made your wife a drunkard. How came she reduced to this dreadful condition? You are well dressed."

"I left her three months ago, and went West to find a place to move to. She said if she could go where nobody knew her she would reform. I left her in a comfortable room, with good furniture and good clothes. Now, where are they? All gone to the pawnbroker's; the money gone for rum—her virtue, shame, everything gone. How, what, and where do I find her? As you see, crazy drunk, in this miserable hole, in Cow Bay. And my boy, starved, made drunk, and—"

"What, have you a child by her, then?"

"Yes, a sweet little boy, six years old. Oh, I wish he was awake, that you might see him."

And he stepped to the miserable bed, and lifted the dirty rag of a quilt, looked a moment upon the pale boy, dropped upon his knees, raised him in his arms, looked again wildly, and fell back fainting as he exclaimed, "Great God, he is dead!"

What little I could do or say to relieve such heart-crushing woe as overwhelmed this poor father of that murdered child—this miserable husband of that wretched, crazy—rum-crazy woman, was soon done. What else could I do than call in a police officer to take her away to prison? whence she went to the hospital, then to the drunkard's uncared-for, unwept-over grave!

Now, strange footsteps are winding up the rickety stairs, which I follow. They were those of Tom and the Missionary, for here lived little Madalina.

The second floor was divided into three rooms. We looked in as we passed. The back room was ten by twelve feet square, inhabited by two black men and their wives, and a white woman lodger, who "sometimes has company." Here they eat, drink, and sleep,—cook, wash, and iron. The latter operation is performed on the bottom of the wash-tub, for there is no table. The front room, eight by fourteen feet, contained five blacks, men and women. Each of these rooms rented for four dollars a month, *in advance.*

A dark centre room, occupied by a white woman, was only six by seven feet, for which she paid fifty cents a week. On the third floor, the dark centre room, same size, was occupied by a real good looking, young, healthy German woman, with her husband, a great burly negro, as black as Africa's own son, and a fine looking little white boy, four years old, as a lodger. We found the door shut, and no ventilator bigger than the key-hole. There *was* a smell about the air.

In the back room, ten by twelve, we found the wood-splitters—the woman and her two boys, a negro and his wife, a woman lodger, and occasional company. The rent of this room is one dollar a week in advance. The total amount of furniture, was not good security for one week's rent.

"Good woman, why do you bring all your great piles of wood up these steep, slippery stairs, to fill up your room?"

"Cot in himmel, vare vould I puts him? In te court? De peoples steal him all."

True, there was no place but in that one room to store up a supply, while the time of gleaning was good. Then it has to be carried down to the court, to be split up into kindlings, and then again carried up for storage. How so many find room to live in such narrow space, if our readers would learn, let them go and make personal inquiry. They will find plenty of just such cases, with slight search.

Up, up again, one more flight of creaking stairs, without bannisters, the thin worn steps bending beneath our tread, and we are on the upper floor of this one of a hundred just alike "tenant houses." Along the dark, narrow passage, opening by that low door at the end, into a room under the roof, ten by fifteen feet, lighted by one dormer window, and we are in the home of Madalina, the rag-picker's daughter. Home! Can it be that that holy name has been so desecrated—that this child, with sylph-like form and angel face, must call this room her home. 'Tis only for a little while! She will soon have another!

In one corner of the room stood two hand organs, such as the most of us city dwellers are daily tormented with, groaning out their horrid music under our windows, while the grinder and his monkey look anxiously for falling pennies or pea-nuts. These stand a little way apart, with a couple of boards laid across the space. On these boards there had been an attempt to make a bed, of sundry old coats, a dirty blanket, and other vermin harbors.

On this bed lay the poor little sufferer. Not so very little either. In her own native Italy she had been counted almost a woman.

We have seen many, many beautiful faces, but never one like this—so angelic.

"It is a bad sign," said Tom, in answer to a remark upon the expression of her face; "it is a sign she will soon be among those she looks so much like. She never looked so before. She is a living angel now, she will soon be a real one."

"Madalina, my good child," said the missionary, "how do you feel to-night?"

"The pain in my breast has been very bad, but it is easier now. It always goes away when you come. I am so glad you came to-night, for I wanted to thank you for a thousand good things you have done for me."

"Are you afraid you will not get well?"

"Oh, no, I am not afraid; I know I shall not, but I am not afraid. I don't want to live, if I must live here; look around. It did not use to look as it does now to me; when I went out begging, and came home tired and cold and hungry, I could lay down with the monkeys on my mother's bag of nasty, wet rags, and go to sleep directly. Now they worry me to death with their chattering. Do drive them down, Tom, that is a dear, good fellow."

It would evidently have been a source of great gratification to Tom, to have pitched five or six of them out of the window. But there were dark eyes scowling on him, out of a dozen sockets of men who come from the land of the stiletto, and looked now as though they could as readily use it as play the organ and lead the monkey.

I looked about, and counted six men or stout boys, and eight women and girls, besides several children, monkeys, tambourines and hand organs. In one corner was the rag-picker's store. This had been the bed of Madalina until this evening, she grew so much worse, that she was lifted up to the bed I have described. But here she had not escaped the torment of the monkeys. They had long been her companions and seemed determined to be so still. They were climbing up and down, or sitting chattering on her bed. Late as it was in the evening there were several fresh arrivals of parties of musicians and rag-pickers from their distant walks. Several were at supper. A long, black table with a wooden bench, on either side, was furnished with two wooden trays, which had seen long service and little soap. Into these was ladled from time to time, the savory contents of a large pot simmering upon the stove. Each guest helped himself with fingers and spoon. Whether the stew was composed of monkey meat, or two days old veal, I cannot say. That onions formed a strong part of the ingredients, we had olfactory demonstration. Some of the party indulged in a bottle of wine, and we smelt something very much like bad rum or worse brandy; but generally speaking, this class of the city poor are not great drunkards. One end of the room was entirely occupied by a camp bed. That is, in that narrow space of ten feet, ten human beings, big and little, of both sexes, laid down side by side. The balance of the family lay around here and there; some on and some under the table, some on great black chests, of which each family had one, wherein they lock all their personal goods from their pilfering room mates. The stove and a few dishes finishes the catalogue of furniture. How many persons are, or can be stowed into this one room, is beyond my powers of computation.

Will some of my readers, who faint at the smell of unsavory food, or who could not sleep but in fresh linen and well aired rooms, fancy what must be the feelings of poor Madalina, who had just begun to taste of the comforts of civilized life, now sick and dying in such a room, where the penny candle only served to make the thick clouds of tobacco smoke more visible and more suffocating?

One of the difficulties in all these close-packed rooms is the necessity of keeping the door always shut, to prevent pilfering, thus leaving the only chance for fresh air to enter, or foul air to escape, by the one small window in the roof.

Having given you a view of the room, and its inhabitants and furniture, let us look again upon poor Madalina, as she lies panting for breath upon her hard pallet. Her face, naturally dark, has an unhealthy whiteness spread over it, and there is a small, bright crimson spot upon one cheek—the other is hidden in the taper fingers of the hand upon which it rests. Such a pair of bright black eyes! Oh, how beautiful! Her wavy locks of jet, are set off by a clean, white handkerchief, spread over the bundle of rags which forms her pillow, by one of her visitors. Now, in spite of pain, there is a smile lighting up her face, and showing such a set of teeth as a princess might covet. Whence this happy smile? Listen how cheaply it is brought upon the face of the suffering innocent. She had said, "I am so thirsty, and nothing to drink but nasty, warm tea." Directly, Tom was missing

THE DEATH-BED OF MADALINA.—*Page* 217.

Now he was back again, and there he stood with a nice, white pitcher in one hand, full of ice water, and a glass tumbler in the other. Now he pours it full of the sparkling nectar—now he drops upon one knee and carries it to those parched lips. Is it any wonder that she smiles? Is it any wonder that that simple-minded, good-hearted boy should look up, as I stood looking over the kneeling Missionary, and say, "Don't she look like an angel, sir?"

It was an angelic smile. It was a sight worth days and nights of earnest seeking, and yet, Oh, how cheaply purchased. Only one glass of cold water!

Would that I had some Raphaelic power to transfer the picture of that scene to this page, for you to look upon as well as read of, for a sight of that face with its surroundings, would do you good. It would make you yearn after the blessed opportunity of holding the cup of cold water to other fevered lips, lighting up other angelic, happy, thankful smiles.

As it is, the artist has only been able to give you a faint illustration of the principal features of this scene. So far as it goes, you cannot but admire his skill—admire the delineator's art, by which the picture is sketched upon the block, and the engraver's skill, who cuts the lines by which the printer spreads the scene out before the admiring eyes of those who read and view. Such is art, and skill, and industry. How much better than the idle life of those who furnished the originals for these "Life Scenes!"

Vainly we pleaded with the mother of Madalina to carry her

to a comfortable room—to my house—to any house—to the hospital—to get a physician—a nurse—some one, at least, to give her a drink of cold water through the next long, long day, when she would be left nearly alone—perhaps quite so—locked in this dreadful room—while men and monkeys, organs and tambourines, beggers and rag-pickers, were all away plying their trades in the streets of the city. It was no use; she was inexorable. The *padre* was a very good doctor—the *padre* was good for her soul—the *padre* would pray for her; and if she was to die, she should not die in the house of a heretic. So we parted. It was a hard parting, for she clung to each one as she said:

"Good bye; I wish I could go with you, but my mother—you have taught me to obey my mother, that all good children obey their mothers—so good bye—good bye, Tom. You will bring me another drink to-morrow? yes, I knew you would, if I asked you, you are so good to me."

There were tears at parting, and they were not all tears of a sick child, or good boy, but strong men wept.

"Tom," said the feeble, sobbing voice, after we had almost reached the door, over the careless sleepers on the floor; "Tom, come back a minute, I want to—want to—say—what if I should not see you again? I want to send something to Mrs. Pease; she was so kind to me; I wish I had something to send her to remember me by; but I have got nothing—nothing. Yes, I will send her a—a little nearer."

And she put her arms around his neck, and imprinted a kiss upon his lips.

"There, I will send her that, it is all I have—it will tell her I love her, for I never kiss any but those I love."

Poor Madalina! Poor Tom! What must have been his feelings at that moment, with the kiss of that angelic, dying girl burning upon his lips, and running streams of lava down into his young heart, while these words, "I never kiss any but those I love," are thrilling through his brain like words of fire?

What he felt I cannot tell. I will not tell what I felt after the first flow of scalding tears had passed away, but I fear there was an unforgiving spirit in my heart; and if the foot which crushed that tender flower had been there then, perhaps it and its fellow had not carried their moving power, the head, "this side up with care." Perhaps that head would have been pitched headlong down these long, steep, dark, and narrow stairs, to the pavement—less hard than its guiding heart.

"We must not kill," said Tom, as we reached the street.

Had he divined my secret thoughts, or was it the response to his own?

"We must not kill those who sell the rum, or kick little children to death, or make brutes of their mothers, but we will kill the business, or else we will prove that all are not good men in this world who pretend to be."

"It is greatly changed," I said to the Missionary, as we came down upon the street, "since you have lived here; as it was some years ago, when I first knew this locality, it might not have been quite safe to walk alone through these streets at this midnight hour; now we have no fear. Good night."

"It will be better two years hence, if you and I live. Good night."

"Good night. Heaven protect you, and bless your labors. Good night, Tom."

But Tom heard me not. "I never kiss any but those I love," was ringing in his ears. He heard nothing—thought of nothing else. Poor Tom! He carried a heavy heart to a sleepless bed that night.

Back, up Anthony to Centre, then along that one block, and I stood and contemplated that great sombre, gray stone building which fills a whole square, looking down gloomily upon the multitude who reek in misery on the opposite side of the street, or pursue their nefarious schemes of crime within the very shadow of "the Tombs." Alas! prisons prevent not crime, nor does incarceration work reformation upon such as dwell in tenements such as we have just visited.

"It is but a step from the palace to the tomb."

True, and so it seemed this night; for ere I had fairly realized the fact that I had passed over the short step of two squares between the City prison—the Tombs—and Broadway, I stood looking into that great palace hall on the corner of Franklin street, known as Taylor's Saloon.

Was ever eating and drinking temptation more gorgeously fitted up? How the gilt and carving, and elaborate skill of the painter's art glitter in the more than sun-light splendor of a hundred sparkling gas-burners. Are the windows open? No. The ten-feet long plates of glass are so clear from speck, it seems as though it were open space. Look in. It is midnight. Is all still? Do the tired servants sleep? No. They are flitting up and down, with noiseless tread, to furnish late suppers and health-destroying luxuries, to a host of men and gayly dressed women. 'Tis the palace of luxury—'tis but a step from the palace to the tombs—'tis but a step beyond to the home of "the Rag Picker's Daughter"—'tis here that the first step is taken which leads to infamy like that of that daughter's mother. 'Tis here that he, whose trade is seduction, walketh unshamed at noonday, or prowls at midnight, to select his victims. 'Tis here that mothers suffer young daughters to come at this untimely midnight hour to drink "light wines," or eat ice cream, drugged with passion-exciting vanilla.

"Ha, ha, ha!" laughed the fiend as we passed on, "rag-picking mothers are not the only ones who traffic away the virtue of young daughters in this rum-flooded city."

"What," said I, as I passed on, "if all the mis-spent shillings, worse than wasted in this palace, were dropped into the treasury of the House of Industry?"

"Cow Bay, Farlow's Court, and Rotten Row, would be no more, and my occupation would be gone," said the fiend. "It must not be. Dry up rum, and murder would cease and misery have no home here. It must not be. *Our* trade is in danger; I must alarm my friends!"

And he clattered his cloven foot down the steps of a near-by cellar, where there were loud sounds of blasphemous words, the noise of jingling glasses, and much wrangling, amid which I heard female voices in one of the "private rooms," and then an order for more wine—then I heard old cloven foot say, "give them a bottle of two-and-sixpenny cider, they are so drunk now they wont know the odds."

Then I understood why the fiend said "our trade"—it is one which none else than such delight in.

I listened again. There was an awful string of oaths coming up out of the infernal regions, where men and women —street-walkers—were getting drunk upon alcohol, carbonic acid, and cider, mixed into three dollar bottles of "wine"—pure champagne.

"Give me my pocket-book, you——"

I cannot repeat the horrid expletives. Why does a man call a woman with whom he associates, such vile names? Why does the woman retort upon him that he is the son of a female dog, and call upon God to send his soul to perdition? Because they have "tarried long at the wine; have looked upon it when it is red, when it giveth its color in the cup." Now "it biteth like a serpent and stingeth like an adder."

Now the woman has picked the pocket of her male companion—I cannot say gentleman; now he utters those terrible oaths; now she pours out such a stream of words as would pollute the very air where virtue lives; now there is a struggle; now a man is stabbed by a woman; now there is a crash of broken glass, a female street-walker is knocked down with a bottle in the hands of a man who has picked her up, and whose pockets she has picked; surely it was no vision of the brain that fancied we saw the incarnate fiend go down there; now there is a cry of murder; now there is a rapping of clubs upon the pavement, and running of men with brass stars upon the left breast of their coats; now the police bear up a wounded man—if Madalina was here her wounded breast would ache with new pain—she is avenged at last; now they drag up a woman, a young girl, on her way to the Tombs—it is Julia Antrim.

Drop the curtain. Surely you would not look into a prison cell, or go into the police court, or with a "vagrant," not yet fourteen years old, to Randall's Island. In some change of the scene you may see her again. *Quien sabe?*

"It was late next morning," said Mr. Pease, "when I woke up, and then I lay in a sort of dreamy reverie, thinking what a world of good I could do if I had plenty of means, until near ten o'clock. Finally, I heard an uneasy step outside my door and at length it seemed to venture to approach, and then there was a timid rap."

"May I come in?"

"Yes, Tom, come in. What is it, Tom?"

"If you please, sir, I want to go away to-day."

"Oh, no, Tom, don't go away to-day, you remember what you promised to do for Madalina."

"Yes, sir, and I am going to do it. I am going to see where they put her, and then I will plant a flower there, and I will water it too, and that is not all, either, that I am going to do with water before I die. I am going to teach people to drink it, and not drink rum."

"Going to see where they put her?"

"Yes, sir."

"Tom, do I understand you?"

"I don't know, sir, she did."

"Tell me, my boy, what you mean. You seem a little wild, your eyes are very red. Did you sleep any last night?"

"Sleep! could you sleep, with those words ringing in your ears all night? Her last words—she never spoke again."

"By this time I had reached the window. I looked out. There was a "poor house hearse" in Cow Bay. A little coffin was brought down and put in, and it moved away. It carried "the Rag-picker's Daughter."

CHAPTER XII.

ATHALIA, THE SEWING GIRL.

"Oftentimes, to win us to our harm,
The instruments of darkness tell us truths:
Win us with honest trifles, to betray us
In deepest consequence."

At the close of chapter nine, we left Athalia standing by the side of her trunk and bandbox on the sidewalk, in front of her now empty home. After paying up the rent, and a few outstanding little bills, she had but a scanty store left in her little purse. Of this she set apart, as a sacred deposit, almost the entire sum, to redeem her Bible and watch—the locket at any rate. Now she wished she could see Nannette, for she was the only instrument she knew, that she could employ in the negociation. She could not go where she lived, for fear of meeting Walter, whom she had determined never to see again. She had sent for a hack to take her away, she really knew not where. She had but few, except business acquaintances in the city; none upon whom she felt willing to call in her emergency. She felt so cast down, that she could not look one of them in the face. She had made up her mind to go to a hotel for the night, and leave the city in the morning; whither she knew not; anywhere to get away. Then she thought that she could not go without seeing Nan nette, and making an effort to regain her valued keepsakes. How should she see her? what should she do?

It is an old proverb, "Wish for the devil and he will appear." Just then a carriage drove up and stopped where she stood. She was so certain it was the one she had sent for, that she did not observe that it contained two ladies, until the driver had opened the door, and one of them spoke.

"Why, Mrs. Morgan, are you going away? How unfortunate. I wanted three or four dresses made. When will you be back?"

When? How could she tell, since she did not know where she was going? She was in a fever of excitement to go somewhere, to get away before Walter should come. She felt as though it would kill her to see him then.

All day she had been calm; she had found it absolutely necessary, in order to keep herself so, to drink two or three glasses of wine. If it had been wine, such as the fermented juice of grapes will make, it had not done her material harm; but it was such as is made in this city, or "got up" expressly for this market; and she began to feel the effects of the alcohol it contained dying away. She felt as though she was dying, too. She did not, therefore, hesitate long, or refuse the pressing invitation of Mrs. Laylor to go home with her and stay all night. Although she began to suspect the character of Mrs. Laylor's house, she did not know it, or her either, or she would have spent the night where she stood rather than in her best room.

She was still further induced to go, when she found that

her companion was Nannette. True, there was a flash, a mere flash of thought across her mind, why so common a woman as Nannette should be in the carriage of so reserved a lady; one who, if she was guilty of slight improprieties herself would not be suspected for the world, and had no charity for the inmates of houses in M—— street.

Little thought Athalia, that Nannette, when she visited Mrs. Laylor's, passed for "a very respectable married lady, who would not be known for anything—it would ruin her;" or else, when dressed in deep mourning, with a thick veil over her face, which nothing could induce her to remove, was a "very interesting young widow, of one of the first families in the city, who was obliged, by necessity, to accept the love of a gentleman—a married gentleman—who visited her house, but would not make the acquaintance of any woman except one in just such a condition as this 'sweet young widow.'"

I know, I speak it boldly, a woman now living in this city, in up-town style, upon money obtained from six dupes, every one of whom she had "on a string" at the same time, and some of whom she used to meet at that very house, under just such guises. I say it, still more boldly and truly, for "old sores must be seen to be healed," that she has thus duped the whole six in one day. I know the woman—I know five of the dupes, and that each one of them has a wife. Two wear the title of Judge; one deals in flour; one in dry goods; and one has another employment I dare not speak so boldly of, for the sake of his children and unsuspecting wife. He drives fast horses, and truth, might drive a good woman to despair.

Athalia little suspected all this; still less did she suspect that she had been watched all day; that her order for a carriage even had been intercepted, and Mrs. Laylor had come in its stead. She did not know then that the stable owner was the paramour of Mrs. Laylor, and Nannette the pimp of this most dangerous woman—dangerous, because she struck her game, both male and female, out of the upper class of society, giving them a fair start on the road down to a cellar in Cow Bay.

We have seen one of the Morgan family that she started on that course, who run a swift race. She is now fishing for another—already has her in her net, for she has ordered Cato to put up the baggage—already has Athalia seated by her side, condoling with her in her afflictions, giving her sweet sympathy, telling her a few truths and many lies—"instruments of darkness" win by such—wondering how she could have lived with her bad husband so long as she had, when she could live so much better—"*by the needle*"—without such a man. She does not propose another now—of course not; she will bide her time for that, when all her plots have ripened the seed she is now sowing.

They were soon at home; before Athalia had half done telling how fearful she was of meeting Walter, and how she wanted to get out of town before he discovered her; and then Mrs. Laylor told her how very private she could be at her house—she would give her the third floor back room, and send her meals up to her, and she need not see a single soul but Nannette and herself, besides the chamber-maid—"none but your best friends."

Why did Mrs. Laylor whisper Nannette, and why did she run in the basement way, and why did they have to wait ten minutes for the door to be opened? And where was Athalia's thick veil, with which she had intended to hide her face so that no one would see her, for the excitement of the day had flushed her cheeks, and made her fascinatingly beautiful, and she had no desire to expose it to tempt the passion of any one who might chance to meet her?

"Where can my veil be, I am sure I had it in my hand when I got in the carriage?"

"I cannot see; perhaps Nannette has gathered it up with her shawl."

So she had. It had been slipped into the folds of it on purpose, for Mrs. Laylor was already working her plans, and counting the hundred dollars that she was going to charge some rich fool for bringing about a meeting with "one of the handsomest women in the city—a dress-maker, fresh from the country." In furtherance of this object of a wicked woman, in pursuit of gain, she had sent Nannette into the house, to station one of her dupes where he could see, without being seen, the unveiled face of Athalia, as she passed in, and up the stairs. For this purpose, the usually dark hall had been lighted, and the veil stolen.

"None but friends," there.

The victim that Nannette went to put in place, was a young

clergyman, like other men in the vigor of youth, possessed of like passions. He would have sought a wife, but his salary would not support one in the style that she would demand, or his congregation expect their pastor to maintain; and so he sought indulgence where he had found out accidentally that some of the members of his own church had sought it for themselves.

He had slipped in, with handkerchief over his face, just before Mrs. Laylor went out. She told him that she was going to the railroad depot to meet a young woman from the country, a dress-maker, whom she had sent for, to come and make a few dresses for her and "my daughter," as she unblushingly, called Nannette, who, she said, "had been away from home, at school."

The words were true, yet the speech was a lie, a wicked lie, made to deceive one who had been unwary enough to put his finger in a trap. She had been away from home, a home where she left a mother, and brothers, and sisters. And she had been at school—a school where language and manners are taught; but, oh! what language, and what ways, and manners. It is a school which is computed to have thirty thousand teachers in this city.

What strange inconsistencies our human nature is possessed of. This Nannette had naturally a good heart. We saw that in the scene where Mrs. Morgan discovers the depth of depravity to which one of those teachers had dragged down her husband. Yet, no sooner is Athalia placed by misfortune in a position to be subject to temptation, than she offers her gratuitous services to Mrs. Laylor, to effect her complete ruin. What for? Who can answer? I cannot, unless the fable of the fox that lost his tail in a trap, will give a cue to the solution. I fear, that we are too apt to wish others no better than ourselves. It must have been some such motive that actuated Nannette: the little pecuniary advantage offered by Mrs. Laylor for her assistance, does not seem to be a sufficient motive for one female, though she herself has lost the priceless jewel of female virtue, to wish to bring another of her sex into that vortex which engulfs all who come within its mäelstrom power, as certain as that upon the Norway coast. Be the motive what it may, she had certainly lent herself this day, as a willing tool, to do a double deed of wrong.

I cannot name the clergyman who was to be made—had been made—the victim in this nefarious plot, because he is still living, and has paid the penalty of ruined health for visiting such a house, and a still greater penalty of a gnawing conscience for the sin, and the lies told to cover it up.

As a *nom de plume*, I will call him, Otis, because it is the most dissimilar to his own, of any one I can think of.

Otis had been tempted to visit this house, as I said before, by a natural strong passion, but that would have been insufficient, had not a sort of Paul Pry friend told him of the delinquency of one of his flock, and urged him to watch him. He did so, saw him enter the house with a woman, certainly not his wife, charged him afterwards, with a view to his reformation, and was met with a plump denial of the character of the place, and even threatened with exposure of his attempt to watch and pry into other peoples' business. Goaded with such an accusation, he retorted upon his informer, and he in his turn reiterated the charge, and urged Otis to "call on a professional (that is pastoral) visit," and satisfy himself.

This he did, and found the house most genteelly and richly furnished; the owner, "a widow, living," she said, "upon the interest of money in bank,"—she meant the interest of bankers' money—a very modest, genteel lady, very much pleased to have him call, and begged him to repeat the visit "some afternoon or evening when the young ladies, her nieces and daughter, would be at home, and if he was fond of music, they would play for him, and one of them could sing beautifully." She could sing the "Mermaid's song." He was completely deceived. Who might not be by such a siren? The truth is, that her penetrating eye had seen at a glance quite down into his very secret thoughts, and that he possessed passions which she could inflame and turn to account, and she laid all her plans to that end. Although satisfied, after one or two visits, that all the inmates of the house were correct, he had his suspicions aroused as to those who visited them, for he could not help noticing the fact, that while he was there one evening, there were no less than five calls, apparently of couples, who were received in a dark hall, with whispered words, and then went upstairs, and after awhile went out in the same quiet way. Twice, he saw through the crack of the door that the ladies were veiled with thick dark veils, such as we meet every day upon the Broadway side-walk. But the most convincing thing of all, was an incautious word spoken aloud by one of the visitors as Mrs. Laylor was letting him out. He knew the voice. It was the man whose conduct had led him first to this house. Then he was so well satisfied, that he told Mrs. Laylor his suspicions, and she acknowledged that she did sometimes let a room to a gentleman and lady, but to none except persons of the highest respectability, such as himself, for instance. That was a cue. He took it and fell into the snare. She agreed "for a consideration," to introduce him to one of the most respectable ladies, upon the understanding that she was to remain closely veiled,—as the whole proceeding was to be veiled from the Argus eyes of the world.

The "respectable lady" was drawn from the same house to which we have before had an introduction; in short, she was the same "lady" in whose room Athalia saw her husband from Nannette's room. With Otis she played the part of "clergyman's widow," and for that purpose always dressed in deep mourning, just as her sisters in sin do now every day in the fashionable promenades of this city; and she played it well, until one night, after having taken one bottle extra between them, for he had not yet learned that wine drinking was but little better than whiskey drinking, "she let out on him," in such a manner that his eyes were opened, and he determined to leave the house. But he had tasted sin, and who that has, but well knows how much harder it is afterwards to resist the temptation?

So he came back. What an excuse he made to conscience

as he did so!—That it was only to upbraid the woman for deceiving him. He deceived himself. First, in trusting himself in a deceitful woman's power; and, secondly, in supposing that after she had deceived him once, she would not again. This last visit was upon the very night in which Athalia was introduced into the house, and hence the lies to inflame his mind, and the art made use of to give him a stolen glance of her face.

It is no wonder that the first man fell, when "tempted of a woman." It is idle to talk of our power to withstand their seductive arts. Otis was entrapped again. The sight of Athalia's beauty inflamed his already wine-heated blood, and he readily offered Mrs. Laylor a hundred dollars to bring about a successful negociation. This was just what she intended—what she expected—she had baited her trap high, and the game was already caught. And he was not the only one she intended to catch with the same bait. She intended to use her as a profitable investment upon all her "regular customers"—for all such houses boast of such—as long as she could make the lie of "fresh from the country," pass as current coin. She little thought, and cared less, how many lies she had to contrive and tell Athalia, before she could accomplish her purpose. It does seem as though, when a woman loses her own virtue, that she imagines all her sex have lost or would lose theirs just as easy as herself.

"I drag down," should be graven upon the brow of every one of her class. Whether man or woman, whoever comes within their influence—and who does not, since they are permitted to go forth at noonday through the thoroughfares of this city, seeking whom they may devour, and all night long they show their brazen faces in the streets, "picking up" poor fools for victims, whom they drag down—true, they go willingly—to their dens of destruction.

It does seem as though when a man loses his balance so far as to fall into the influence of such a woman, that he is "ready to believe a lie even unto his own damnation." How else could Walter Morgan—there are a great many Walter Morgans—leave such a wife as Athalia for such a Jezebel as he did? How else did such a man as Otis, whose business it was to watch the fold, allow the wolf to enter and carry off the shepherd? Why, after he had found out how much he had been cheated, did he believe the lies of the cheat again? Who can answer? I cannot. I can only say, that in this branch of intoxication, the only safe rule is that of the teetotaller, "touch not, taste not, handle not;" and it must be more rigidly applied in the one case than the other. A man may possibly touch liquor and drink not. Can he play with a harlot and not fall? Otis should have preached a sermon, not to his congregation, but to his own conscience in his own closet, from this text:

"For a whore is a deep ditch: and a strange woman is a narrow pit.

"She also lieth in wait as for a prey, and increaseth the transgressions among men."

She certainly had increased the transgressions in the case of Otis, and she lay in wait for Athalia as a prey.

Otis would have sought an introduction immediately, for wine had mastered reason; wine, that is made expressly for such houses, had inflamed his blood.

This the master-piece of iniquity knew would never answer. But she promised him that for the sum named, she would bring about the desired interview.

"To-night?"

"Yes. At least she would try."

"To-night or never! To-night is the last night that I shall ever set foot in your house. I have registered a vow in heaven to that, and I will keep it."

So he did. He had good cause to remember that night.

Mrs. Laylor saw that he looked as though he intended to keep it, and as he had been fool enough to tell her so, she at once determined to fool him to her own profit. So she promised him that he should have his utmost desire, and upon that she ordered up another bottle of wine, urged him to drink and amuse himself with the young ladies, while she went up and "smoothed the way."

There is but little need of smoothing the way that leads nearly every young man, who visits such places, to destruction. But she had a way to smooth. It was her last chance with this victim, and she determined on profit and revenge.

In due time she came in, and reported favorably.

"The lady would see him, in consideration of his profession, upon one condition—that he would not seek to learn her name, or anything about her, and that he should not see her face."

What did he care for that, since he had already seen it, and it was daguerreotyped upon his heated imagination, so that he would know her whenever he should meet her afterwards in the street.

Let the curtain of night fall. The sun shone into an eastern window of No. — H———n street the next morning, while Otis still slept. Its bright rays awakened him to the startling consciousness of having over-slept himself after a night of debauch. How should he get away without being seen? The thought troubled him sorely. But he soon determined what he would do; he would steal the veil from the face of the sleeping beauty to hide his own, and then slip out by the basement door, perhaps unseen. What harm could it do to her, since he had seen and knew the face so well?

He dressed himself hurriedly, then gently drew the veil away, with a salvo to his conscience that he would not then see her face, he would look the other way. His conscience would have been more easy afterwards if he had kept that resolve. He could not. The glance at Athalia's beauty the night before had maddened him, and he turned, as he was going out of the door, to look back where she slept, and steal —"Thou shalt not steal"—he had forgotten that—steal one more glance. He did, but instead of the face of Athalia, he saw that of a common street-walker—a young harridan—and he rushed from the room with the full weight of a burning conscience for his folly, with a feeling of self-degradation at being victimized a second time by the same deceitful woman; hating himself and everybody else; dreading to meet any one he knew, and, finally, encountering in the basement hall, striving to get out in the same sly way, the very man whom he had first taken to task for visiting this den of infamy. What a recognition! Neither could speak, so intense was the thought in the mind of each that the other might ruin him by simply revealing the truth. Strange that neither thought how little the other would dare to speak, least it should be inquired, "How did you know he was there? Where was you?"

Otis said afterwards to an acquaintance of mine, a physician, whom he was obliged to consult in consequence of that sinful night, that he could not conceive any agony more intensely painful in this life than that which he endured the next Sabbath, when he arose in the pulpit and looked down upon the congregation, but saw nothing, could see nothing, but that one pair of eyes glaring upon him just as they did the morning he met them in the hall of that house where he had been so disgraced.

"I little knew then," said he, "as I did afterwards, that he felt just as bad as I did, for he told me that it seemed to him that I was about to denounce him to the whole congregation. So intense had this feeling become, that he was on the point of seizing his hat and rushing out when the words burst from my lips, 'if thou knowest aught of thy brother's failing, cover it up from the rude gaze of the world, for it can profit them nothing to know of his faults.'

"'Go to him privately and speak kindly, and he will reform!' So he did, to our mutual benefit."

This relieved the mind of Otis, but it did not save him from the sad effect of a poisoned, neglected system, but it cured him from visiting places where he was ashamed to show his face. It taught him that "the way of the transgressor is hard." He had one more trial. He had not paid Mrs. Laylor the hundred dollars promised while heated with wine, for he felt that she was not entitled to it, and he had no such sum to spare. Late one Saturday night he received a note from the lady, requesting immediate payment, and threatening exposure in church the next day if he failed to make it instanter. He had not so much money in the world, and knew no way by which he could get it immediately. He was in an agony of fear all the evening. The only man to whom he dared apply either for money or advice, the man who was equally guilty, was out of town. What should he do? He did what every Christian should do. He opened his Bible, and the first words, that his eyes fell upon were, "ask and it shall be given you."

He did ask, and ask earnestly, what shall I do? Before he had done asking, the door bell rang and a letter marked "private—by express," was laid upon his table. A glance at the superscription told him it was from the man he was so anxious to see.

He opened and read:

"MY DEAR FRIEND OTIS,

I have had a sort of presentiment upon my mind that you were about to be distressed for that hundred dollars, and as I am well aware that you never would have been placed in jeopardy if I had not first done wrong, I beg you to accept the enclosed check for that amount.

"I need not say who it is from."

How strange, how opportune, how quick the answer to his asking had come back. What a load it lifted off his mind. It is not the first load that prayer, earnest, sincere prayer, has lifted. He was relieved in more ways than one; he had repented of his folly, and had become a better and a wiser man. Gold is refined of its adhering dross by fire. Otis still lives, and every day he warns some one, not only of the folly and sin, but the danger, of visiting that class of houses, if only from curiosity. They are all traps for the unwary, and gulfs into which the soul sinks blindfold down to perdition.

We have lost sight of Athalia. Let us return to her—she will need all our sympathy, for she stands upon the very brink of a precipice, over which though many have fallen, few ever returned.

Mrs. Laylor manifested the greatest sympathy for Athalia that one friend could for another. She gave her the most private room in the house, and assured her that she should be welcome to it just as long as she pleased; "but of course," she said, "you will not remain a moment, after you get your things from that wicked woman. Now what can I do to assist you?"

This was said in such a kind, sympathizing manner, that a more suspicious mind than hers might have been deceived; and she answered, "Oh, you can do a good deal. I am afraid to go out, particularly to go to that house, or that woman, and I want my keepsakes. I have got seventy dollars, and I will give it freely if I can get them again."

She did not see the glisten of the eye, or the avaricious clutch of the hand, as that miserly woman thought, "I will have that." She only heard the soft tones of her voice as she said, "my dear Mrs. Morgan, I will take it and see what I can do, but I am really afraid it is not sufficient to induce her to part with them, as you say they are actually worth more money."

"What shall I do then? I feel as though I could not part with them, and in such a way too, that is worse than all. I would have sacrificed them in a moment for that man, if he had been sick and suffering, for want of food or medicine."

"Well, well, my dear friend, do not worry yourself. Remember that you have friends, kind sympathizing friends, who will do more for you than they would for themselves. I will go directly and see what can be done if you will give me the money."

So she did, and by dint of threats, and coaxing, and promises to Josephine, to try and get something out of "the poor fool's wife," for her, she gave them up, and Mrs. Laylor, before night, had them safely locked in her own iron chest.

"Why did she not give them to Athalia at once?"

Simply, because she intended to keep both money and things. So she told Athalia, that Josephine had not yet returned from Coney Island, where she knew she had gone with her husband, wearing her watch, passing for his wife, spending her money, which he had collected for the making of the dress that he had stolen away without her knowledge.

But she had come back; where was Walter?

Somewhere with his set. He had not yet dared to face his injured wife. He intended to skulk home late at night. In the evening he went to see his dear, sweet, amiable mistress. She was in about the same state of mind after Mrs. Laylor left her, that a female tiger would be, on arriving at her lair, after a little pleasure excursion, in which she might have killed a couple of Indian children, but was driven off before her appetite for blood was satisfied, and now found that some other equally ferocious animal had despoiled her of her own young.

Walter and she had had "a good time" together, and parted lovingly only a few hours before. How he was surprised as he entered her room carelessly, to hear her tell him with a terrible oath—oaths are ten times more terrible in woman's than in man's mouth—to leave the room or she would take his life. At first, he thought she was in sport. One look was enough to convince him of his error. Then he thought she was mad, because he had entered without knocking, and found her engaged in dressing for the evening debauch and usual scenes of dissipation, and began to rally her on her Eve-like appearance.

That was more than some more amiable women can bear. No matter how ill dressed or undressed, a woman does not like to be rallied on her personal appearance.

It was more than such a human tiger could, or would bear. She darted at him, and proceeded vigorously in the task of reducing him to the same state, so far as his toilet was concerned, as herself. It did not take long. First, she crushed his hat. His dress coat was fine, and it was tender, for it was old, and she tore it into ribbons, in an instant. His vest and shirt followed, and she made vigorous efforts at the remaining garment, and then he broke and ran from the wild fury. She overtook him at the top of the stairs, gave him a vigorous kick that sent him, naked and insensible, down to the lower hall, where he was picked up by the police, and carried to the station house; there he had his bruises attended to, and there he would have got a passport to "the Island," only that he happened to be known, and when he told where he lived, one of the officers said, that was the fact, that he knew his wife, and a most excellent woman she was, and it would be a pity, on her account, to send him up this time, and so he volunteered to go home with him, and get some clothes and see what his wife wanted done with him. Walter found his trunk and all that he could claim as his own—it was not much, hardly enough for present necessity—where Athalia had left it, in the next-door shop, and there he learned the facts about the sale, and his wife going off in a carriage with two ladies, and a Negro driver; but he did not learn why she had gone, he needed no words to tell him that, a monitor within spoke louder than words.

"A guilty conscience needs no accuser."

What should he do? It is easy to say what a man should

do. He should go and find his wife, and fall down upon his knees; yes, bow his face into the dust, pray for forgiveness, and promise reform. And he would be forgiven. That is woman's nature. The Forgiver of all sins, is not more forgiving.

"What did he do?"

That is just as easy said. He sold his last good shirt—one that his wife had just made—to procure the means of getting drunk.

"What a pity that there should be any places where such a man could get liquor; or that such places, if they do exist, should be kept by wretches who will take the shirt off the back of the poor inebriate for rum."

Yes, it is a pity. It is the cause of ruin of more men than all other causes.

From this last fall Walter never recovered. He went down, step by step, to the final termination of almost every young man who surrenders his reason to such vile influences. You heard Reagan say what that end was. Let his epitaph be,

"Requiescat in Pace."

With various excuses, Athalia was kept in daily expectation of recovering her property, until continued disappointment made her heart sick. In vain she begged for something to do. Everyday it was promised, and every day the promise broken. She was kept from going out of the house by continual tales about her husband watching it day after day, and night after night. Of course this was all sham. He had been told that she had gone out of town, and he believed it; he never got sober enough to think of inquiring or caring whether she was dead or alive.

Finally, when Athalia could not be kept any longer upon such lying promises, Mrs. Laylor told her "that she had finally got Josephine to consent to give up the watch, and chain, and locket, and the Bible, for a hundred dollars."

Where was the poor girl to get the other thirty. She knew it was more than they were worth to anybody else, but she felt as though she would give it freely if she had it. To add to her distress of mind, just at this time she overheard a conversation in the next room between Mrs. Laylor and one of the girls—it was got up on purpose—to this effect:

"To be sure she will pay for her board. Of course she cannot expect to have the best room in the house ten weeks for nothing. But I shall only charge her seven dollars a week."

"Seven dollars!" thought Athalia; "that takes the whole of my seventy dollars, and my watch and Bible still remain in the hands of that red-headed——Oh, dear! what shall I do?"

The two continued their conversation.

"But, Aunt, you have promised to give that seventy dollars, and thirty more with it, to redeem her traps; how are you going to get seventy dollars more? or if you take that for her board, and let the watch go, what is she going to do in future? she has got no money, and don't work any."

"Don't work any," thought she. "How can I work shut

up here? I would work, if I had it to do. I could have earned that sum before this time." And again she said "Oh dear! what shall I do?"

It was just what they wanted she should say. Mrs. Laylor replied:

"Do! Why, she must do what other folks have to do. Frank Barkley is dying to do for her, the fool that she is; he would give her any amount of money, if she would be a little more agreeable when he calls. It was a long time before I could persuade her to drink a glass of wine with him. Some girls would have helped me to sell two or three bottles every evening. I shall tell her to-day that she has got to do something. I cannot keep anybody in the house this way much longer."

What a dose of gall and wormwood was this to poor Athalia! This was boasted friendship. Forced by one specious pretence after another to remain; purposely kept without work, that she might get in debt, for that would put her in her creditor's power; and robbed of her money—worse than robbed; and yet she was only served just as innumerable poor girls have been served before, and will be again; it was enough to make her cry out, "What shall I do?"

And then to be accused of being ungrateful. That was worse than all. Then she thought that perhaps she had been. Mrs. Laylor had told her several times how much wine some girls could induce gentlemen to buy, and how much profit she made upon every bottle; and more than that, she had hinted very strongly how much money such a handsome woman as

Athalia could make, if she was disposed to; and then she told a story about a young clergyman that used to come there, and what a great fool he was when he drank a little wine, and how she made a hundred dollars out of the simpleton, and a great deal more; but she did not tell her how she cheated him, nor how she had cheated Athalia out of her seventy dollars, nor that Frank Barkley had paid her board, which she was now trumping up an account for, so as to drive her to the seeming necessity of selling her body and soul to escape from the tangled web which this human spider was weaving around this poor weak fly.

In the course of the day, after this overheard conversation, Mrs. Laylor came to tell Athalia "that she had succeeded at last in obtaining her watch and Bible, by paying thirty dollars out of her own pocket, although she did not know how in the world to spare it, but she supposed Mrs. Morgan would repay it almost immediately."

Repay it! How could she? And so she said bitterly that she had no hope. Her heart was almost broken. Mrs. Laylor, of course, condoled with her, soothed her, reassured her of her pure friendship, took out the watch and put the chain over her neck, sent down and had the Bible brought up, and with it a bottle of wine, one of the half brandy sort, and insisted upon her drinking of it freely, and driving off the blues; and then, after she had got her into a state of partial intoxication, and fit for any act of desperation, sent for Frank Barkley, who had just arrived, to come up to Athalia's room, and play a game of cards. She had never before consented to that, but now Mrs. Laylor was there, and she desired it, and so he came. It had been all previously arranged that he should, and that he should order another bottle of wine—mixed wine—and then Mrs. Laylor was called out, and went suddenly, saying as she did so:

"Let the cards lie, I will be back in a minute."

That minute never came. That night was the last of conscious purity which had so long sustained Athalia through all her trials.

For the next six months she never allowed herself to think. She was lost. The instruments of darkness had betrayed her into the deepest consequences.

The scene shifts.

Shall we see Athalia again?

Wait.

CHAPTER XIII.

THE LITTLE PEDLAR.—MORE OF ATHALIA.

"Wisdom and goodness to the vile seem vile,"
And thus at this may laugh the scoffer.
"Let those laugh who win."

WE started in the first chapter of our volume of "Life Scenes," to take an evening walk up Broadway. How little progress we have made. We turned off at Cortland street, to follow Mrs. Eaton and her children home, and then we went with the crowd to the fire. Then we came back to listen to the cry of "Hot Corn, hot corn! here is your nice hot corn, smoking hot!" that came up in such plaintive music from the mouth of Little Katy, in the Park. Then we followed her to her home, and to her grave. What a ramble I have led you, reader. Occasionally our route has led us back again and again into this great, broad, main artery of the lower part of this bustling world, this great moving, living body, called New York. There are several other broadways in the upper part of the city. We have but one in the lowest portion of it—that is for carriages. There are a good many broadways of the town, through which pedestrians go, where they "put an enemy in the mouth to steal away the brains," an enemy

"Whose edge is sharper than the sword: whose tongue
Out-venoms all the worms of Nile; whose breath

Rides on the winds, and doth belie
All corners of the world; kings, queens, and states,
Maids, matrons," all in one fell swoop,
To earth struck down.

Such a broadway may be seen, nay, must be seen, by all whc enter the great, high, oaken doors of the granite portal of one of the best of the great Broadway hotels in New York, for the way is wide open, inviting the weary traveller to enter the great, dome-shaped "exchange"—exchange of gold, health, peace of mind, domestic blessings, for a worm that will gnaw out the very soul; a worm with teeth, "whose edge is sharper than the sword."

That granite pile is a creditable ornament to the city. Its walls have a look of solidity as enduring as the hills. Yet it contains an element within that has settled the strong built fabrics of a greater Master Builder than the architect of that house, down to the very dust, in a few short years, carrying with it marble palaces and granite walls.

That building was erected by one who sprang, from a class as lowly as the day laborer who helped to rear its walls, to almost immeasurable wealth, by a life of industry, free from the vice or misfortune of drunkenness.

At first it did not contain that great broadway to death. True, death had his abode there, but he kept in a cave out of sight. He did not thrust his hideous visage into the face of every guest, as he does now. The place of his "exchange" was then a place of green grass and flowers and sparkling fountains, upon which all the interior windows of that great caravansery looked down with joy and gladness, smiling o'er the perfumed atmosphere, and beauty admired beautiful flowers, and listened to love-inspiring songs of birds, and pattering of falling water in the great marble basin. Ah! that was a court, worthy of such a traveller's home. But it did not produce the profit that flows to the owner through another liquid channel, where that fountain once leaped, played and sparkled in the sunshine. Lovely eyes still look down from the surrounding chamber windows, not upon the flowers and birds and crystal waters, but upon an unsightly dome, and in fancy through its roof, and there they see their husbands, brothers, fathers, friends, putting an enemy in their mouths to steal away their brains. How fancy will work; how it will send sharp pangs to the heart; sharper than a two-edged sword; how the feeble wife will look down upon that roof, and pray for it to give up her husband. Other wives have prayed the tomb for the same object, both equally effective. Both will pray to both again, and both will feel that hardest of all pangs for a wife to bear, the pang that tells of a lost husband; lost in one case almost as sure as the other; the loss more hard to bear, when lost while living, than when lost by death.

I was sitting, one night, in the corridor of this, with the exception of its drinking "exchange," really good, well managed hotel, looking over the balustrade. at the in-coming and out-going throng, counting the numbers that went rum-ward as three to one, to those who went up the solid stone steps, already deeply worn by the constant dropping of feet, and trying to read the varied countenances of the ever-changing, varying scene before me. It is a useful study, to study our own kind; it is a good place, in the corridor of a great hotel, to practice. Every now and then, a face beamed out from the mass which made me sensible that it was not new, but whether an old acquaintance, or one seen before in some other crowd, I could not tell. Once only I was sure that the face which riveted my attention was that of one I had called friend, yet, for my life, I could not tell when or where. It was one of those faces which we never forget. It was one which a child would approach with confidence, to ask for a favor. It was one, which a stranger in his walk through the city, would pick out among a hundred, to ask for a direction to a particular street. Ten chances to one, he would not be satisfied to give that stranger a direction in words, but would turn round, and go a little out of the way to show the inquirer the best route, or stand upon the side-walk until one of the right line of stages came up so as to be sure that he went right. There are a few such faces, which go far to redeem the mass from the charge of coldness or selfishness, which does seem to be the distinguishing mark of the majority.

I followed this one up the steps, and as far as the vision extended, as he walked away to one of the parlors. He was an elderly man, silvering with age, neatly, but plainly dressed, and I could not help feeling that he looked in everything about him, as though it would rejoice his very soul to have a chance to do a good action. I was not mistaken. You will not be if you read on. I could not sit still after he had passed up. I went into a long train of thought upon the mental question, the one absorbing question, "Who is he?" The argument grew intensely painful, and I became so much absorbed in it, that I almost forgot for a moment where I was, until I was brought back to consciousness by a little voice in my ear, of, "Please to buy these, sir." I almost said, no, without deigning to look up at the quasi beggar, as the frequency of the question, in all public places, is such that it is somewhat annoying. But there was a something in the tone of the voice that sent its magnetic power through me, and put down that spirit which gives the cold shoulder to the poor, and bids them "call again to-morrow."

"There is a Providence in all things," many a pious heart will aspirate, as the truths of this little incident are made manifest. It does, certainly, seem a little singular that this little pedlar girl should be the chosen instrument of connexion between me and that benevolent gentleman, whom I had been vainly endeavoring to recognise in thought, and also another character, with which the reader is already acquainted.

What is there in a word, or tone, the mere sound of the voice, that sends a stream of magnetic fluid through the system, to repel or attract the speaker?

What singular means are used to bring about strange results! I was magnetized by that voice. What the result was, you shall see. But after the fluid had once entered my brain, I could no more repel the voice, or its owner, or drive it away, than the iron can disengage itself from the magnet.

I looked up, and a little girl with a basket upon her arm was standing by my side, holding up a pair of suspenders while she uttered the "Please buy these, sir?" close to my ear. She was a pretty child, between twelve and thirteen years old, rather precocious in appearance; was neatly dressed, and possessed of such a mild, sweet voice, that the mocking-bird might imitate it in his dulcet notes.

I could not say, no, in such tones as would send her away, and so I replied, pleasantly, "No, my girl, I do not wish to buy them."

The timid take courage at mild words. Was she too, attracted by mine? There is magnetism in the human voice.

"Then, perhaps, you will buy a box of matches?" "No." "Or a comb." "No." "Oh, do buy something, sir, it is getting late, and I am so anxious to sell a few shillings' worth more. Will you buy a pair of gloves? you wear gloves, don't you? Oh! do let me sell you a pair, you look as though you would buy something of me if you wanted anything. Will you buy a shirt collar? There is a nice one, sir, one that my sick mother made, sir. Will you buy that?"

"No, my girl, I never wear collars, but I will buy a pair of gloves, if you will answer me a few questions."

"Will you? Well sir, if they are such as I may answer, I will, and I don't think you would ask me any other—some men do, though."

"That is just one of the questions I wanted to ask you."

"Oh, sir, I wish you would not ask me what some men

say to me, it is so bad ; only yesterday evening, one very bad man—but I cannot tell."

And she burst into tears.

" Well, then, don't tell if it distresses you so."

" It won't now, and I want to tell you, because I should like to let you know what a good man that grey-headed old gentleman is that came in just before I did."

" What, the one with a gold-headed cane ?"

" Yes, sir, a tall man, with a grey frock-coat, and such a good-looking face."

"Then, I do want you to tell me, if it is anything about him. I think I have seen him before."

" Then, I hope you will again, for he is one of the real good men. Well, sir, yesterday evening, I was here, and I offered to sell some things to a young gentleman, and he talked so clever, that I felt glad to think how many things he was going to buy, for he picked out a pair of gloves and six shirt collars, and several other things, and told me to come up to his room, and get the money, and I went up ; I did not think it any harm, for I had been up several times before to gentlemen's rooms, and they never acted bad to me, but this one did, and I was so frightened that I screamed, and then he caught me, and put his handkerchief to my mouth, and I don't know what he would have done, but just then I heard a rap at the door, and somebody demanded to come in, but the door was locked, and he could not, and so the man that held me told him, but it did no good, for he was a strong man, and he burst the lock off in an instant, and how he did talk to the one in the room, and he made him pay me for all the things he had picked out, and then he told him to pack up his trunk, and leave the city by the first boat or railroad in the morning. And then he told him how he had watched his manœuvres, and then he took me in his room, and talked to me so good, so kind, and asked me all about my mother, and where she lived, and what she did, and why I went about peddling, and all that; and then he asked me if I would not like to go and live with some good family in the country? and then I told him that I should like to live with him, for, indeed, sir, I loved him, he talked so good to me. Then he gave a little sigh, and said, 'Ah, my girl, I wish I had a home to take you to, but I have none; I am a lone man in the world, but I will go and see your mother, and see what we can do for you, as you have grown too big for such work as this. You must quit it, or ruin is your doom,' and a great deal more, he said."

"And why have you followed it till now?"

"Because my mother would not let me quit it—in fact, sir, I do not see how we could live if I did quit, for I make about three dollars a week, and that is more than my mother can make with her needle, and work every day till midnight; and then she is sick sometimes, and so I must do something, for mother is very feeble and says she is almost worn out, and that I shall soon have nobody but myself to work for. I am sure I don't know what will become of me then; do you, sir?"

I thought, but dared not give it utterance. And I almost

wept at the certainty of her sad fate, if she remained in the city; a fate she could not escape from, without abandoning her helpless mother, one of the poor sewing women of this pandemonium.

"Now, will you buy the gloves, for I have answered all the questions you asked?"

"One more. What is your mother's name?"

"May—Mrs. May. If you should want any shirts made, sir, there is her name and number on that little card."

"Is that your mother's writing?"

"Yes, sir; don't she write pretty? I can write too, but not like that."

"Well, I shall call and see your mother, if I want work. Here is the money for the gloves."

"I cannot make change; have you got the change, or shall I run out and get it changed? I will if you will keep my basket."

"No, no; I do not wish any change. You may keep it all."

"Oh, that is just the way that good old gentleman said last night—keep it all. Ah, me!"

And she gave a little start of surprise as she looked at the individual who seemed to be standing behind my chair.

"Why, here he is now. I do wonder if he has heard me talking all about him? I hope I have not said anything wrong."

"No, no, nothing that you need to blush for. I am glad you have found another friend to talk with; one who is willing to pay you for the time—time is money—that he keeps you from your business."

It was my turn to start now. I had heard that voice before. In a moment I could fix it in my memory, though it was a good many years since I had heard it, and then it was in the wilds of the West. I offered him my hand, and said:

"We have shaken hands before. Your name is—"

"Lovetree. And now I know you. I thought it was some one whom I had seen before. I saw you in such earnest conversation with this little pedlar girl, that I could not help drawing nigh to hear; I must own I wished to see if she would tell you the same story she did me. I think now she is a girl of truth. What can we do for her? Shall we go and see her mother?"

"I wish you would to-morrow. She is not at home to-night. She has gone—at any rate she told me she would go to see a lady, a real good lady, who is worse off than my mother, for she is in a bad house, and she wants to get away; she told me so to-day, and they will not let her. She is one of the best women in the world. She is a dress-maker, and she used to live so nice in Broome street, close by my mother, with another good girl, and that girl got married and moved away off out West, I don't know how many thousand miles; and this girl got married too; and, oh dear! her husband used to get so drunk, and go to bad places, and his wife used to work and work; my mother used to work for her, and she was good to my mother, and that is what makes me so sorry for her now."

"How came she in the bad house you tell of, and how did you come to find her there?"

"Oh my, I cannot tell you all about it, I don't know; I know she had an auction, and she went away in a carriage, and I felt so sorry, and I did not know where she went; but to-day, I saw that same carriage, and saw her with that same woman, and I followed it home, and then I went up to the door, and I told the girl I had come to see Mrs. Morgan; that was no lie, for I had, if I did not know before that she was there; and that Mrs. Morgan wanted to buy some needles; that was a lie; but what should I say, I wanted to see her so bad; and then the girl said, she was not there, that there was no Mrs. Morgan in the house, and then I felt bad, because I knew she was there, and I was afraid something was wrong, and I began to cry, indeed, sir; don't laugh at me, I could not help it, I would have cried my eyes out to see her, but the girl said, she was not there, and I said, I saw her come there in the carriage, just a minute ago; and then another girl told the servant girl, it was Lucy, Lucy Smith, that I wanted to see; but I knew it was not, but I thought I would go up and see Lucy Smith, and may be she would tell me about Mrs. Morgan; and so I went to Lucy Smith's room, and I rapped on the door, and somebody said, come in; I thought I should go off, for I knew the voice in a minute, and I opened the door, and then it was not Lucy Smith, they only called her so for sham, and so that nobody would know her; it was Mrs. Morgan. How glad I was to see her, and how glad she was to see me; how she did hug me and kiss me, and call me her little pet; and then she told me—but you don't want to hear—why did you not stop me before—my mother says I always talk too much when I get a-going; I am sorry that I have talked so much, but, oh, how I do wish you would go and see Mrs. Morgan, and help her to get away from there; I will give you all the money I have made to-day, to help you, and I am sure my mother would give it as soon as I would, for she cried and took on so when I told her. Oh dear! I know well enough she never would be a bad woman, unless they made her."

"I do not understand this matter at all; do you?"

"Oh, yes, I replied, perfectly. Some poor unfortunate woman, with a miserable, drunken husband, has been driven by necessity, probably to take up her abode in some house of sin, where she finds her life miserable, and is anxious to escape; I suppose that is it."

"Anxious to escape! Why, sir, you confuse me worse than ever. No one is obliged to stay in such houses, are they? If she wished to go away, she could go; it is her own sinful choice that she is there."

"Friend Lovetree, how long have you lived out West?"

"Well, some twenty-five years, I suppose. You have a short way of turning a corner. Was I talking anything about the West?"

"No. Twenty-five years. This city has changed some in that time, and you have got behind the times. You don't know as much as this little girl about this matter. Ask her."

"How is it little girl—what did you tell me was your name?"

"Stella, sir, Stella May."

"Well then Stella, what is to hinder this Mrs. Morgan from coming away if she wishes?"

"Because she is in debt, sir."

"Debt, sir, debt! do private citizens imprison their fellows for debt? Are women compelled to live in houses of prostitution in this city, a city where the Bible is read and gospel preached, against their will? Preposterous, I will not believe it."

"Nevertheless it is gospel truth, as much as the Bible itself. The keepers of such houses sometimes inveigle innocent young girls into their dens, board and clothe them, and get them in debt, and in fact make them slaves, as sure as those who are bought and sold in southern cities. They cannot leave unless they leave naked, with the mark of their owner branded, not upon the surface of their bodies, but burnt into the inmost recesses of the mind.

"Sometimes those who go there voluntarily, repent afterwards most bitterly, most gladly would leave, but the door is closed against them, they are shut out of the world by the mark upon them, and shut in by their creditor mistress, or kept in such a state of intoxication that they have no time to redeem themselves from their life of slavery.

"From this little girl's account I venture to say that this woman is some one of the thousands of poor seamstresses, who stitch and starve in this city, who perhaps in very despair after a long struggle to live with a drunken husband, has been tempted into one of these places, and is now repenting grievously, and would gladly get away, but has not the means to do so; for she lacks a small sum to pay her greedy landlady some iniquitous charge, and a few dollars and some friend to assist her in her immediate necessities. Thus she will live a short life of excitement, and go friendless and unwept to an early grave."

"She shall not. She shall not. I have money, useless, idle, more than I shall ever want, and I have no friends. I will be her friend, I will rescue her, and she shall be mine."

Stella, the little pedler, had stood as though transfixed, during all this time, drinking in every word, until she found that her friend, poor Mrs. Morgan, would have some one to care for her, some one to love her as she loved her, one who had money, "more money than he wanted," to assist her, and then she grew as enthusiastic as Mr. Lovetree. She caught him by the hand, and as the tears ran down her cheeks, tears of joy, blessed tears, that drop like honey upon the lips, sending sweetness through every channel of sensation in the whole system, she said, "Will you, will you give her money to get out of that place? Will you go and see her? Will you love her? Oh I am so happy! I must run home and tell my mother, and that will make her happy too. Now I am so glad I told you all about it."

"And you will do it," said she, looking up in his face so earnestly, "yes, I know you will, you don't look like one of those kind of folks who say one thing and mean another."

Yes he would do it, I knew that; naturally enthusiastic, though not easily carried away by sudden flaws of side winds, when he once said, "I will do it," it was half done.

"Now I will run home and tell mother, for I want her to be as happy as me. Good night."

"Stop, stop a moment, you have not told us where the poor lady is that you wish us to go and see, nor what her name is."

"Oh dear, I forgot that. Yes I told you, Mrs. Morgan, but you want her whole name; well that is such a pretty name; I love pretty names; have you a card, I will write it for you."

"What, can you write?"

"Oh yes, sir, before we got so poor, I used to go to school. I would like to go now, but I have no time. You ought to see my mother write; she can write so pretty."

I saw what was working in the benevolent old gentleman's face, while Stella was writing. He had heard her say, "I would like to go to school now," and he was resolving in his mind, "Why not? Why should I not send her there? I have none of my own to send." It was a good resolve.

"There, that is it. 'Mrs. Athalia Morgan, at Mrs. Laylor's in H———n street.' I don't recollect the number, but you can find it easy enough; mother says it does seem as though the evil one always stood ready to lead folks to such houses. But you had better inquire for Lucy Smith. They don't know her by any other name there. Shall I go now? Good night. I am so anxious to tell mother."

"Athalia!—Athalia!" said my friend, as he spelt over the

name on the card. "Athalia! oh, pshaw! that is nonsense, yet it might be—why not? I say, my little girl, you knew her before she was married. What was her name then?"

"And what is that, 'why not,' and what about that name? The little girl is well on her way home, by this time, if she kept on at the speed she went down stairs. Her earnestness makes me begin to feel a good deal interested in that woman."

"Nothing, only a thought, a mere passing thought, and yet I cannot shake it off. It is rather an unusual name. I had a brother—yes, I had a brother, whether I have or not now, I cannot tell; yet he was not exactly a brother either, though we called the same woman mother, and the same man father, and whether he is living now or not I cannot say, but think not. He did very badly, drank up all his property, and took the usual course, and I suppose he is dead, and his wife too, and then his children are orphans, and why not this be one of them; it is the same name. Athalia—it is not a common name; if it had been I should not remember it, for I never saw her but once, then a little girl not as big as this one just here. I wish she had not run away so soon, before I could ask her a single question. What shall I do now?"

"Go and ask Athalia herself."

"What! to-night? It is now ten o'clock, time all respectable citizens were in bed. It is too late."

"No, it is never too late to begin to do good. It is just the hour that the lives of the inmates of such houses, as we propose to visit, begin. From this till one or two o'clock, drinking, carousing, swearing, and all sorts of revelry and debauchery, and then —— it is well that night has curtains. Now this house where we are to go, however, I take, from its location, to be one of a different character, one that maintains a show of respectability, yet is one of the most dangerous, for its victims are drawn from among a class just as good as Stella has described Mrs. Morgan."

"You think, then, that we may go there safely, at this hour of the night?"

"As safely, as respects our persons, as to church. As dangerously, as respects our morals, as the poor weak bird fluttering within the charmed circle of the fascinating serpent."

"As to that I fear nothing."

"So has said many a one. I say,

'He must have a long spoon that must eat with the devil,'

or he will soon come to such familiarity that he will eat freely out of the same dish. No man is proof against the fascinations of a designing woman. But as we go doubly armed, for our cause is just, let us go, go at once, for I see you are excited about that name. It would be strange, if it should prove to be your niece."

"Yes and stranger still, the way that we have been brought together, and to a knowledge of her, through our mutual sympathy for this little pedler girl, such an one as we may see every hour in the streets, without exciting a passing thought. What a mysterious power governs all our actions, and how we are influenced and turned aside from the path we had marked out, by the most trivial circumstances. I had seen this little girl come in here and offer her little wares a score of times, without paying any attention to her or her movements, except to wonder how any mother could trust such a child, bright, good-looking, free spoken, forward—that is, precocious—among so many fops and libertines, who would take advantage of her some day, and by deceit and money work her ruin. Last night I had put on my gloves and hat, and was just walking out as she came in with her "Please to buy this, sir," and why I did not go out I cannot tell, but some unaccountable influence turned me back, and I picked up a paper and sat apparently absorbed in its contents, while my ear was open and mind awake to every word and movement of the libertine rascal who made a pretence of buying liberally, to induce her to go up to his room to get the pay. I followed, watched him to his room, heard the key turn in the lock, heard all his conversation, his vile proposals, and her virtuous rejection, with an energy, 'that she had rather starve and see her mother dead;' and then I heard a struggle and I knew the villain was using his brutal strength upon a weak girl, and then I burst the door, and then—you know the rest."

"Why did you not strike the villain dead at your feet?"

"That is savage nature."

"Why not arrest and punish him, then, for his attempt at rape?"

"That is civilized nature."

"What then did you do?"

"I forgave him, and bade him repent, and ask God to forgive him, as I did."

"Lovetree, give me your hand, I give you my heart; I stand rebuked. I understand you now, that was Christian nature. Let us go."

Reader, walk with us. We threaded our way along the crowded side-walk, passing or meeting, between the Astor House and Canal street, not less than fifty girls; some of them not over twelve years old, many about fourteen or fifteen, some of them superbly beautiful, naturally or artificially, and all, such as the spirit, hovering over the poor shipwrecked mariner upon the stormy ocean, cries wildly to, as they sink, down, down, to death, "lost, lost, lost!"

"Why, why, tell me why they are permitted to roam through the streets, plying their seductive arts? Where are your police? Where your city Fathers?—guardians of the morals of strangers and citizens! How can anything, male or female, remain pure in such an atmosphere of impurity? Where are your laws? laws of love that lift up the fallen. Where all your high-paid, well-fed city guardians, who should watch the city youth, to keep them from becoming impure?"

Echo gave the answer, and it reverberated back and forth from granite wall to freestone, from marble front to red-burnt bricks, from dark cellar to gas-lighted hall, from low dens of death to high rooms of wealth and fashion, from law makers to law breakers; echo came back with that one word, "Impure, impure, impure."

How the throng go thoughtlessly onward. Do they ever

think—think what a sirocco blast from the valley of the Upas tree, is sweeping over this city? Do mothers ever inquire, ever think whether it is possible for their sons to escape the contagion of such company as they keep in the great evening promenade of this mighty Babylon? Have New York mothers no feeling of fear for their sons? or has "the pestilence that walketh in darkness," obtained such strength that this is overcome? or has the plague spot grown so familiar to their eyes that they no longer seek to wash it out? If they have given up their sons, if they have surrendered the great street to the almost exclusive occupancy, at night, of painted harlots; have they also given up their daughters, surrendered them to the wiles of the seducer? do they let them go out without fear, even in company with their male friends, to be jostled upon the side-walks by midnight ramblers, and seated at the same table, at some of the great "saloons," side by side with those who win to kill, whose trade is death, whose life is gilded misery, though enticing as the siren's song? Have they forgotten that we are all creatures of surrounding circumstances, subject to like influences, and liable to the same disease as those who breathe the same atmosphere, and if that is impure, those who breathe it may become so?

Even now, while I write, the "New York Daily Tribune," gives this "Item" to its readers:—

"Mysterious Disappearance.—On Sunday evening last, between six and seven o'clock, Miss G. C—— left her father in Spring street, near Broadway, to go to her brother-in-law's (Mr. B——), No. — Spring street, since which time nothing has been heard of her, and it is feared that she has been dealt foully with. She is seventeen years of age, good-looking and rather tall; dark complexion, and dark eyes; lisps somewhat when in conversation. She was dressed in plaid, light and dark stripe; Talma cape; straw bonnet, trimmed with white outside, and green and white inside. Her disappearance has caused the deepest affliction to her family, and any information that can be given will be gratefully received by her aged parent, No. — Spring street."

"It is feared that she has been foully dealt with." Yes, and it ought to be feared that "good-looking, rather tall" young girls, are foully dealt with in the streets of this city, every night in the week. It is feared she is not the first girl of seventeen, whose "mysterious disappearance has caused the deepest affliction to her family."

"Any information will be gratefully received." Yes, any information will be gratefully received by the author of this book, which he can use effectually to awaken aged parents to the fact, that each one of these girls who wander the streets at midnight, or who fill up the dens of infamy that line whole blocks of some of the best streets in this city, is somebody's child; some "mysterious disappearance," that has caused deep affliction, and will cause more, for she is now influencing others to disappear from the path of rectitude, in the same way that she did.

Perhaps, yea, it is probable, more than probable, that Miss G. C—— has been inveigled into one of these dens where worse than cannibals live, for they only eat the body, while these destroy the soul.

How long would a house be permitted to stand, where

human flesh was served up as a banquet for those who delighted to feast upon such dainty food? A house where young girls were driven in by force or fascination, to be cooked and eaten by young epicures and gouty gormandizers. How the city's indignation would boil over, and how the storm of wrath would beat upon that house, until there would not be one stone left upon another.

Yet how calmly that same public sleeps on by the side of a thousand worse houses, where victims are worse than cooked and eaten every day—they are roasted alive.

How coldly parents will read that "mysterious disappearance;" they will never think that girl has been destroyed by cannibals, far worse are here—they belong to savage life.

How carelessly, how thoughtlessly mothers will read this page that tells how their daughters may be influenced to ruin themselves, by such unfortunate associations as they must meet with in their walks through the city, while our municipal government permits the streets to be monopolized by the impure, because it is itself just what the echo answered.

How I would rejoice if I could make the truth manifest, as regards this matter, that, "to the pure all things are pure."

Now, let us walk on.

You need not stop to drop anything into the hand of that woman with a child on her lap. True, she looks like a pitiable object, with her opium-drugged infant wrapped in that old blue cloak, but she is not. She is a professional beggar. I have known her these three years. That child is not hers. It is hired for the purpose. It draws a share of the benefit, as it does the sympathy of those who are attracted by that well-put-on, appealing look. That child is kept by a woman who keeps three others "to let." They never grow too big. Laudanum is not the food that infants grow upon. They will die young, and others will be begged, borrowed, or stolen, for the same purpose.

There, the sixpence you have given that little child, will go into the till of that "family grocery," before we are a block farther on our way. I know her.

It is hardly charity to give to that man; I know him too, and where he lives.

"But, he is blind."

I know it, and that is his fortune. With it he supports himself and family of great idle girls and boys, better than many others live who labor. He is a stout, rugged, hearty man, capable of doing much useful labor, if he had any one to direct him.

"Well, here, what of this?"

Yes, you may give there; no, give me the quarter, see what I will do with it. I will buy two smiles.

"Good evening, Joseph, how do you do this evening?"

"Oh, very well, sir, thank you. How are you this evening?"

"Very well. How is trade with you, Joseph? Do these gay people buy your bouquets?"

"Well, some do, sir, but these big boys and stout men can run about and forestall a poor black man who has got no legs."

"Joseph, has that sewing woman been down this evening;

the one who always stops to give you a kind word and look, and smell of your flowers?"

"What, the one that looks so pale, the one who makes shirt collars; the one you gave the bouquet to, sir?"

"Yes; and I want you to give her another, here is the money."

"I wish I had known it a few minutes ago, for her daughter went by; she stopped a moment just to admire this one, and said, how she did wish she could afford to buy it for her mother; and then she said, it did not matter, she had such good news to tell her, and she picked up her basket, and away she ran."

There was a queer idea came into my mind, when he said basket, just as though there could be but one girl out to-night with a basket. I was about to drive away the idea as a foolish one, when something whispered me, "Ask him." So I did.

"A girl with a basket? Who is that girl with a basket; do you know her name?"

"Oh, yes. We call her, the little pedler. She is a nice girl. Her mother's name is May."

The queer idea was a true one after all. And so this woman, whom I had often seen speaking pleasant words to this poor legless Negro man, who sits night after night, upon the Broadway side-walk, selling bouquets, is Mrs. May, the little pedler's mother.

"Do you know where she lives?—could you get anybody to carry this to her to-night?"

"Yes, sir, here is Tom Top, he will go in a minute; he will do anything for me, or for a lady; he is ragged and dirty, but he is a good boy; it is a pity he had not somebody to be good to him. Tom, will you go to Mrs. May's for me? Stella, the little pedler's mother, you know where she lives?"

"Yes, sir, shall I carry that? Is that for Stella?"

"No, that is for her mother."

"And this," said Mr. Lovetree, picking up another beauty, "this is for Stella. Stop, Tom. Here is a shilling for you. Don't tell who sent you. Now let us go on. You know this poor black fellow, then, do you? What is his name?"

"Joseph Butler. He was a sailor. He was shipwrecked, and lost his legs by freezing, fourteen years ago. He has been to sea five years since, as cook, hobbling around on the stumps. Now, he supports his family by selling bouquets. Did you ever see a finer face? Always cheerful, intelligent, and polite; it is a pleasure to buy flowers of him. It is a wonder that ladies and gentlemen do not all feel it a duty and pleasure both, to buy all their bouquets of this poor cripple."

"It is because they never think. If they did, they certainly would."

"Then, I must ask them to think. I must try and awaken the sympathies of the benevolent to look at this poor unfortunate black man as they pass, and see if they do not think him a fit subject for honest sympathy. He is not a beggar. He gives a fair equivalent for your money. At least, give him a kind word, or pleasant look, and he will return you the same."

How we do linger in our walk. So will you, reader, if you come to New York, and undertake to see all the curiosities of Broadway, in one night.

At length, we reached Mrs. Laylor's. It is a handsome house, in a quiet street. My friend hesitated about entering. He thought I must be mistaken. It did not look like what he had conceived of such houses. Then he was afraid they would suspect us, and would not let us in.

"For the fact is, we do not look much like the class of men who visit such places," said he.

"That shows how little you know of life in New York. Let me manage this matter, and I assure you, they will think us two old rakes, rich ones, too, out of whom they may make a harvest."

So we went up the broad, high steps, and rang the bell with a jerk, that said, as near as bells can speak, that is somebody that has been here before. The lady, as is the usual practice, came herself to the door, unlocked it, and opened it a little way, where it is held by a chain, so that she could reconnoitre, and if the company did not suit, or if a stranger applied, she would refuse him, particularly, if she had plenty of company, unless he could give very good references.

I thought of that, and so I said, with the same confidence that I had put into my pull of the bell, "Good evening, Mrs. Laylor, how do you do this evening? You were unwell the other evening when I was here. This is Mr. Treewell, from the South." That was an "open sesame," that undid the chain directly, and we walked in as old acquaintances. True, she could not exactly locate us, but our easy assurance carried us through.

"Walk into the parlor, gentlemen, there is nobody there, we are quite alone this evening. Or, will you go in the back room; the young ladies and I were having a little game of whist together, to drive off the dullness."

Yes, to drive off the dullness, thought I; to get rid of the horror of thinking. That is the greatest curse that this class of women have to endure. They cannot bear to think. They must have something "to drive off the dullness." If they have no company, they must play cards, or something else to keep away thought. If they have company, wine is the panacea. They cannot afford to buy it themselves, but they often persuade gentlemen to do so, pretending to be very thirsty, when they have just been drinking, because that is a part of the contract upon which they are kept by the mistress of the house. If a girl had any conscientious scruples about coaxing a gentleman to buy, or about drinking, or wasting all the wine that all of them would buy, she would be trained into the work, or turned out of doors. So that it is a very rare thing for one of them to go to bed sober. In the morning, or rather towards night, when they wake up, they are almost unable to dress themselves for the next scene in the round of dissipation, until they have sent out and got a little cheap rum, "to bring them up."

Those who have studied the life of these poor, wretched

women as carefully as I have, will not wonder at the shortness of it.

Of course we accepted the very polite invitation to go in where the young ladies were. We had an object in doing so. Neither of us knew Mrs. Morgan, and if we should inquire for her, if it suited the convenience of madame she would palm off any other one that she thought she could make pass. I adopted my plan of operations very quickly. I thought if they had had no company yet to-night, they had had no wine, and consequently would not be in the best of moods to be communicative. As soon as we were introduced, I ordered a bottle of wine and thought I would find out if either of the three girls present answered to the name of Lucy, and if she did, I intended to whisper one word in her ear, and that word should be "Athalia," and watch what emotion it produced.

It would be entirely impossible for a stranger to form an idea what an emotion the very name of wine caused among them. They were fairly longing for it. We were in the good graces of all the household at once. I pleaded headache not to drink. Lovetree took his glass with them. I fixed upon one that I thought perhaps might be Athalia, but soon found that she was called Nannette.

Another was Belle, and the third was Adelaide. The latter was one of the most perfectly beautiful girls in face and form I ever saw, and she had really pretty red hair. I have often met or passed her since that in the street and never without admiring her beauty and thinking of her mother, and how she must mourn "a girl lost."

I was now satisfied that Athalia was not in the room, and I said carelessly. "Where is that other girl I saw here, with brown hair and blue eyes, not very tall?"

"What was her name?"

"Oh, confound names, I never can think of names."

"Oh, I know who he means," said Adelaide, "it is Lucy, Lucy Smith."

"Yes, yes, that is it. It is Lucy at any rate."

"She is in her room. She has got the dumps—the blues—I should not wonder if she was all melted by this time, she has been crying these three days."

"Crying, why what has she to cry about? I should not think anybody need to cry in this house, you never cry, do you?"

The very question almost brought a tear, but she drove it back.

"Well, Lucy must come down and have some wine. Get her down, and we will have another bottle."

"She won't come. We are all tired of trying. She has got the pouts, because Mrs. Laylor took her trunk away from her to keep for her board. She don't make anything. All she ever did make was out of Frank Barkley, and that she gave to redeem her watch and a good-for-nothing old Bible I don't see what she wants of that."

"Well, I am going to have her down—I have no opinion of having any girl in the dumps. Where is her room?"

"Third floor back room. That is right, go and bring her out whether or no. She has hardly been out for a week till to-day Mrs. Laylor took her out riding with her, to try to put a little life in her, for fear she would die on her hands, and she would have to bury her for charity."

"Well, well, I will bring her down, see if I don't. Come, Treewell, if she will not come without we will bring her."

So away we went upstairs, now satisfied that we were on the right trail, and that we had completely lulled all suspicion that we wanted anything of Lucy Smith, except to compel the poor heart-sick woman to join in a Bacchanalian revel, at which her soul revolted. Up, up we went, passed three "private rooms," in which we will not seek to look, for they are occupied by those who come veiled and in the dark. Here is the room we want. We knocked but received no welcome "come in."

How quick she would open the door if she knew who was waiting for admission. Tired of knocking, we enter unbidden, and find the room empty. The prisoner has escaped.

The truth flashed upon my mind in a moment. She has gone off with Mrs. May. Mr. Lovetree thought not, for Stella said they would not let her go out except some one in the house went with her to watch her.

"No matter. I am almost sure that woman has got her away. These women are great at contrivance. Very likely she came prepared for it, as Stella told her of course, all that Mrs. Morgan had told her."

We made a light and the first thing that Lovetree saw was

the Bible, and Athalia's name—her age and birth-place and the age and names of her father and mother and grandfather and grandmother, a complete family record. I thought the man would go crazy. It would have made him nearly crazy if he had found her an inmate here, as much lost to shame as those we had just been carousing with, and now to find that she was not here put him into a perfect agony. He thought he could not live till morning without seeing her. At first we thought of going directly to Mrs. May's but then we recollected we did not know where she lived and could not find out, for I had lost her card that Stella gave me.

Finally we concluded to go down and talk a minute in the same kind of sang froid manner, to keep up our assumed characters and then go home and await coming events.

We were rallied as we entered the room with a jeering laugh at not being able to bring one woman between us both.

Then I pretended to get angry at being sent upon a fool's errand, to a room where nobody was at home. At that Mrs. Laylor started.

"Was she not in the room?"

"No, nor has not been lately. You are playing tricks with the wrong persons, trying to fool us."

"Indeed, gentlemen, upon my honor it is no trick."

She rang the servants' bell violently. "Martha, do you know where Lucy Smith is? She is not in her room. Have you let her out to-night?"

"No, ma'am. I have not let anybody out but that sewing woman."

"Where is Kate? Send Kate up. Kate have you let anybody out to-night?"

"Yes, ma'am. I let that sewing woman out."

"You let her out! Martha says she let her out."

"So I did."

"And so did I."

"Both of you."

"I did."

"Well, I did."

"You have let out the ——. Get out of the room, you stupid Irish ——s. You have let out the sewing woman, sure enough. I have lost my bet which I made with Frank, of a hundred dollars that I would keep her here till she would not want to go away."

And there was such a string of oaths as I never heard before, and hope I never shall hear again, particularly from female profane lips. None but a drunken slave driver, ever poured out such a stream of awful language, full of oaths, anger and billingsgate expressions, at the escape of one of his victims, as she did at the escape of a woman whom she had determined to debase to her own level, until she had brought her to that condition that she would feel degraded in the eyes of the world, would know that all her own sex had closed and barred the door against her, so that she could never return to the paths of virtue, and she would be to her mistress a "profitable investment," for she would be attractive, by her beauty and manners, and "draw custom to the house." But she had escaped—gone off too in a temper of mind which might send retribution back upon the head of one who under the guise of friendship had first robbed, then by pretended debt, enslaved her mind, coaxed and almost driven her into intoxication, and then prostituted her most shamefully. It would be idle to pretend that Athalia had escaped without sin. She had not. She had sinned deeply. She said afterwards while claiming some extenuation, though by no means trying to justify her fall, that her mind was so wrought upon by her disappointments of life, by her lone and friendless condition, by the accumulation of debt, by the terrible treachery of those she had entrusted herself with as such disinterested friends, by her anxiety to obtain her valued keepsakes and get money enough to redeem them, and then escape from the pandemonium she found that she had unwittingly entered, that she had determined to drown her thoughts in wine, and then she accepted the oft-repeated proposals of Frank Barkley to redeem her watch, which he honorably did, but which another *friend*, one of Mrs. Laylor's friends, whom she forced her to accept, and which cost her the friendship of Frank, robbed her of, and carried off so that she never saw it again; whether he kept it or gave it to Mrs. Laylor, she never knew.

Often she intended to fly, but it seemed to her that she could not get away; she was kept in one constant whirl of excitement so that she could not reason with herself long enough to determine what to do. What deterred her most, was that she had nowhere to go to, no friend to call upon for counsel or assistance, and thus she went on from day to day, adopting one plan in the morning to discard it at night.

Frank was very kind to her in a certain measure. He liked her, but it was a very selfish liking. He did not like to hear her talk about leaving. He liked her there, and he was almost as much her jailer as Mrs. Laylor. He took her out to all manner of dissipation, theatres, saloons, late suppers, balls and frolics, in which strong drink—not Athalia Morgan—acted as wild a part as the wildest. But he offered her no means of escape. She began to have a sort of fondness for Frank. What woman can avoid liking one who is devoted to her? But this devotion to one was not what Mrs. Laylor wished. It was not what brought the most money to her iron chest. She would like to negotiate the charms of Athalia to some rich libertine every day, whenever she could meet with one fool enough to pay her well for her influence with the "young widow."

Among the most determined of her suitors, was a young Frenchman, who used every art which he knew well how to use with words and money, to win Athalia's favor. As a last resort, he pledged a splendid diamond ring to Mrs. Laylor, if she would accomplish what he could not.

When all other arts fail to work ruin and misery in a woman's mind, there is one left, one which concentrates all the power of all the lies of the father of deception. It is jealousy.

There is a little story in "Othello," about the arts of a villain, to produce mischief by that power. It is nothing compared with the villainy and lies invented to produce jealousy between Frank and Athalia, so as to let in the Frenchman, and win that ring.

Villainy is too often successful in this life. It was in this case. Jealousy, a feeling of revenge, drives more women to infidelity towards those they love, than all other causes.

It did its perfect work with Athalia, and then the fiend who had accomplished the work, laughed at her, and told her how she had been fooled, thinking it would have the usual effect, to make her careless of what she did in future. It had an entirely different effect upon Athalia. It was this that produced the state of mind that Adelaide called the dumps, the blues, and the tears that Stella saw her shed. Stella had told her mother much that Athalia told her, much that the child did not understand, but the mother did, for she knew how girls were inveigled into those houses, and kept there as prisoners.

I have lately witnessed a scene, highly illustrative of this fact. It is one of the "Life Scenes of New York."

Coming up one of the streets west of Broadway, about one o'clock at night, I saw a fellow hovering near a house, whom I recognized as a Negro wood-sawyer that I had seen the day before, engaged at the same house, putting wood down the cellar grate. I knew him or thought I did, as a poor but honest man, and I felt pained with a fear that I had been deceived, that he had left the grate unfastened, and now was about to steal something from the cellar. I passed on around the next corner, out of sight, and then turned back and crossed over, where I could have a full view of his operations. There were no lamps burning, because there should, or might have been moonlight, if it had been clear; as it was, it was a fitting time for the burglar's trade. Directly, the fellow approached the grate, opened it carefully, and drew up a trunk. My heart beat with excitement, fear, and sorrow. I was just on the point of calling, "Watch," I must own with a view of letting the fellow escape, and saving the trunk, when I saw a bonnet, then a shawl, and then a full suit of woman's clothes follow the trunk up from that dark recess. My mind was somewhat relieved; my honest wood-sawyer might be honest still, though he was probably assisting a dishonest woman; else why did she leave that house, to all appearance, an honest house, for all that I had ever seen in passing it a hundred times, in such a clandestine manner. The Negro walked on with the trunk on his shoulder, and the woman followed. It was a scene of such frequent occurrence, that it would excite no suspicion or question from a policeman. He would think it was a passenger by the train, from Boston, or Albany, or the Erie railroad, all of which make midnight arrivals.

On they went, block after block, and I followed, till I thought the chase likely to prove a long one, and then I stepped up to the woman, and laying my hand upon her shoulder, said, "Stop!" She uttered a little cry of alarm, and said, "Oh, don't take me up, please don't."

The Negro stopped, looked round, and set down the trunk hastily, evidently supposing that a star had nabbed her, and that the better part o' a fight consists in running away. There was a light here, for the lamp-lighters were just going their late rounds. He gave one glance back before he started, to be sure he had good cause to run, and instantly burst into a most merry fit of laughter, very unlike what might be supposed that of a caught burglar.

"Ha! ha! ha! ki, missee, you don't know dat gemman? You nebber seed dat gemman 'fore? You tink him a star? Look at um. You tink he look so he hurt you? He wouldn't hurt a child, much more a woman. I know dat gemman. Ki, I mighty glad to see him. 'Spose tell him all about um? Spec he say a body has a right to steal he own trunk, and run away from such a house as dat."

"Such a house as that, Peter; is that not a good house?"

"Well, spec him house good enough, but spec he folks dat lib dare, not 'zactly straight up and down like dog hind leg."

"Why, Peter, what do you mean? Is not that Mr. Ingram, whose name I see on the door, and whom I know as apparently a gentleman of wealth and leisure, for I have often seen him associating with gentlemen about the hotels; is he not the gentleman of the house?"

"Gentlum! Lord, sir, he is dat woman's man, her pimp, she gives him all dem fine clothes and gold rings, and he gets fellows to come an see her gals."

"Mercy on me! The outside of the platter is made clean, while the inside is full of dead men's bones."

"Dat's just what Agnes says; she says, she find dead men's bones in the ashes, and buttons, and bits of burnt woman's clothes in a pile in the cellar, and she seed woman's ghost dare, and she won't stay in dat house no how can fix um, and dat's what it mean 'bout I got dis trunk; did you see how I get him, massa?"

"Yes, I did, and I want to know something about why you 'get him' at this time of night out of that cellar. The ghost story won't do; if she was afraid of ghosts she would not go down into that cellar at night any more than she would go down to her grave. It won't do."

"Oh, sir, the ghost goes upstairs every night, to stay in the room where she was seduced. None of the girls in the house will stay in that room. They gave it to me when first I went there. I did not know it was haunted then, but I found out afterwards that it was, for she told me so, and how she was shut up in the coal cellar, and starved, and suffocated to death, and then cut up, and part of her body burned, and part buried in lime and ashes, and how, if I would look in one corner of the cellar, I would find some of her bones, and I did; and then I determined to run away, and that is why I am here."

"And what are you going to do now?"

"I am going home with Peter, I have got nowhere else to go, and then I shall try to get a place."

"A place! Why, Peter, is not this one of the girls of that house?"

"Why, no, not 'zactly; but 'spose you go wid us in my house, he close by here now, and she tell you all about herself. I spec she not a bad gal, sir."

"Go ahead then;" and he shouldered his load, and went a few steps farther, and then turned into a dark alley, where I should have hesitated about following the burglars, but now followed the honest, good-hearted wood-sawyer, and his protégé with delightful pleasure, up the long, dark alley into the centre of the block, and there was a tenant house, inhabited by the better class of blacks. Compared with some of those full of foreigners, it was a little paradise. Up, up to the sixth story, that is where the poor live; here is where the poor legless Negro flower-seller lives, with his nice little family; a door opened as we approached, and a light shined out, and a voice said:

"Is dat you, Peter? Has you got hër, Peter? Thank God for that!"

It was Peter's wife, rejoicing at the rescue of a woman from perdition. One of a poor, down-trodden race, a member of a Christian church, yet considered unworthy to sit by the side of white skinned (thin skinned) Christians, doing a most Christian act, such an one as many of her sisters in the church would consider beneath their dignity to do.

We entered Peter's home. It was but one small room, scantily, yet neatly furnished. There was a little stove, and all necessary cooking utensils, and plenty of dishes, a table, a bureau, a carpet on the floor, a stand in one corner covered with a clean white cloth, and on this a large Bible, covered with green baize, lying open, with Phebe's spectacles on the page, indicating her employment while waiting and watching for Peter to return, as she expected, with company—one more than she expected. There was a bedstead in one corner, from which a portion of the bed had been removed and made into a nice pallet upon the floor, in readiness for an expected lodger. Agnes met a warm welcome from Phebe. We shall see Phebe again, out on another errand of mercy. In some of these ever shifting scenes, we may have another glimpse of Agnes. Peter explained to Phebe, how I happened to be in company, and then we all sat down to hear Agnes's story. I shall not tell it now. But I will tell here another little story, which will give a clue to what she said about the haunted house.

It is a story about "a girl lost."

The "Tribune" one day published an appeal to the kind-hearted of the city, to give a distracted family some information of "a girl lost."

She was "a good-looking, rather tall girl, seventeen years of age, dark complexion and dark hair. She was well-dressed, and started to go from her father's house in Spring street, near Broadway, to her brother's in the same street.

"And she was lost!"

Some stranger who reads that simple announcement, one who has spent a night at one of the three great hotels on the corners of Spring street and Broadway, may wonder that a girl should be lost in such a respectable neighborhood. He does not know that the guests of one of those great hotels look down from one side upon one of the worst gambling hells and police-permitted gambling lottery offices in the city, and on the other side upon still worse premises; houses which the vocabulary of infamous language has no words black enough to describe; houses which are ever open for innocent young girls to enter—from which innocent young

"'SPEC A BODY HAS A RIGHT TO STEAL OWN TRUNK."—*Page* 285.

girls never return. They are "lost." This is not the first girl lost in New York. These are not the first parents who have been deeply afflicted; who have appealed in vain through the press for any information of "a girl lost."

I have a little incident to relate of a girl lost. A few years ago No. 000 Church street, was accounted the "luckiest house in the street." There are a great many unlucky ones in that street now, and that particular one is esteemed the most unlucky of all of them. It should be so. It was in that house about three years ago, that a girl was lost. For the sake of her parents, brothers and sisters, and large family of relatives, I will not give her true name. You may call it Julia Montgomery. She was just such a girl as the one described in the "Mysterious Disappearance!" She was tall and handsome, just seventeen, with dark hair and eyes, and well dressed. She lived in one of the river towns, and came down upon one of the barges that float down such a multitude of things produced by farmers, in company with her father and mother, who brought some of their own produce to market. On the same boat were two young men who had been up the river, they said, on a sporting excursion. This was true. But they might have added, "What is sport to us is death to you." They were gamblers. On the passage they made the acquaintance of Julia, and by their bland manners completely won the confidence of the old folks. When they arrived, they were very anxious that Julia should go home with them and see their sisters. They were not so anxious that her mother should go, but they insisted very hard that she should, because they knew she would not; she had her butter and eggs and chickens to sell, and lots of shopping to do, so Julia went alone. She came back to the boat towards night to tell her mother what nice girls the Miss Camptowns were, and that they wanted she should go with them to the theatre, and then as it would be late, stay all night. The mother consented, as Mr. Camptown was such a fine young man. After the play they had an oyster supper and wine, and Julia became very much elated. Then they went home, to Mr. Camptown's home, which was no other than that notorious Church street den, and the "sisters" the most notorious sinners in it. Of course more wine was drank, and Julia became oblivious of what transpired. She waked to consciousness next morning to find herself—"a girl lost." Almost delirious, she flew from the wicked scoundrel at her side to the street door, to find it barred against her. In vain she begged and prayed, and cried to be let out. The soul incarcerated in the infernal regions might as well pray for egress. She finds in both cases only scoffing at the victim's agony. Then she grew wildly furious, and then they tied her hands and feet and carried her down into the coal cellar, "to let her get over her fit, and keep her out of sight till the old woman was out of the way." For three days, Camptown watched her father and mother, and then they gave up and went home with heavy hearts, for "a girl was lost." Yes, she was "lost." Then Camptown went back to enjoy his "country beauty." She was lost to him also. In some of the pullings down and diggings up in that street, all that remains to earth will make another "Item" in a daily paper. It will be headed "Human bones found."

The inmates of that house soon left. It was no longer a lucky house. The ghost of that murdered girl walked through every room. One in particular, it never allowed any one to occupy. It is said that that ghost still haunts that house. It is still an unlucky house. The old harridan who kept it—well known in that street when that girl was lost—went off to New Orleans, lost all her property, and then was lost herself. Camptown still lives. I saw him a few days ago, in the very street where that girl was lost, noticed in the "Tribune." Has he any connection with her loss? Reader, there is a girl lost. Ask where and why? Rum and gambling can answer.

Now, let us leave Agnes in the hands of the wood-sawyer and his wife, those good-hearted, kind Christians, that despised, because black-skinned, brother and sister, more worthy than many of the despisers, and return to Mrs. May, and see how she effected the rescue of another prisoner.

What Stella told her mother was sufficient to give her the most intense anxiety about Athalia. She was so well acquainted with the ways of the wicked in this city, that she felt satisfied that her friend wanted good counsel, and perhaps assistance, and she determined to give it to one who had often given such to her. As soon as it was sufficiently dark, she slipped on a shawl and hood, and went into a neighbor's and borrowed another just like her own.

"What in the world do you want of it?" said the woman.

"No matter, it shall come safe back to you, in the course of the evening."

So it did, and with it came Athalia, who, by that double, had eluded her jailers.

Lovetree went to his hotel in a state of mind not to be envied. He had found the strongest evidence that his niece had been in a house which pollutes all who breathe its atmosphere, and he had heard vile women speak of her as one of themselves, and he knew not how far she was like them. He had witnessed an exposition of character that night, such as he never had before conceived possible. He first saw Mrs. Laylor, a specimen of a high-bred lady,

> Bland as the dewy morn
> That opes the buds to flowers.

Then he saw her furious as the winds,

> By Boreas rudely driven,
> Wild as the storm, when Jove hurls down
> His thunderbolts from Heaven.

He trembled with fear that she would pursue Athalia, and drag her back, and perhaps hide her where he could never find her. Undoubtedly she would have exercised her vindictiveness upon Athalia in some way, if she had known where she was. Lovetree had heard Mrs. Laylor swear that Athalia had robbed her, and that she would have her punished, and although he did not believe a word of such a charge, he believed that vile woman wicked enough to swear away an innocent girl's life.

He was quite mistaken. She was furious at her disappointment and loss of gain, for gold she worshipped, but after all she would not have done a thing to put the life or liberty of Athalia in danger of the law. The restraint she had put upon her, was one of policy, all in the way of her business. Lying and cheating were a part of her trade; it is of some others. She had been outwitted by one whom she thought too tame to resent an injury, or protect herself. Lovetree did not know that like a furious wind it would soon blow out, or that a portion of her apparent anger was put on for effect, for one of the other girls was held by a slender thread, and it was an object to deter her from taking the same step that Athalia had.

It is a great object—great as it is with the merchant to get new goods—with all this class of houses to get new girls; those fresh from the country are objects of great importance; hence the effort to keep them until their conscience is obliterated from hearts made for virtuous actions, and then they stay willingly—often have to beg for the privilege of staying, for "old goods" in this branch of trade are a greater drug in the market of seduction, than old dry goods upon the merchant's shelves. They are more like old meat upon the butcher's stall; nobody wants to buy, though all may admire its fatness, and remark how good it had been, but when they examine closely, an odor cometh up to the nostrils, which giveth offence to the stomach.

Men treat all these poor girls as children treat toys. The fresh and beautiful are admired, then barely tolerated, then kicked aside to make room for a fresh set. Hence all the arts that cunning vile women know of are used to obtain new toys for their customers.

Lovetree slept but little that night. How he did walk up and down the corridors of the Astor house the next morning, watching every one that entered, hoping it might be the little pedler girl. She was at home and asleep. She got home before her mother and went to bed, so that she knew nothing of the coming of Mrs. Morgan. All slept late, and Stella's mother saw her daughter sleeping so sweetly that she could not bear to wake her for her daily task until breakfast was ready. How delighted she was to see Mrs. Morgan! "Oh, mother, mother, let me go and tell that gentleman; I will bring him right here. He will be so glad to see Mrs Morgan."

"So glad to see me, Stella, who is it that knows me?"

"He don't know you at all. But when I told him about you, he and that other gentleman said that they would go right off to Mrs. Laylor's, and get you away."

"Why, Stella, my daughter, who are you talking about? We do not understand a word you are saying."

"Don't you, no, you do not; I had forgotten that I had not told you about those two nice gentlemen that I met at the Astor house last night. Oh, mother, where did you get those bouquets? As I live there is the very one that I looked at and talked about with Joseph Butler, last night. Did you buy them, mother?"

"No, Tom Top brought them here just as we got home, and

said that an old gray-headed gentle[illegible] m of Joseph, and gave him a shilling to bring [illegible] and one for you."

"Oh, my, that must be him, who else cou[illegible] then, only think of it, his name is just like Mrs. M[illegible] fore she was married."

"What, Lovetree? Is his name Lovetree? How rema[illegible] able it would be if he should turn out to be my uncle from the West."

"So it would. Now I think of it, he does look like you. No, no, I cannot eat now, I must run and tell him, that you are here, it will make him so happy.

So it did. There was another happy person that day; ah, two or three of them, for Mrs. May and Stella were almost as happy as Athalia; when he came they saw how quickly she recognized him, and how overjoyed he was to see her, and how he hugged her and kissed her, and then he took Stella in his arms and kissed her, and told her that she should never go out peddling again; that he would set her mother up in a little shop, and Stella should be her clerk, for he felt that he owed all that he now enjoyed to her, and he owed her mother a great debt for her kind intention and goodness of heart, in getting Athalia away from that house; and then he told them all about his visit to Mrs. Laylor's, and Mrs. May told all about how she worked her plan to get Athalia away; how she dressed her up and sent her down first, and then she watched until she saw the other girl in the hall, and then went down herself. Then Stella said, she must run and see

Joseph, she wanted Joseph to tell that other gentleman; and so she did, and Joseph told "the other gentleman," when he came by and stopped to give the poor crippled black man a kind word, which always lighted up a pleasant smile upon his fine face; and in the evening the two gentlemen, and the two ladies, and the dear little girl, all sat down in Mrs. May's little parlor, to such a supper, as, perhaps, never had been set in that room before. This was one of Mr. Lovetree's whims. It was a thanksgiving supper, he said, for the prodigal returned, and he wanted to eat it there, all by themselves; and so he went out and ordered the best of everything that could be provided sent there, and then as happy a party sat down as ever enjoyed a supper in New York. Athalia and her uncle had talked all day, and she had told him all the secrets of her life, and he had forgiven her everything, and told her that he would love her as long as she would love him. Then he asked Stella to go out and get him some writing materials, and then her eyes fairly danced with joy as she ran and got her own little portfolio, one that she had made herself out of some colored paper, and asked him if he would use her pen and paper. He did so, and then wrapped up the little home-made article in a newspaper, and carried it away with him, without saying a word. Stella thought it very queer that he should do so, and she almost dropped a tear at the thought of losing it, for it had cost her a good many hours of busy work to make it. After awhile a boy brought it back, wrapped in the same paper, but as it had her name on the outside, she thought she would open it, to see what he had put in it; "some paper, I dare say, in place of that which he had used." That was not what she found; she found in place of her old one, the most beautiful portfolio that could be found in New York, filled with all sorts of stationery that could be desired.

After supper was over, of course Stella had to get her portfolio, and show it, and talk about it; and then Mr. Lovetree talked about what he had written with Stella's pen—it was his will.

"I have made," said he, "Athalia my heir. I adopt her as my daughter, and shall always treat her as my child. I hope she will always feel towards me as she would if I were her father in fact. She is an orphan, and she is —— a widow."

"A widow—a widow?"

"Is Walter dead?"

"Is that so, uncle—father?"

"Yes, it is so. When I went to the attorney to see if I had got my will all right, and when he came to the name of Athalia Morgan, he said, 'Oh, that is Walter Morgan's widow.' Then, I said, widow, widow, just as you all did a minute since. And he told me, that was the fact; and a good thing it was that he was dead, for he got to be a terrible sot. And now, Athalia is my heir, and my executor. When I am dead she will do what she pleases with what I leave, and get married again if she likes; she has promised me that she never will while I live. There is one little clause in my will that I will read now, for I like to make people happy, and I am going to make a mother happy, free from anxiety about what her child will do when she is gone. This is the clause, 'To the owner of the pen with which I wrote this will, I bequeath five hundred dollars.' "

"Why, what is there in that to cry about? Bless my heart, I thought I was going to make you all happy, and here you are all shedding tears."

"Oh, uncle, uncle, you have made us happy. These are tears of joy and gladness. How noble, how generous, how good!"

"Just like him," said the other gentleman.

"This to me! Oh, Mr. Lovetree, this to the poor widow! This to my daughter!"

"To me, mother, to me? Does it mean me? Yes! Oh, mother, may I kiss him?"

Before anybody could say no, if they had been disposed to, Stella was in his arms, and who shall say, that to one of his wealth, that moment was not cheaply purchased for five hundred dollars. Happiness is contagious. Those who feel it, feel as though they would like to make everybody else feel just so. Stella did, for she reached out one hand and drew her mother to the same enfolding arms, and then Athalia enfolded them all, until it seemed to my dim-growing eyes that four exceedingly happy people were blending all in one. Feeling how useless is a fifth wheel to a vehicle already having four, and feeling too a sort of choking sensation, as though the air of the street would be beneficial, while this scene was on, I went off.

When I had breathed the fresh air long enough to recover my equilibrium of thoughts, one came into my mind that I might do something to increase the happiness of the full hearts I had just left. With this new idea in my mind I took my way directly to Mrs. Laylor's. Of course I found the storm had passed. A May morning could not be more calm and pleasant. Of course I was a welcome visitor. I had ordered a bottle of wine the night before, that paid my footing. I had spent money for one sin, and apparently seemed willing to spend more for another, and that always makes welcome guests, because profit can be made out of such visitors. I had an object in my course the night before; I had nothing of that kind to accomplish to-night, and so I ordered no wine. I looked serious, earnest, determined, and asked Mrs. Laylor for a private interview. It is not necessary to inflict the particulars upon my readers; it will be only interesting to them to know that one of the results of the talk did add to the happiness of those whom I had just left already very happy, for just as Lovetree was in the act of kissing good-night to Athalia, there came a rap to the door, it was a porter's rap; his load was a trunk, a bandbox and a square bundle. The bundle was opened first, its contents were now doubly dear, and Athalia longed to show it to her uncle. It was the old family Bible. Everything had been sent but the watch. That was irrecoverably lost.

As I was leaving Mrs. Laylor's, with the porter and Athalia's trunk, I met Frank Barkley and had five minutes talk with him. As we parted, he said: "Depend upon it I shall claim my bet, and the stake is in the hands of a friend who will fork over."

The next morning Athalia met with another surprise. The three had just finished breakfast, and sat talking over the strange events of the last day or two, congratulating each other upon their singular good fortune, and laying out plans for the day, while awaiting the momentarily expected arrival of Mr. Lovetree. Mrs. May and Stella were to go out and look up a place for the "little shop," which was to hold an assortment of just such goods as she had been accustomed to sell out of her basket, to which her mother was to add her nice shirt collars, and perhaps the work of some other poor woman who might be in need of assistance; and Athalia and her uncle were to go "house hunting," a very common employment in New York, for he was going to set her up in a business that she could live by, and have a house for herself and him too, when he was in the city, and pretty soon he hoped that would be all the time; it should be as soon as he could get his Western business settled up; but she should have a house and take a few boarders, and always keep a room for him, and he would always call that home; "and we shall be so happy," says she, "and if he is sick I will take care of him, and if I am sick I know he will be kind to me, he looks just as though he would; don't you think so, Mrs. May?"

"Indeed he does; and you will be so happy, but I do not know as you will be quite so happy as Stella and I shall be, when we get a-going. I am happy now, only one thing troubles me a little, I do not know what I am going to do for a little money for present necessities. I had just paid my month's rent, ten dollars in advance, and bought a piece of linen for my work, and Stella had laid out all of her little stock, and now we are quite out. If you had money as you once had, I should know very well what to do. I should ask you for a loan of five dollars. and I know very well what you would say ; no, you would not say anything, you would jump up and run to the little drawer, the left-hand top drawer of the bureau, I can almost see it now, and then you would say, 'there, there it is, go along, I don't want you to stop to thank me.' But that time has past away. I suppose I shall have to do what we poor folks often have to do, go to the pawnbroker again."

"Your trouble, Mrs. May, is just mine too; I want a few dollars so bad that I do not know what to do, and I was about to ask you ; I do not like to ask my uncle, so soon, and would not on my own account, but will on yours."

"No, no, no, do not, I can get along very well, I can pawn the linen, I shall not want that for a few days."

"Yes, I will, do not say anything more, I have made up my mind, and here he comes, so it is too late for argument."

There was a rap, and as they did not expect anybody else, of course it must be her uncle; who else should it be? but it was not. It was the same porter who was there last evening. He did not bring any trunk or bundle, he simply brought a letter and a very small package; a letter addressed, "Lucy Smith."

Athalia was on the point of denying it, but then she thought that Mrs. May and Stella both knew that was the name she was known by at Mrs. Laylor's. Still she blushed and trembled. She blushed to think that she had once said of her first name, "I never shall change that." It is a sad thing for a girl to change that. She trembled at the thought of having any of her old acquaintances, who knew her by that name, write to her or speak to her as friends, for they were only friends of days which she would gladly blot out of memory—days of sin and shame, which she looked back upon with horror, as she felt their deep degradation. She trembled still more when she opened the letter, and saw that the signature was Frank Barkley. She felt faint, and her eyes grew dim, for she felt that she was still pursued—"the guilty flee when no man pursueth"—by one with whom she had sinned, and she felt that it was a renewal of the proposition to sin again. She saw the name, and the "Dear Lucy" with which it commenced, she saw no more, she could see no more, and so she handed the letter to Mrs. May, with an "oh, dear!"

Mrs. May read it, and then *she* said, "Oh, dear," but it was a very different "Oh, dear," from Athalia's. It was an "Oh, dear, what a fortune," and then she handed the letter back to Athalia, and said, "read, you will not find it very bad." Her joyous smile reassured the fainting, trembling Athalia, and she read:

"My Dear Lucy.

"Dearer to me now than ever. I have heard from a mutual friend all about it. First, forgive me for the wrong I have done you. I shall not do it again. Blush not to meet me in the street or church, for by no look or word will I ever seek to renew our acquaintance. I know you now, I never did before, and I feel that I am not worthy to renew that acquaintance. I am a man of the world, and enjoy what my own class call pleasures. I have enjoyed pleasant hours with you, but I never enjoyed a night as I have the last. I have been alone in my room all night. I have been thinking. I have thought how much myself and my associates have done to swell the class of females whom we look upon with contempt, as they pass us in the street. I have found that it is good to think. I have thought a great deal of you, and of your history, as I gleaned it partly from you and partly from Mrs. Laylor, but the last and best part from your friend. Believe me when I say that I am most sincerely glad that you have escaped from a life which I had persuaded you to adopt. I was selfish then. I am sober now.

"Of course you know I have won my bet. I have got the money. I do not need it, you do. It is your due and much more from that avaricious woman who deceived you so bitterly. You lost your watch. It was partly my fault. If I had not believed the lies told of you, it would not have happened, for then in a spirit of retaliation, I had not been false to you, nor you to me, and you would not have made the acquaintance of the gambler who stole your watch. I cannot return that, but I send one in its place. I also send you my check for the money won, and the same sum which was staked against it. If you are ever in need hereafter remember your real, truly sincere friend,

"Frank Barkley."

She looked up with tearful eyes, and simply said, "Mrs. May, you will not have to go to the pawnbroker's to-day. Take this check and go to the bank, or I will write a note to a friend who will cash it in a minute, it needs no endorsement, it is payable to the bearer, and you shall have one hundred and I the other. Now let us look at the watch." They did look at it, and of course admire it, and then Mr. Lovetree came in, and then the letter was read again, and then he said, "the fellow has got a heart after all, it has only been spoiled by bad associations; he has got a good start now in the right path, and I shall make it my business to look him up and help him along. Do you know, Athalia, where he lives?"

"I have his card, sir, in my trunk."

"Very well, give it to me at your leisure, and we will let him know that the pearls of that letter have not been cast before the very worst sort of pigs."

Then Stella was going out to get the check changed, and then he said, "Never mind, give it to me," and then he put it in his pocket-book very carefully, and put that away in his left-hand pocket—he had a place for everything; and then he put his hand into his right-hand pocket, and took out fifty dollars in gold, and handed that to Athalia, with the remark that he would bring her the balance to-morrow, that that was as much as she would want to-day; and then he said, as he saw her slipping it slyly into Mrs. May's hand, "Oh, that is it, is it?" and then Mrs. May said, she *must* tell, and then she did tell all about her want of money, and how she used to go to Athalia when she was in want, and now, when neither of them had any, it did seem as though the good spirit had opened the heart of that man to repentance and good works, just when it was most needed."

And then they all went out, Mrs. May and Stella to hunt for the shop, which they found and had in operation in a week, and which was the foundation of a fortune, for it prospered wonderfully. The ball only needed a start, it would accumulate at every roll. It is accumulating still. I wish a few more benevolent old gentlemen would take each one of them a little girl out of the street, and set the ball to rolling.

Good bye, Mrs. May—good bye, Stella. We may never meet again, but we never shall forget you, good-hearted little girl, and kind, blessed, good mother. Thy good works have their reward.

Athalia and her uncle found a house. We have heard of that before, from Maggie; we shall hear of them again, in some of these shifting " Scenes."

I shall draw the curtain now. It may remain down for one or two or more years, what does it matter to the reader? It is facts that he wants, he cares nothing for time, or which scene comes first. If the reader is a woman, she cares neither for time nor facts, so that the story is good.

What next?

Look in the next chapter

CHAPTER XIV.

NEW SCENES AND NEW CHARACTERS.

"There is some soul of goodness in things evil,
Would man observingly distil it out."

THAT was well exemplified in the last chapter. It may be in this. If any of the readers of these "Scenes" suppose the writer lost sight of the chance to do good, and the right time to do it, that the death of "Little Katy," offered, they are quite mistaken. Although he may not be able to do with his own purse, he has a way of procuring others to do a part that is so much needed to be done. He found that Katy had an aunt in the city, who was able to do for her sister, and he took the preliminary steps to restore the poor, lost sheep to the fold from which she had strayed. That he should have lost sight of her for a little while, in the busy whirl of city life, is not surprising. That the reader has been left in suspense, while he has had many other scenes before him, the author hopes he will not regret. We do not travel old, beaten paths, in this volume.

As the subject is new, so is the way of illustrating it. Now, let us walk on.

"There has been a black woman here twice this evening after you, and she says, she must have the sight of ye afore she sleeps, any how."

This was a piece of Irish information, which met me as I opened the door, one night, in rather a melancholy mood, for I was as yet supperless, tired, sleepy, and about half sick, from breathing fetid air four or five hours, while visiting the poorest of the city poor, the denizens of Cow Bay.

Now, it must not be understood that Mrs. McTravers intended to tell me that the Ethiopian female, who had twice called at my abode, and declared that "she must have the sight of me before she slept," had the least desire to gouge out my eyes. On the contrary, she was only anxious to have a sight of the ugly visage I own, and come within speaking distance of me.

"What for? What did she want, Mrs. McTravers?"

"Sure, your honor, it's not the likes of me knows what a lady wants with a lone gentleman at this time o'night."

If I did not swear, I had some very hard thoughts at the blundering awkwardness of this woman, or her entire inability to convey ideas by language, so that I could understand them "at this time of night."

She proceeded to give a most minute description of "the black woman," how she looked, and talked, and dressed.

Who could it be? I run over in my mind all of my African female acquaintances—not large—but not one of them answered the description given by Mrs. McTravers.

I was about proceeding up stairs, when she said, "ye'll surely go and see the sick lady." I had a slight internal intimation that I was nearly losing my patience.

"Mrs. McTravers, what is it about a sick lady? You have

not told me a word about anybody, sick or well, except a negro woman, and you have not told me what she wanted."

"And sure, then, I thought you knew all about it. The wench said you knew the lady."

"I know a good many, but how can I tell which one of my acquaintances this may be?"

"Why sure, then I thought you would know when I told you where she lived."

"In the name of common sense, Mrs. McTravers, if you know who the sick woman is, or where she lives, or what she wants, why don't you tell me?"

"Wasn't I going to, only you put me into such a flusteration? There, sure, that'll tell you all about it."

And she handed me a piece of paper, on which was written, in a very delicate lady hand, though evidently nervous, "Madame De Vrai, 53 W— street."

I am sure I must have looked like a living specimen of confusion worse confounded. The name I had never heard before. The street was an unknown locality. I only knew it was a street on the west side of the city, somewhere, and whether it had such a number as "53," was entirely too much for my arithmetic. I determined not to go. Still there was a mystery, that natural curiosity prompted me to solve. Who could it be? "Did the black woman say that I was acquainted with the lady?"

"She did that, and that you had been very kind to her. God bless you for that same, for being so to a stranger and a foreigner too at that. The black woman said you was a blessed good man to the poor lady, and a father to her childer, dead and alive."

Was anything ever so provoking as the stolidity of an Irish servant. Every word she uttered made the mystery still darker. I knew no Madame De Vrai; never heard of the name before in my life—took no credit to myself for any special act of kindness to the poor in general, and certainly could not call to mind any act of my life that would warrant me in appropriating the blessing so heartily offered for my acceptance. As to being the father of the poor woman's "childer, dead and alive," I declared emphatically that it was just no such thing. I would not own them. So I called for something to eat, and determined to go to bed, fully satisfied that African blunders and Irish ditto, duly mixed, had made one this time too large for my mastery, either with my very common name, or by a mistake in the street or number; or else somebody else had undertaken to father this family, and now desired to shift the responsibility; certainly I had not, could not, would not father them. So I sat munching and musing over my bread and butter and cold water, of the scenes of the evening which I had witnessed.

"Would to Heaven I knew what had become of her," I thought aloud.

"Who?" said a kind voice at my elbow. "What lady are you so anxions about now. Any of your Five Point protégés?"

"Yes. You have guessed it exactly. None other."

"Is that what you have been looking for to-night. Do tell me of your visit. What have you seen?"

"More of human misery than I ever saw before in one night. Would you like to hear the detail?"

"Yes, it may do me good to hear how others live, and if worse than I do, it may make me more contented with my own lot."

"Worse than you do? Why, madam, have you not all that is necessary to make life comfortable around you. A neat, airy, well-furnished house, plenty of room, plenty to eat, good bed to sleep on, good baths for evening ablution or morning renovation, and above all the other luxuries of city life, plenty of that greatest of New York's blessings, the Croton water? Now listen how and where others live. In a close, dirty, pent up court, are piles of old bricks and frame houses, perfect rat harbors, filled with human beings, men, women, children, from cellar bottom to garret peak, poor beyond the power of imagination, dirty to a degree that is sickening to behold, criminal through necessity——"

"No, not necessity. Nobody is necessitated to be criminal."

"You are simply mistaken. I repeat, criminal by necessity. So educated from childhood, that they know of no way to live, but by the beggar's trade, or pilferer's, or prostitute's crime. Such are the parents, such must be the children. There is no hope otherwise. They are sent out in infancy to beg, and early taught to "pick up things;" the place of education is the street, the watch house, or city prison."

"Why don't their parents send them to school?"

"Why should they? They never went to such a place

themselves, and care not that their children should go. They care for nothing but rum, and that the builders of prisons, and hangers of murderers, take care they shall have the means of getting. The imprisonment and hanging, is the sequence of the license system."

"But you were to tell us what you saw this evening."

"Human misery. The houses of the city poor. The locality is Cow Bay. It opens upon Anthony street at the North West angle of the Five Points."

The first *home* we entered was a cellar room twelve by twenty feet, quite below the surface, and only just high enough to stand up under the beams of the floor over head, while at every step the water oozed up through the boards we trod upon. At one end was the narrow, muddy stairway and door, by which we entered, and at the other a fire-place.

On one side two windows with places for three panes of glass to each, gave all the light and ventilation afforded to the four families who occupied the room. These consisted of two men and their wives, two single women, an old woman and her three boys, and a young girl as a boarder. There were four sleeping places, called beds, upon forms, elevated above the floor, for none could sleep on that on account of the water.

"Do you always have the water as bad as it is now?" I inquired.

"Bad is it? An I wish then you could see it after a big rain, when the water is over the floor entirely fornent the the door."

"Have these women husbands?"

"These two with the young children have."

"What do they do for a living?"

"One of them jobs about—but he is on the Island now."

"What for?"

"Just nothing at all, yer honor, he is as kind a husband as ever lived, only when he takes a drop too much once in a while."

"Hoúld your tongue now, Ellen Maguire, you know your husband is drunk every time he can get liquor, and that is as often as he can coax anybody that has got money into that dirty hole at the corner—Cale Jones's grocery. He is a burner, sir?"

"A burner. What is that?"

"He asks some one to go and take a drink with him, and then tells him to call for what he likes, and so he drinks and drinks, thinking all the time it is a treat, till he gets ready to go, and then the fellow who keeps the shop stops him and makes him pay for all the liquor the company have drank."

"Don't he refuse?"

"What's the use? He is burnt, and must stand it. If he refuse, they will take his coat, or hat, or shoes. If he gets off with his breeches on he is lucky."

"What does this woman's husband do to support his family?"

"Deil a bit can I tell. It is not for me to pry into peoples' business who pay the rint like honest folks."

OLD PLATO COOKING HOT CORN.—*Page* 321

"The rent. How much rent do you pay for this room?"

"Fifty cents a week for each of us—that is two dollars in all, every Monday morning in advance; sure, you may well believe that, if you know Billy Crown, the agent. It's never a poor woman that he lets slip; if she was dying, and never a mouthful of bread or drop of anything in the house, the rint must be paid."

"Well, these women what do they do?"

"What should a lone woman do? she must live. There is but one way."

"Have you a husband?"

"The Lord be thanked, no. It is enough for me to live with me boys. What would I do if I had a drunken husband to support out of me arnings?"

Sure enough. What should any woman want of a drunken husband? Let us look above ground. Perchance misery only dwells in dark, low, damp cellars. Up, then, to the very garret of the same house. It is divided into three rooms, one is ten feet square with one window, without fire-place or stove. What may be inside we know not, for a strong hasp and padlock guard the treasure. Back of this, through a two feet wide passage, is another room, eight feet by twelve. This is partly under the roof, has a dilapidated fire-place and broken window. This is inhabited by a black man and his wife. There is a bed, a table, dishes and two chairs, and an air of neatness, contrasting strongly with the cellar.

By the side of this is another room inhabited by a negro

and his white wife, and a white man and wife. Did you ever see four uglier beasts in one cage? The white man is a hyena; his wife a tiger; the negro a hippopotamus; his wife a sort of human tortoise; the dirt, representing the shell, out of which the vicious head poked itself, glaring at the intruders upon her premises, with a look that plainly said, Oh, how I should like to bite and claw you, and strip off those clean clothes, and spoil that face, and put out those eyes, and make ye as dirty and ugly and miserable as I am. The black man was social, courteous and intelligent. He was a cobbler, and diligently plied his hammer and awl. With a kind master and well cared for, he would be a faithful, good servant. He has no faculty to take care of himself. By nature the slave of one of nature's strongest passions, he has sunk down into slavery to this hard-shell woman, and the tool of his designing hyena and tiger room-mates. The white man looked as if he were counting the contents of our pockets, and what chance there would be for a grab at our watches.

The shape of this room was peculiar. Take a large water-melon, cut it in quarters, cut one of those across—the flesh sides will represent the floor and one wall—the cross-cut the end, where there is a fire-place—the rind is the roof and other side of the room, through which at the butt end, there is a window. There is no bedstead, or place for one. There is no table, or occasion for any. Two boxes and a stool serve for chairs. The bedding is very scarce, but the floor is of soft wood, and the weather is warm. Each of these rooms rents for three dollars a month, always in advance.

Now let us go down the rotten stairway to the next floor. Though what we have seen is bad, we may yet say:

> "The worst is not
> So long as we can say, 'this is the worst.'"

What have we here?

Something worse. Yes, for coupled with poverty and crime, is fanatical hatred of everything that is not worse than itself. Let us rap at this door. A gruff woman's voice bids us enter. We are met by an insolent defiant scowl and an angry "what do you want here?"

"Good woman, is some one sick here?"

"Yes. What of that. Nobody wants the like of you, with your pious faces and 'good woman,' prowling about at this time of night. You're after nothing good, any one might swear that."

"Perhaps we can give you some good advice for your sick child."

"Give your advice when we ask it. Haven't we got Father Mullany to give us advice, and he a good doctor too. I tell you we don't want any miserable heretics in the house and me child a dying. And who have I to thank for it?"

"Surely, madam, we cannot tell. Perhaps you can, or your husband, where is he?"

If a dog were thrown among the whelps in a wolf's lair, it would not arouse the dam quicker than these words did this human she-wolf. She sprang towards us, foaming with rage. A stout cane in my strong right hand caught her eye, and she stood at bay.

"What was she so mad at you and your companion for? Did she know either of you?"

"She knew us by sight, or rather she knew him as one of the active helpers of the Missionary, Mr. Pease, the House of Industry, and the Five Points Mission. What more should she know to hate us? She knew we were not of her faith; that we believed not in the efficacy of holy water and confession, to work out sin; that we did not kneel and receive a consecrated wafer with 'extreme unction', and so she hated us with all the fervent rancor of religious hate. She hated us for our mission of good; for she knew we hated what she dearly loved—drunkenness and all its concomitant evils. She hated us with that envious hate of depravity, which would sink everything to its own level. She knew that we would take her dying child to a clean bed and airy room, and give it food and medicine, and nurse it into life, and she hated us for that."

"How could she? How could a mother be so wicked to her poor sick child? I am sure if I could not take care of mine, I would trust it with anybody who would save its life." Thus will say more than one Christian mother.

Think—be careful—be not uncharitable—good mother. Would you let it go with those who saved its life to be reared with them—taught their creed—perhaps to hate yours? Certainly if taught the principles of temperance—virtue—

neatness—her child could not love its drunken mother, in her rags and dirt and life of sin.

"But then the child would be brought up by religious teachers, and taught to be a Christian."

Yes, a Protestant Christian; she is a good Catholic. Would you willingly give up your child if it were to be reared a Pagan, a Mahometan, or even a Jew?

"No! I would let it die."

There spoke the Five Points mother. Sooner than it should go into a Protestant house, she would see it die.

Alas! poor human nature; yes, poor human nature, sunk down into these depths of misery and degradation, yet every one of them are our brothers and sisters, who are rearing up children like themselves, as true as like produces like, while we look on, shrug our comfortably-wrapped shoulders, and "Thank God we are not like one of these," and yet never give, out of our abundance, one cent to make one of them like one of us.

"Well, what of her husband?"

"My husband, is it?" she said, as she stood glaring at us; "my husband? Go, look in your city prison, you old gray-headed villains, where ye or the likes of ye, murdered him without judge or jury. Did you try him for his life? No. Had he been a murderer? No. Had he done any crime? No. You licensed him to sell liquor, and he drank too much —I drank too much—what else can you expect, when you set fools to play with live coals, but they will burn themselves? What next? What is the natural consequence of getting drunk? A quarrel. I know it. Don't ask me what I get drunk for; I know you did not speak, but I saw it in your eye—yes, your eye—turn it away—I cannot bear it, it looks right into my soul. Don't look at me that way, or I shall cry, and I had rather die than do that. It would kill me to cry for such as you, who murdered my poor husband. You licensed him to sell rum, in the first place, to make other wives miserable with drunken husbands—mine was not drunken then, and I did not have to live in such a hole as this—look around you, ye murdering villains. What do you see?—poverty, filth, and rags; starvation, misery, crime—on that bed is my dying boy—that is nothing. Let him die, I am glad of it—the priest has made it all right with him. Now, look in that bed, rum-selling, licensing whelps that you are—that is worse than the dying boy in the other—see what we have bought with our money paid to your excise office. See what a mother is sunk to by rum. Yes, I do drink it—why do your eyes ask the question? I do drink, and will again. What else have I got to live for? What lower hole can I sink to? Me, a mother. A mother! Mother of that shameless girl, do you see her, there in that bed, before her mother's eyes?"

"Yes, and a pretty looking, bright-eyed girl she is."

"Bright-eyed. Yes, bright-eyed. I would to Heaven she had none—that she had been born blind. Her bright eyes have been her ruin—a curse to her and the mother that bore her—they are a curse to any poor girl among such villains as you are. Ye are men—how many hearts have you broken?

—withered, trampled on?—there, go, go. I hate the sight of all men."

"Who is this man I see with your daughter; is he her husband?"

"Husband! husband! Do the like of her get husbands? Where is my husband?"

"We cannot tell, can you?"

"Tell! who can tell where a man is that died drunk—died—murdered in your man-killing city prison, and the priest not there to give him absolution. What had he done? What crime? Drank rum that you licensed him to sell—beat me because I drank too. What next? Next come your dirty police—the biggest scoundrels in the city—mad at my husband because he would not 'touch their palms,' and drag him to the Tombs—a right name—good name—true name—Tombs indeed—a tomb to my husband."

"Did he die there?"

"No! he was murdered there. Look here. Can you read? Yes, yes, I know ye can. So can I. Do you see that account of prisoners dying by suffocation—poisoned by carbonic acid gas—there, read it,"—and she thrust a crumpled paper before us—"read how ye reform drunkards—shut them up in prison cells, and in spite of their prayers, and groans, and dying cries for air, ye let them die. Are ye not murderers? Do you see that name? That is—that was my husband. Ha, ha, ha! Now, what is he, where is he? Don't answer—I know your answer; but if he is in hell, who sent him there? Who, who, who?"

And she sank down upon one of the pallets which were spread over the floor, in a paroxysm of wild, delirious grief and rage, speechless as her dying boy, lying unheeded and unheeding, by her side. What could we do? Nothing here; much elsewhere; and we looked up and registered a vow, that much as she hated us for what we had not done, yet had permitted our fellows to do without crying out against them, that she should be avenged. If we could do nothing here—if we could not pull down the sturdy oak by taking hold of its topmost branches, yet, although its mighty strength defies our weak efforts thus applied, we can and will dig around its roots—we will take away the life-sustaining earth—and that strong tree shall be made to feel our power—it shall wither, dry up, and die, and time shall rot down its strong trunk, and the place that once knew it, shall know it no more.

This then is our pledge, made over that dying boy, and, worse than by murder, widowed mother, and here now we redeem it. Here we expose the hydra-headed monster—the orphan and widow-maker—the property, health, and virtue-destroyer. Sad, harrowing as these scenes of wretchedness and misery are, they must be laid open to the gaze of the world. "Wounds must be seen to be healed." Weak nerves tremble at the idea that physicians cut and carve the dead, talking, aye laughing, as freely over the quiet heart and still nerves in the dissecting-room, as the butcher over his beef upon the market house block; yet without the dissecting of one and butchering of the other, how should the maimed be healed, or meat-eating multitude be fed? So let us on with our panorama of scenes from life in New York.

Let us open this door. Ah! we have been here before.

The room is seven by twelve feet, under the roof, which comes down at one end within a foot of the floor. There is a broken, dirty, window in the roof, at the right hand of the door as we enter on the side. No fire-place or stove, no table, only two broken chairs—a very old bureau—a dilapidated trunk—a band-box—a few articles of female apparel—some poor dishes and a few cooking ustensils—used upon a little portable furnace standing in the room—a poor old bedstead and straw bed in one corner—a child's cot and a doll; and yet the only occupant of the room is an old negro man, who sits of nights upon cold stones, crying Hot Corn. We look about wonderingly, peering in here and there, but except the old man we see no one.

"She gone, massa, clean gone—cry old eyes out when I come home next day arter dat one, you know massa, which one dis child mean—sad day—don't like to mention him, massa—give me chaw terbacca, massa—come home and find her and little sis—nice child dat—

"You found her."

"No sir, found her gone—done gone entirely—key in old place where I knew where to find him—everything all here—no word for old Plato—what I give to see her once more—to see little Sissee—Oh that I knew where she was. Oh, oh, oh."

"And would to Heaven we could tell what has become of her."

"Who?" said the lady who had been listening with intense interest to my narrative.

"True, I had forgotten to tell you that we stood in the chamber where little Katy died. Where that last sweet kiss of an angel was given—where the candle seemed to the dying innocent to go out—where she said, 'Good bye—mother—don't drink—any more—good b—' but before the word was finished, there was another angel added to the heavenly host around the throne of God."

It was here that the scene, which the artist has so touchingly illustrated upon the opposite page, transpired. Turn your thoughts a moment from this page to that and look upon the picture. Turn back to Chapter VI., "The Home of Little Katy," and read over the story of the death of that poor innocent, and you will better appreciate the description and illustration of that home and that dying scene.

'Twas then and there that that fallen mother was touched by a power greater than human strength—'twas then as she knelt over her dead child, she had said, "never, never, never, will I touch that accursed poison cup. Oh, God," she prayed, "take my child, my wronged and murdered child, and I will not repine; I will thank thee; I will praise thy name as my mother taught me to praise thee; as she loved and blessed, and prayed for me all her life, even after my fall, although hastened to her grave by my sin. Oh, my mother, forgive me; oh, my child, forgive me; oh, my God, forgive me, but let me live to repent, and be a mother and a blessing to my living child. Oh, my sister, where are you, cold and unforgiving sister. but for you I had not been here—why could you not forgive. Oh, God, canst thou?"

What was that still small voice that seemed to say in our ears, as she ceased speaking, and lay sobbing upon the breast of little Katy?

"Yes, sister, he can, he will, he has; rise, thy sins are forgiven thee."

Did she hear it too? Else, why did she instantly rise up, with dry eyes and calm, almost happy features?

It was then that I gained from her the secret of her sister's name, upon a promise that I did not keep—I could not keep—it was not my duty to keep it. But where has she gone? Has her sister got my letter?—has her heart at last been touched?—has she taken her away? If so, why has she not told me where. Long days and nights of anxiety have come and gone, and she comes not back to her home. Has despair worked its wonted result, and does the ocean wave roll over the mother and her child, in a suicide's watery grave?

"What would I give to know?"

"You must wait," said our sympathizing friend.

Yes, we must wait. Yet "Hope deferred maketh the heart sick."

"Have you been to see the woman who sent for you today?"

"No! It is nobody that I know. Some mistake."

Yes, it was some mistake.

"But she sent her name by the black woman, when she came the second time."

"I know it, but it is no one that I know. The name is utterly unknown to me. It is a French name. Some mistake." There was a mistake.

What prompted me to look again at the name? I knew it as well as I should if I looked at that paper a hundred times. Yet I was prompted to look at it once more. The desire was irresistible. Who has ever felt a longing after something unseen, unknown, unheard, undefined, something that he feels as though he must have or die, yet knows not how to obtain, may realize the intensity of my desire to see that paper once more. Where is it? This pocket, and that is searched, turned wrong side out, and turned back again; the table, floor, books, papers, hunted over, but nowhere can it be found. What has spirited it away? It could not blow out of the window, for there is no air stirring.

"It must," said the lady, "have gone down on the tea-tray —I will call Bridget."

A woman is worth a dozen men for thought, and this time she thought truly. It had gone down that way, and gone into the slop-bucket, and into the street.

"Bridget, will you take a lamp and go out and see if you can find it."

"Yes, sir, certainly, and I think I can."

Blessed hope. My friend was curious to know, what in the world I wanted of that piece of paper? "You say, you remember the name and number perfectly, and yet you act as though it was of the utmost value. I recollect seeing you once when you had lost a twenty dollar bill, as cool and careless as though it had been as worthless as this little scrap of paper. Now you act strangely, what can it mean?"

"I don't know—I know I want to see that paper. I cannot tell why."

"Well, you will soon be gratified. She has found it. Do wait, don't be so impatient to meet her at the foot of the stairs."

I did not wait though. I gave one glance at the soiled scrap —it was enough—the pen and ink name had faded out, but there were three words—talismanic words—in pencil marks, evidently added as an after-thought by her who had first written her name in ink—words which sent me out of the door, and half way to the next street, before that voice, sent after me from the stair-head, of "Do stop him, Bridget, he is crazy, to go out in this rain," had reached my ears. It did not stop me—I was gone beyond the reach of her voice. The girl stood amazed. She looked at the scrap of paper with about the same degree of astonishment as did the savage tribe at the white man's paper talk.

"Bring it to me, Bridget."

"He is gone, ma'am."

"Yes, yes, I know he is gone, bring it to me."

"I can't ma'am, he is gone."

"Not him, Bridget, the paper, the paper. I want to see what is on it, that has driven that man out at this hour, in such a rainy night."

The girl looked at the door just closed, shutting the man out in the rain, then she examined the corner where the cane and umbrella usually stood, to be sure they had gone out too, that she had not been dreaming all the while; then she gave a glance at the table to satisfy herself that the hat had gone with the cane and umbrella; then she looked again at the paper, to see what magic power that might possess, to do such midnight deeds. Papers have great power. Poor Bridget, she could not read, but she could feel, and she knew that there was a cause—the effect she had seen.

"Bridget, what is the matter? are you frightened to death?"

"Yes, ma'am. No, ma'am—only speechless. Did you ever see the like? that that little dirty scrap of paper, I picked out of the gutter, should send the gentleman out of the house faster than I ever saw him go before in the year and a half I have been with you. What does it mean? Will you please to tell me, what these little marks mean? What does it read? There now, you can see them good. Please, read them to me, ma'am."

"Little Katy's Mother."

"Is that all?"

"Yes, and quite enough. I wonder not he went so quickly. I almost fancy I can—

> 'By the lamp dimly burning, or the pale moonlight—
> See where he goes —— '

almost past whole house fronts at a single stride. If a cart is in the way at the crossing he will not go around—

two steps and he is over. If there is a bell at the door, take care, or the wires will crack. If a knocker, it will thunder loud this night. Woe to the watchman, who, thinking he may be a runaway burglar, puts out a hand to stop him in his walk. The bull, that butted the locomotive, made equal speed in his intent. He went down—the steam went on."

"Is he mad, ma'am?"

"No, Bridget, only enthusiastic. If he is mad,

'There is method in his madness,'

he is only very much interested about a woman."

"Oh, yes, ma'am, I understand it now. I have seen gentlemen often mad after women. I suppose little Katy, then, is his child."

"Oh, no, Bridget, you are all wrong. She is not his child."

"Oh, well, ma'am, then, I suppose, she is somebody's else child. And if her mother is an interesting woman, I don't see as there is anything so very wrong about the matter. What am I all wrong about, ma'am?"

"Little Katy is dead."

"Oh, is she? I am sure then I am very sorry. Can I do anything about helping to get her ready to be buried?"

"No, she was buried long ago. You may see her grave some day in Greenwood Cemetery."

"I don't see, then, what was the gentleman's great hurry, if nobody is sick and nobody to be buried."

"Perhaps the mother is sick—perhaps in want—perhaps

some unknown power has drawn him to her assistance. I have seen stranger things than that. This is a strange world."

"Indeed it is, ma'am. And there is a strange noise in the street." And she looked from the window.

"What can it be, Bridget, there is a crowd around our area fence, and see, there is a woman under the steps by the basement door. Go down and see what is the matter. Are you afraid? Well then, I will go with you; it is somebody that a parcel of brutal men and boys are persecuting. No matter who, or what she is, she is a woman, and should be protected."

So down they went and she said to them, "Oh men, men, where is your manhood, thus to hunt a woman through the streets? Have you forgotten that mothers bore you in pain into this world? Have you no daughters, no sisters, are you savages—wolves—is this a lamb or stricken deer, that ye trail by her bloody track?"

"No, ma'am," said a bull pup looking boy, "she is drunk, and we is just having a little fun with her, that is all."

God of mercy! Didst thou make man in thine own image, and yet leave him void of that heavenly attribute—mercy? Why, "a merciful man is merciful to his beast," and yet these images of their Maker hunt this poor woman through the streets of a Christian city, as savages hunt tigers through the jungles of Africa—for fun. What for? "She is drunk." A potent reason, surely. Who made her so? How came she drunk? Who is she, what is she? No matter, she is a woman, in distress at a woman's door, and she must, she shall be protected. There is a commotion in the crowd. The human blood-hounds are about to lose their prey—They want more *fun.*

"Bring her out Bill, never mind the women—it is none of their business—bring her out and let us see her run again. She is a real '2.40' nag."

And they shouted and screamed like so many wild Indians.

What but savages are they? True they had white skins and Christian clothes, and spoke the language of a civilized nation, and dwelt in "one of the first cities in the world." Yet they pursued a poor, young, helpless female, like a hunted hare through the streets, and now press hard upon her two protectors; one a delicate, sickly lady, the other a timid servant girl, with a cry to Bill, the leader, to "bring her out"—to drag her by force from where she has sunk down upon the very threshold of a house which she hopes may offer her protection, yet she dares not ask it. Shame has overcome her, she buries her face in her hands as she sits crouched up in a corner, but neither looks up nor speaks. The crowd press forward, the servant shrinks back, the lady stands firm, with a determination to protect or perish.

Can she do it? What can a woman without strength, do against a pack of loosened blood-hounds, already licking their chops with delight at the sight of their prey?

"Drag her out, some of ye, down there, why don't ye," screamed a human tiger, in the rear of the crowd; "don't mind that woman, she is no better than the gal. Let me in and I'll bring her."

A strong hand is laid upon the poor girl's arm, and for the first time she looks up, but ventures not a word. The look was enough. It appealed to a woman's heart for protection—an appeal that never failed. How can she protect the helpless with her feeble strength, against the brutal force of rum crazed men and vicious boys, who shout, "drag her out, drag her out."

Will they do it? They heed not the appealing look of their victim—their object of sport—*fun*—fun for them, death to her. They heed not the appealing words of her who would protect. God help you, poor soul, you have drank wine—you are drunk in the streets at midnight—you have none but those who are as weak as yourself, to save you, poor, timid, stricken fawn.

"Drag her out, drag her out." How it rung in her ears! How those terrible words went down into her soul!

Succor is at hand.

There was a shout, a yell, a horrid scream of anguish, a few hurried oaths, a pushing, shoving, care-for-self-only struggle among the crowd, as a shower of smoking water fell among them, and they were gone.

The lady turned her eyes, and there stood Mrs. McTravers, in her night cap, pail in hand, her effective engine of war.

"Oh, Mrs. McTravers, how could you scald them?"

"Did'nt they deserve it, the brutes?"

"Yes, yes; no, not so bad as that. I am afraid you have put out their eyes."

"Oh, never fear that. Didn't I timper it, like 'the wind to the shorn lamb,' just warm enough to wash the faces of the dirty spalpeens, and give them a good fright? How the cowards did run. What were they afraid of? I had spent all my ammunition in the first volley. This is nothing but cold water, and that never hurt anybody. It is a pity the scurvy dogs did not use more of it every day, and nothing else. They would never chase poor girls through the streets, if they drank nothing but water."

"Come, young woman, you can get up now and go home, if you have any to go to, and if you have not. what are you going to do with yourself?"

"Why, Mrs. McTravers, we will take her in and put her to bed, and let her sleep till morning."

"Take her in? What, take a common street-walker in to disgrace your house?"

"Indeed, my dear, good, kind lady," said the object of their conversation, now for the first time speaking. "I am no street-walker—I am not what you take me for. Do not—pray do not, force me to go into the street again to-night. Let me lay here on the door-sill till daylight."

"Never! It shall never be said I refused to give shelter to one of my own sex in distress, no matter what she is or has been. Mrs. McTravers, she must have a bed in the house to-night."

"I should like to know then where you will find it. Every bed in the house is full."

"I will give her mine then, and sleep myself on the floor."

"No, no, no, let me sleep on the floor—on the hearth—on the stones in the back-yard, rather than go in the street again, but I won't sleep in your bed."

"Well, well, come with me to my room. I will make you a bed on the floor, and you shall sleep there."

"Sure, sure, Heaven will bless you; and if you knew all you would forgive me, for I am not so bad as you think I am, or as that woman thinks I am."

"Oh, never mind what she says, she has a good heart after all. Come, come along with me."

"Did you ever see the like of it. She is going to take that thing to her room, a miserable tramper; I dare say the house will be robbed before morning. I will pick up the spoons, and lock all the closets, before I go to bed again. Dear me, did anybody ever see such a woman as that? She never sees a woman in rags, but she wants to pull off her shawl, and give her. I dare say, she won't let this girl out of the house to-morrow till she has all her draggled clothes washed and fixed up, and may be then will send for a carriage to take her away. It is a great plague to anybody to have such a tender heart. It is all the time getting them into trouble.

"There, now I believe the silver is all safe, but mercy knows what will become of this night's adventure. So much for getting drunk. What does anybody want to get drunk for? There was McTravers, the brute, always getting drunk. I am sure, I love a little bitters to clear my throat in the morning, and a glass or two of wine at dinner, and a little hot stuff as I am going to bed, but as for getting drunk—bah—I hate anybody that gets drunk. Oh, dear, this night air, I wish I had not wasted all the hot water on the drunken dogs, for I do feel as though I wanted a dram now, and no more water—what will I do? I must take a little cold, or I shall not sleep a wink to-night. Bah, how I hate drunkards."

What for, Mrs. McTravers, why should you hate your own manufacture?

Let the reader reflect; there is a night before him.

When the curtain rises, we shall see what the author saw last night.

CHAPTER XV.

LITTLE KATY'S MOTHER.

"A true devoted pilgrim is not weary,
To measure kingdoms with his steps."

WHEN Mrs. McTravers told me that Mrs. De Vrai had sent a message for me, I was too weary to measure steps along a few blocks; but when I read those three little magic words, weariness had gone. Bridget thought so too. "He is gone, ma'am." Yes, he was gone, gone abroad at midnight with a merry heart.

"A merry heart goes all day,
Your sad one tires in a mile."

A mile was soon told, and I felt no tiring. Up this step and that, peering at the blind numbers on the doors; how could I tell one from the other? The almanac said there should be moonshine at this hour, the clouds and rain put in their veto. No matter, the almanac had said it, and that was enough for the gas contractors. If the moon chose to get behind a cloud, it was none of their look out. They would not light their lamps, though darkness, thick, black darkness, spread over the earth. Why should they? It was not in the bond. So the traveller plodded on in the dark. How could one see the numbers? Not by city light, but by city license. Here burns a "coffee-house" lamp, where rum alone is sold. More improvident than his city fathers, this one lights up his lamp, of dark, rainy nights, whether the moon is in the almanac, or city fathers' brains. His number is plain enough. 'Tis an even number—I am on the wrong side of the street. Now, cross over, and here is, 47, 49, 51, 53—this must be it, and yet it cannot be. It is a neat, two story, brick house, with basement and attic, in a row of the same sort, in a clean, wide street.

It is a very unlikely place for such a home as we have seen, for the home of Little Katy's mother.

How, are we deceived again? It must be in the number; perhaps we can not see it rightly by the dim glimmer of the grog-shop lamp. It is the first glimmer that ever came from such a place to any good.

There is no bell, but there is an old-fashioned iron knocker upon the door; shall I use it; what if it wakes up some strange sleeper and brings a fever-heated night-capped angry head out of the upper window, with hasty words, perhaps cross ones of "who is there?" I have no familiar "it's me," to answer. No one will say, "wait a moment, dear, and I will open the door."

All is still within. It were a pity to disturb the quiet sleepers for nothing, nothing but the gratification of idle curiosity; to make the inquiry if—if—Mrs. Mrs.—what was her name? Now that is gone—faded from my memory as easily as it was washed away from that paper. Whom could I inquire for? Should I inquire for "Little Katy's Mother?" I should in all probability be told to go across the street and inquire there, where I got my liquor, upon which to get drunk. Or else, perhaps, to go home and inquire if my "mother knew that I was out;" or told that she might happen to wake up, and find her green gosling of a son gone—gone out in the street to inquire after little girls' mothers—no doubt she would be much alarmed. It was well that the moon was veiled, or else the man in it would have seen how sheepish I looked as I sneaked down the steps, with a weary step, that could not have gone the half a mile without tiring.

How I did rejoice that no watchman was in sight to see how crest-fallen I went away and stood up in the shade of a lamp post! A few minutes afterwards, I would have given gold for the sight of a brass star.

What for? Why did I not go home? What prompted me to keep watch at that lamp post? My object in coming had failed. I had acted upon the momentary spur of a nervous temperament, heated into a state of excitement by what I had seen in the early part of the evening, connected with some of the scenes of the last few weeks' exciting life, which had driven me, without consideration, to start off chasing an ignis fatuus, in the swampy, Jack o'lantern producing air of this city, and it had led me here and left me leaning against a lamp post. Was ever poor wight led into a deeper bog? "Go home," reason told us. If the lamp post had been a repelling magnet, I should have gone. It was the contrary, and I could not break the attraction.

A NEW YORK STREET SCENE.—*Page* 341.

That iron lamp post may possess a very strong magnetic power, yet it is hardly possible, or probable—nay, it is very improbable that it was that power which had drawn me hither and kept me waiting "coming events."

They do "cast their shadows before," for the shadow, and then the substance of a man came round the corner. Like half of those who walk the streets at this hour, he was drunk. Just then there was a moving light in No. 53. The intoxicated night-walker caught the sight of it just as he came opposite the lamp post, and he stopped and laughed one of those horrid laughs, which give the blood a chill and send it with a pang and fluttering fear to the heart.

The last sad remains of a gentlemen—no—a roué, stood in the dim light of a lamp which had been to him the guide to ruin.

"Ha, ha, ha, my old bird, you are astir I see. It is a long time since I have seen you, but I have caged you at last. You would not speak to me, ha, in Broadway, but I tracked you home, and now I am going to roost in the old nest, or I will blow you out of your fine feathers, my lady. Won't let me in? Won't let me in? Then I will break in. Hold, here comes a star. I'll keep dark while it shines." Back he went around the corner, the star went carelessly onward down that way, and I went eaves-dropping. I was impelled to do it. I saw a light come in the front room and heard voices, and felt that there was some strange connection between this house and that man, and perhaps myself, and that the mystery must soon be solved.

The blinds were closed, but the sash was up. I stood close under the window, and the voices dropped down upon my ear through the slats, clear and distinct as though I had been in the room.

The light-bearer with a noiseless step, as though afraid of awaking some sick sleeper, approached a bed, shading the light with her hand.

It was no use. The timid start easy. There was a rustling sound, as though some one started up from an uneasy pillow and sleep-disturbing dreams.

"Will he come?"

That voice, those words. Do I dream, or are there spirits near? Oh, how familiar—how painfully familiar—reminiscential of things past. What can it mean? But one voice ever spoke those words in that tone, and that voice will never speak again. The dreamer is in the street. It is my brain that is disturbed. Hark! Again! I heard aright.

"Oh, no, he will not come. Why should he? What am I to him? Yet I wanted to see him a moment. It seems as though it is he only who can protect me from that dreaded man. Oh, Phebe, Phebe, what should we do if he were to come here to-night? He has sworn to have revenge upon me for leaving him; yet how could I live with a man who threatened my life every day in his drunken fits? Long after I went to Paris, he wrote to me that he would rob me of my child—his child, if he died in the attempt. I long thought—nay, hoped that he was—that is, that he never would return from Cuba. I heard of him in the dungeons of the Moro, and now he is here."

"Yes, ma'am, I is sure he is here. Dat am de fact. Jis sich man, stout, red face, black hair, and such eyes. I is sure he is a wicked man."

"Only when he is drinking."

"Well, dat all de time wid some folk."

There was a groan of anguish in the bed.

"But, Phebe, you describe his looks just as I saw them to-day. Have you seen him?"

"Oh, yes, ma'am—thought I wouldn't tell you though—but it come out when I didn't know him."

"Where? Has he been here? Has he tracked me home?"

"Why, you see, ma'am, when I goes to the door to let Agnes Brentnall out, I sees him over the way, by de lamp, and when she goes down the street, he walks after her, and dat am last I see of him dis night."

"Poor girl, then she is lost. If ever he fixes his basalisk eye upon her beauty, how can she escape. Poor girl—God protect thee—man will not."

There was a sobbing that told of tears—tears that told of a kind heart, crushed by a cold and careless world.

Then I was about to enter, but something said, "not yet," and I stepped down into the shadow by the high steps, till the footfall I heard upon the pavement should go by.

It did not pass—it came directly up to the door, familiar as a burglar with its night latch key. Why had they not bolted the door? It opened as though to one who had a right to enter. The intruder—it was the dark-visaged man I had seen five minutes before—closed the door gently after him without latching it.

There was a thin lace curtain before the window, through which, as I looked in between the slats of the blind, I could see him as he approached the bed. Phebe had left the light and gone into the back room. The lady had buried her face in the pillows—nothing but her raven locks, hanging loose in her neck, were visible. The villain looked at her for a moment, then, satisfied that she was asleep, he reached over her, and lifted a beautiful little girl from her side.

"Mother! mother!"

The light shone in her face—the mother started at the appealing cry for help—sprang up—Heavens, what do we see? It is little Sissee—Little Katy's sister and her mother!

What a sight for that mother! The man she so much dreaded—the man who had so disturbed her dreams—with her child, her last, her only child, in his strong arms, and no one near to protect, to save.

She sprang towards him, and fixed her feeble hands in his hair. Of what avail? He flung her from him reeling, fainting, across the room. The noise brought the faithful Phebe from her couch—too late. The mother saw her child disappearing in the dark passage—she heard her screams for help—she heard no more. One look of his terrible eye, as he bore away her struggling child, was enough to kill one of a stronger form than hers. One look of satisfied revenge—revenge of a man upon a feeble woman, and his hand is upon the door. One step more and he is in the street. One step more and he fell, beneath a blow of a stout cane in a strong man's hand, and lay trembling across that threshold, quivering like a bullock felled by the butcher's blow.

"Here, Phebe, take the child; take care of the mother; tell her all is safe; the Lord watches over the truly penitent; he will protect; he will save."

I dragged the unconscious mass of human flesh down upon the pavement, and struck three sharp blows upon the stones, with the broken cane—broken in avenging a feeble woman. It was answered right and left, up and down, and again repeated. I peered into the darkness for the coming succor.

Will it come? Will it come in time? For a strong hand has seized my only weapon, now he has it in his. There is a momentary struggle—the prostrate man is up and the other one down.

A large Bowie knife, the midnight prowler's fashionable weapon, is gleaming at my throat. A moment more, and all my debts were paid and duties done.

Moments fleet fast, but all too slow for the assassin's knife, when it is not the will of Him that giveth life, that life should fail. The knife fell, but not with a blow—it fell from a broken arm.

The watchman's club had done the work. The watchman had heard the call, and had come in time to save the avenger. and punish the assassin.

"Take him away. You know me and where to send when I am wanted. I have another life to save inside this house."

What was said or done need not be told. The reader is dull of divining power, if he does not already know. I cannot tell. I only know that I awaked from a short nap, next morning, in an easy chair, with a sweet little girl, some three years old, clinging her arms around my neck and nestling her cheek up to mine. Had mortal ever sweeter dreams?

"What time is it, Phebe?"

"Don't know dat, sir; sun up yonder."

"Is it? And she sleeps quietly? Very well, let her sleep. I will send a doctor, on my way home, to look at her. Good by. Bon jour, Sis. One more kiss, there."

"You will come again, when mamma wakes up?"

"Yes—Good bye."

CHAPTER XVI.

AGNES BRENTNALL.

"Every inordinate cup is unblessed, and the ingredient is a devil."

So it proved that night to Agnes Brentnall. But who is she? That we have yet to learn.

We have only heard the name once, during the conversation, between Madame De Vrai and the black woman, Phebe, overheard in that eaves-dropping midnight scene described in the last chapter, unless this Agnes is the same one that we saw in a previous midnight scene. Perhaps it is, for now we remember there was a Phebe in that. At any rate that name, from both of these night scenes, had become deeply impressed upon my mind, as belonging to a beautiful girl, followed in the street by a night-prowling wolf, with a canine instinct which snuffs in the breeze the far-off scent that leads him to some wandering female.

Mrs. De Vrai had said; "Then she is lost."

What had become of her? Had the woman-devouring monster consumed the innocent girl and come back for more prey? He will prey no more, soon; he has met his deserts at last. The stony walls of the Tombs' prison, will hold him safe, and when he recovers from his broken arm, the law will have its course. He will make a good Sing Sing worker in stone. It will not break his heart, for it is as hard as the stone he will hammer.

But what of poor Agnes? Would that I knew. Did she fall before his basalisk eye? Such thoughts were upon my mind as I entered the door of the house I called my home, after such a night of strange adventures as I have just made the reader acquainted with.

"Where have you been?" was the anxious question that met me as I entered.

"What in the world took you out and kept you out all night? Did you find that woman? How is she? Is anything the matter? I do think you might write quite a romance out of your adventures."

There is no occasion to write romance, it is only necessary to give the real pictures of life—real scenes as they occur in New York, to make up a volume more strange than wildest romance.

"Where have I been? Where I saw strange sights. Where it does seem as though some mysterious influence led me, to meet with another adventure."

"You might have had one at home, sufficiently interesting, I should think. A young girl, wickedly made drunk, for the basest purpose on earth—'tis a horrid tale—you shall hear it by and by—unprotected—alone in the street, at midnight—staggering to and fro, chased like a dog by a crowd of boys and half-drunken men, taking refuge in our basement area, within ten minutes after you left the house."

"You took her in? Yes, yes; I see, I see—a heavenly deed produces a heavenly smile."

What was it shot through my brain? A thought. A strange thought. What could have sent it there. Is it true? We shall see.

"What is her name?—where is she? You have not sent her away?"

"You shall see—come up-stairs. She is not up yet. She has been distressingly sick—she is better now, almost well, though very feeble. The doctor says, she was poisoned."

"No doubt, if drunk, of course she was. Every drop of drunkenness-producing liquor is poison, of the most subtle kind—slow, but sure."

She was still in bed. Her kind protector had furnished her with a clean, white bed-gown and cap, and a prettier face, indicating about sixteeen or seventeen years, never looked up smilingly from a downy pillow.

"She is very pale now. She vomited terribly all the latter part of the night. Her color will soon come again."

"Oh, yes, ma'am, I feel quite well now. Do let me get up and dress myself, and go home—I cannot bear to be a trouble to you any longer. Oh, sir, she has been a mother to me—more than a mother—if I had such a mother ——."

"Well, well, my girl, never mind now. You cannot get up yet. You must keep quiet to-day. To-morrow, we will see you safe home."

"Oh, sir, I cannot possibly wait till to-morrow. What will Mrs. Meltrand think?"

She shall know all about it before night."

"Oh, no, no, no! not all, not all! I should die with shame."

"Well, then, only that you have been to see a friend, and was taken very sick."

"Yes, I have been to see a friend, a dear friend, a poor unfortunate woman. Indeed, I must get up. She is sicker than I am, and besides, I promised to go, too, and see a friend for her. It is a gentleman that she thinks a great deal of, sir,—one who was very kind to her when she was very bad, and lived very miserably, and she thinks he was sent by Providence to save her from total ruin. That, sir, was before her little daughter died. Did you ever read about that, sir? it was published in 'the New York Tribune.'"

"I do not know; that paper publishes so many stories. I read the most of them. Then, you want to see Mr. Greeley. You need not go there for that, you can ——"

"Oh, are you Mr. Greeley, then?"

"No, but I shall see him soon, and I will tell him what you want. If it is to assist some poor distressed widow, you may depend upon it, he will do all he can afford, for he is a good man; his worst enemies acknowledge that."

"No, sir, it is not Mr. Greeley, that I am to go and see, it is another gentleman in the office of his paper."

"Who is it? What is his name? I know all of the gentlemen in that office; I can take your message to any one of them, and will do so with pleasure. Is it Mr. Dana? he is the next principal editor to Mr. Greeley."

"No, that is not the name. I cannot recollect it, now. But he is one of the editors."

"One of the editors! Why, my girl, that paper has a dozen editors. Perhaps, it is one of the assistants. Is it Mr. Cleveland?—no—Mr. Snow?—no—Mr. Fry, Mr. Thayer?—no—Mr. Ripley?—no—Mr. Ottarson?"

"No, I think not, but that sounds something like it."

"Why, my dear girl, there are a hundred men, editors, reporters, compositors, pressmen, book-keepers, and all, in that office; now, how are you going to find one that you do not know, and say you have forgotten his name?"

"May be I shall recollect it when I get there. Don't you know how names come back to us sometimes? Do you never forget names?"

"Often, but I never forget faces. I have seen yours before, but I have forgotten where, just as you have forgotten that gentleman's name."

"Oh, sir, have you? well, I do not remember your face, but it does seem as though I had heard your voice, and, perhaps, if the room was not so dark, I should know you. The lady said, I must keep it dark, and sleep this morning. It is no wonder that I should forget everything, I was so badly frightened last night."

"Well, I don't see how you are to find which one you wish to see, among so many, unless you can recollect his name."

"Oh, that will be easy enough, sir. I will ask one of the gentlemen. I am sure any one of them will tell me, for I am sure they are all gentlemen, real gentlemen."

"I do not see what it is that you are to inquire for, or who, or how to find out which one, or anything about it."

"Oh, sir, it is the one that wrote that little story about her daughter."

"Her daughter?"

"Yes, sir, Mrs. De Vrai's daughter."

A light began to dawn in my mind, and I said carelessly, "her daughter?"

"Yes, sir, her daughter. Little Katy, in that pretty story of Hot Corn. She is Little Katy's mother, sir, and she wants to see the gentleman that wrote that story. She did not know his name until yesterday. She thought it was Mr. Greeley, and he was out of town, and she had never seen him since Little Katy was buried, and she had moved away from where she used to live, without letting him know where she was. Yesterday she found out her mistake, and sent Phebe—you laugh—do you know Phebe?"

"Yes, yes, I know Phebe, and I know you now; I know you for a kind-hearted, good-natured girl. Your name is Agnes."

"Oh, yes, sir, has Mrs. Morgan told you."

Now the reader is surprised. Yes, it is Mrs. Morgan—Athalia. It was she that faced the crowd of savages that cried "drag her out." It was she that took poor Agnes in and gave up her own bed, and nursed and watched her all night, and sent for a physician for her. It was Agnes, the girl that you have seen in the picture with the negro wood-sawyer, and at his home when Phebe divided her bed to give the poor girl a lodging. There is some goodness yet in human nature. It was Phebe that Agnes went to see, while nursing Mrs. De Vrai. It was the latter for whom she was now so anxious to get up out of her sick bed, that she might go and tell the gentleman who wrote the story of "Little Katy," that Little Katy's mother was almost dying to see him. It was by that token that she would find him.

"Did Mrs. Morgan tell you my name."

"No, she has not told me; you told me that a long time ago."

"Me, sir? Do you know me, sir?"

"Yes, better than you do me. You have forgotten the gentleman that stopped you in the street one night with old Peter?"

"Oh, dear me; yes, no, not forgotten, but I did not remember. Oh, oh, how singular that I should come right here to this house, where you live, and this dear good lady lives. Oh, I wish I was good; but I am not a good girl. Oh, sir, has this lady told you how bad I was last night? But it was not all my fault, sir. If you only knew, what a poor unfortunate girl I have been—but sir, upon my word, I have not been what folks call a *bad* girl."

"We believe you. There, don't cry, keep yourself quiet to-day, and we hope to see you quite smart this evening."

"Oh, do let me go and find that gentleman, for Mrs. De Vrai. If you only knew what a good lady she is now, now she don't drink any more. But I am afraid she won't live very long. She has got a dreadful cough. And she was worse last night, for she saw somebody in the street yesterday —some man—a bad man—I believe they are all bad—no, no, I don't mean all—but a good many of them."

"I am glad that the sight of bad men in the street, don't make every lady sick who sees one; if it did we might turn the whole city into a general hospital. But what about that man?"

"I don't know what, but she was dreadful 'fraid of him, and that he would come where she lives."

"So he did, but he will not come again, soon."

"Then you know him, too?"

"Yes. And that is not all I know. I know you left Mrs. De Vrai's last night about half-past nine o'clock, on your way home; that soon after you started you were overtaken by a stout-built gentleman, with black hair and black whiskers, who said, 'Good evening, Miss, how did you leave Mrs. De Vrai, this evening?'"

"Mercy on me, his exact words. Did you hear them? I am sure I did not see anybody else near us at the time."

"No, I did not hear him—was not in that part of the city."

"He has told you then. I am sure I never did."

"No, neither have told me."

"What then?"

"What then? why, then you answered, 'Oh, sir, are you acquainted with Mrs. De Vrai?'"

"So I did; why how strange that you should know it all."

"And then he began to talk to you about the danger of such a pretty girl going home alone—"

"Yes, sir, and then he offered me his arm; and, and, and I thought as he was a friend of Mrs. De Vrai's I might take it, and he said so many pretty things that"——

"That you were deceived by a villain, and——"

"Oh, sir, for mercy sake don't tell all before this dear good lady, she who saved my life last night. Don't tell all."

"Why, Agnes, I cannot tell all. How do you suppose I know all?"

"I don't know, sir, but I am sure you do. What is it makes you know it; is it what they call animal magnetism, or what is it? Are you a medium?"

"Yes, I hope so; a medium of glad tidings, that will bring great joy to the world. But not a spirit medium, as they are called."

"I don't know then how you know all about me, but I am sure you do."

"No, I do not; I never saw you but once before, in my life—never heard of you since except to hear your name mentioned once last night, and that you had been at Mrs. De Vrai's in the evening, and that that man followed you from there, and I guessed his wicked purpose."

"Yes, yes, wicked indeed."

"I know nothing more. I do not ask you either to tell more, yet I believe it would be a relief to you to tell it, and that it will be a burden off of your mind."

"Yes, yes, it will, it will; but I am afraid that you will not believe me, or that you will despise me, or laugh at me for being so simple, to be so deceived by a stranger; but then how could I tell that he was a bad man, and the streets so dark?"

Poor child, could she have told any better if it had been as light as noonday, that the soft-spoken, smiling gentleman, with his sweet words, only used them to cover up a heart full of bitterness and lying deceit?

"And so he told you he was an acquaintance of Mrs. De Vrai's, a friend, and then he offered you his arm."

"Yes, sir, and I thought I might take it—that it was so kind of him—for he told me that he was just going in to see her when he saw a lady come out, and he thought he would step along and ask her if Mrs. De Vrai was up, and how she was this evening, and if she had gone to bed, he would not disturb her; perhaps too, he might be of service to a friend of hers, by walking home with her. And then he asked me a great many questions about Mrs. De Vrai, how long she had lived there, and who lived with her, and who else lived in the house, and about little Sissee; he asked such a heap of questions—if she was pretty, and how big she was, and where she slept, and where her mother slept, and oh! I cannot tell you how many things; and then he told me how he knew her in Paris, and what a pretty little girl she had—that was Katy, sir,—and then I told him that Katy was dead, and then—but I did not think of it then—he did not seem a bit sorry about it, while I could not help crying, only thinking about it—and that she should die just then too, when her mother was going to be a good mother, and when some good men were just going to begin to be good to her. Oh, sir, it was sad, very sad for her to die then, was it not? But I suppose it is all right—that everything is for the best—Mr. Pease says it is. Do you know Mr. Pease—has Mr. Pease ever told you about her; has he told you how Mrs. De Vrai used to live in the Five Points, and how little Katy used to sell hot corn?"

"No, nothing, but never mind that now. You were going to tell us about the stranger you were walking and chatting with so cosily."

"So I will."

"Yes, so I was. But when I talked about Little Katy's death, I got off my story. Well, sir, we walked on towards Broadway, and he said we would go through Canal street, it was lighter there, and so it was, a good many shops were open, and all the places where folks go to drink, and the ice cream saloons were open, and there were such crowds of pretty girls walking arm in arm with nice gentlemen, looking so proud and happy with their beaux, and I suppose I looked just so, too, for I could not help thinking how poor I had been, and now how well dressed I was, and that I had a beau, too; and when I saw others going in to get ice cream and good suppers, I almost wished—well, I did feel tempted' and I suppose all girls do, who see such things; and I suppose he must have guessed what I was thinking of, for he said, 'we won't go into any of those public places, there is a nice place just round the corner—real genteel—it is the —— Hotel—we will go there and have some ice cream and good cool ice water—you don't drink anything else?' said he, sort of inquiringly—'no, sir, not now, I have taken the pledge,'—'so have I,' says he—'that is right—all girls ought to take the pledge.' So we turned up Broadway, and then I should think just round one corner, but I don't know certain, it was so light, and so many finely dressed gentlemen round the door, and one of them said, 'look there, Jim, what a pretty girl De V. has got; and that made me blush, and feel so confused I did not know which way I went, and so I clung to his arm, for I thought with him I was safe, and the first that I knew, we were standing close behind some ladies and gentlemen going in at a door—I saw 'private door' on it, and did not quite like that, but I did not exactly know what it meant, and hung back a little, and then he spoke so sweetly, and said, 'don't be afraid,' that I thought it was all right, or else what would so many ladies and gentlemen go there for? So we went in, and the gentleman says to the nice-looking waiter, in his clean white apron, 'No. 6, Bill.'

"'No. 6 is occupied, sir, but I will give you another room—all right.'

'All right.' What could it mean? What could it mean that most all the ladies I saw, wore thick, close veils, so that nobody could tell who they were, old or young, ugly or pretty? But I had not much time to think, for we walked very fast through the passage, between I don't know how many little private supper rooms, and pretty soon we went into one ourselves. There was a table, four chairs and not much else in the room. The waiter made the gas light burn bright and then stood a moment for his order.

"'What shall it be, Miss—I do not recollect your name.'

"How should he? I had never told him, he never knew it. I answered, 'Brentnall.'

"'Oh, yes, Miss Brentnall, what shall we have?'"

How easy poor, weak girls are flattered. It was the first time, perhaps, she had been thus addressed. What would she have? She did not know.

"I was hungry, real hungry, and, so I told him, when he insisted upon it, that I was so; and then he said, how fortunate that two hungry persons should happen to meet, and that they had come to such a good place, where they could get everything that the heart could wish. Did I like crabs—soft crabs—then we would have a supper of soft crabs. 'And I say, Bill, while they are cooking, bring some ice water, a chicken salad, and, let me see, you drink nothing but water, I drink no liquor, no wine. Are you fond of Heidsick?' I could not tell—I did not know what Heidsick was, only that it was some kind of drink that the fellows used to call for at that house where you saw Peter help me to get away from. I thought it was some kind of soda water, it used to sparkle and foam so, when they poured it out, but I would never taste it then; I wish I had not now. I would not, only that the gentleman said it was like water.

"'It is a sweet, pleasant French drink,' said he, 'not a drop of spirit in it—about like ginger pop, or soda water—you will see how it flies when I draw the cork.'

"It did fly and foam and sparkle, as he poured it out, and looked so good. He handed me a glass with such a smile, how could I refuse? How could I know I should break my pledge by tasting? It tasted so good, how could I help drinking. The salad was very good, and that made the drink taste better still, and so we eat and sipped, and sipped and eat with a silver fork. It was delightful.

"After a while the crabs came, and then we eat them—how good. Was it any wonder that so many come here to eat, and drink 'Hiedsick?' And then the rooms were so quiet. Still, the partitions are very thin, for I overheard a woman in the next room say to a gentleman, 'now quit that, or I will tell my husband. You had better not do that again.' And then I heard a little scuffle, and then she said, 'Are you not ashamed of yourself?' "

Why was she not ashamed of herself? She would have been "mortified to death" to have her husband know that she was in that room, eating late suppers and drinking wine, at least, once a week. No wonder she wore a thick veil. She was yet a little ashamed, for fashion's sake, ashamed to be seen going into a private room, at ten o'clock, at night, with a *cavalier servante.* She is on a quick voyage to a shameless harbor, and will soon arrive there—perhaps, just such a harbor as the home of Elsie Morgan, where the rats harbored with her in the same cellar; or the home of little Katy, and her mother in Cow Bay. She would have been ashamed to have her husband know, that under pretence of going to visit a sick friend, she had come with *a friend* to sup in a "private room," in a "fashionable eating-house." So, too, would that husband have been ashamed to have his wife know, that under pretence of going to call on an old friend at the hotel, he was actually, at that moment, enjoying himself with that friend in the next room, and that that friend was a friend of his wife, too—the fashionable Mrs. Smith, whose husband is in California, toiling to earn money, which he remits to her, which she is using to procure a divorce from him, that she may marry a man she is already playing the harlot with, and whom she will fool in the same way she does her present poor simpleton of a husband. In fact, she is already fooling her paramour, for she is here with another man; and that man is the husband of a lady, whom she addresses as her "dear friend." Ah, well! *C'est la vie* in New York.

"So we sat and talked, and eat and drank, a long time, for time went merrily on, and at last he poured out the last of the good bottle, and we were just going to drink it and go, for I said, 'I must go home, I have a good mile to go yet,' and he said, 'Oh, I will see you safe home.' So as I was lifting the glass, he caught my arm, and said, 'Stop, there is a fly in it;' and he took my glass and began to look about for something to take the fly out.

"'Oh, this will do.' And he took a little folded piece of paper out of his pocket, and stooped down a little under the table. as though to throw it on the floor."

"What for?"

"Do you think he could have put anything in the glass out of that piece of paper, just in the moment he had it? I thought there was a bitter taste. I wish I had thought so at first. But I drank it, and then started to go home. When I got in the street, I did not know which way I went. I should have gone up Broadway, but we did not. Everything seemed so strange. I felt as though I could fly almost. I never felt so before. I clung to his arm, I could not walk without it. I felt as though I could almost hug him. And then he put his arm around my waist; I am sure I would not have let him do that if I had known what I was about; and so we went on, I do not know how far, or which way, but it could not have been a great way, and then he went up to a great fine house, with a silver plate on the door, with a name on it in great letters, it was Phillips or Brown, or something, only one name—just as though they were ashamed of the other, or else did not want to be known, or something. I said, don't go in there, what will the folks think? and he said, 'Oh, this is a friend of mine lives here, a very nice lady, and we will stop and rest a little while, and then I will go home with you. I guess the Hiedsick has got in your head a little, and we will go in here and wait awhile, till you feel better.' Well, I did feel as though I could not go home, until I got over my dizziness, and when he said, he knew the folks, and that they were nice people, I thought I would go in a few minutes. So he rung the bell, and then a woman came and opened a little blind in the door, so that she could see who was there, and then he said, 'Open the door, Leta,' and then she said, 'Oh, is that you?' and then I knew he was acquainted there, and in we went, and he whispered something to her, and then she called the servant girl and told her to show the gentleman up to No. 6. There it was, No. 6 again. And there it was again, for she said, 'there is a gentleman and lady in No. 6 now; I will give them another, all right.' I am sure, I never shall hear that word again without believing it means all wrong. But I scarcely knew right from wrong; I just held to his arm, and went wherever he led me. It was a very nice room that she showed us in. There were beautiful pictures on the walls; I could not see very well what they were, but I thought they looked like some I had seen once before, such as I am sure never should be hung up anywhere. There was a great mirror, and marble-top tables, and washstand, a very rich carpet, and such a splendid bed, and chairs and rocking chairs, one of which I sat down in, for I felt so tired and sort of sleepy; and then he told the servant to bring in some water, and when it came, he poured out a tumbler full, but I do believe it was half wine, and I drank it down, and then I felt, oh, I never can tell how I felt, or what happened after that; but I know more happened, and that more was—was—what I never can tell."

"Villain, black-hearted villain; who laid his snares for a poor, simple-hearted girl, to work her ruin. I wonder that you ever got away, ever got out of that house. How did you do it?"

"When I came to a little, I ran down stairs as fast as I could go, and he ran after me, and cried, 'Stop her,' and two other women ran out in the hall to do it, but just then the door was opened, and two gentlemen were going out, and I ran right into the arms of one of them, and he carried me clear out, in spite of them, and then the other one said, 'Let her go, she is drunk—now run.' I did run and they hallooed, and then the boys took after me, and, oh, dear, you know the rest."

CHAPTER XVII.

THE INTELLIGENCE OFFICE.—AGNES.

"All things are pure to those who are pure."
"Wisdom and goodness to the vile seem vile."

PERHAPS some of my readers have been sufficiently interested to inquire, "Who is Agnes, and what of her?" Perhaps there may be some, who, like Mrs. McTravers, think she is not a proper character to introduce into a respectable family, coming as she did from a house which gives an air of taint, spoiled, lost, ruined, to every character that is found within its walls. I am aware that there is room for suspicion, but suspicion is not proof. In the case of Athalia, her acknowledged sin is no more proof of moral turpitude than any other act of a deranged mind. A lunatic may kill, yet it is not murder. A drunken husband may beat his loving wife, and love her still. It was not the man who struck the blow, it was the demon Rum! It was not Athalia who lost her virtue, it was the worse than demon who robbed her—intoxicated her—destroyed her reason—enslaved her mind—but he did not, could not, destroy her virtuous, benevolent heart. Her conduct toward Agnes, is alone sufficient to prove this. And if she had known as much as I did of Agnes, that there might be some ground of suspicion against her, it would have made no odds; she would have taken her in and taken care of her in the same way, if she had known that she was a great sinner; that is the true way to work reformation; and then she would have said, "Go, daughter, and sin no more."

But she knew nothing against Agnes; even after I had told her of the trunk, she said, all may yet be right. She was unwilling to believe that all was wrong. How triumphantly she met me as I came home in the evening—how a woman does love to triumph over us in a good cause, proving herself what she is in all the purest qualities of the heart,—our superior.

"I told you so," said Athalia. "I knew there had been some base deception, some wickedness practiced towards that poor girl to inveigle her into that house. Come up stairs, and you shall hear her story from her own lips; she is quite smart now, and able to sit up and talk, and looks so pretty—she is pretty, and that has been the great cause of her trouble. But she is a good girl; I have heard a good deal about her to day, besides what she has told me. Phebe and Peter, have both been here, and such a meeting, oh! it would have done your heart good to have been here, and to see these poor blacks' conduct towards this girl, after I had told them the story of her adventures last evening: they hugged her, and kissed her with as much affection as though she had been one of their own; and then Peter went to see the lady where she had been living, at the place he got for her, the next day after your first interview with her, and the lady was terribly alarmed about the poor girl, and so she would not let Peter come back until she had the carriage up, and then she took him in—only to think, such a sweet, nice, pretty lady did not feel herself in the least disgraced to ride with a poor, old, negro wood-sawyer in her fine carriage, to visit a poor sick servant girl. And so she came, and such a time! why, if she had been her own child, she could not have been more affectionate. And then Agnes told us her story, and then I told Mrs. Meltrand, that is her name, about Mrs. De Vrai, and how that same man, who treated Agnes so badly, tried to steal Mrs. De Vrai's little girl, and then she said, 'how singular,' and then of course I said, what is so singular?"

"Ah me, it is a long story, and would not interest you, but I was robbed of a dear little girl, fifteen years ago, in England, by just such a man, in just the same way, but it could not have been this man, his name was Brentnall."

"Brentnall, why that is my name," said Agnes.

"Your name, why you never told me that before."

"No, ma'am, you never asked me, and I did not suppose that you cared to know anything about me, only that I was a good girl, and did your work well, and answered to the name of Agnes."

True. How little interest we all take in our servants; they come and go and we never know that they have any name but one that is most convenient to call them by, and we take no interest in them, hardly enough to know that they possess souls as precious as our own.

"And so, your name is Brentnall, what was your father's name?"

"I don't know, ma'am, as I ever had any, or mother either."

"But you must have had both."

"Oh yes, I suppose I must, to have been born, but I mean I never saw any."

"Where did you live, and who brought you up?"

"I lived with an uncle, near Belfast, and came over with him and his family, and every one of them died of ship fever on the voyage, and when I landed here in this great city, I was utterly alone, and almost penniless. Oh dear!"

"And then Mrs. Meltrand, said, 'Oh dear,' and she went away feeling sad. I do wish I knew what it could be in that name that made her feel so sad. Some reminiscence connected with the loss of her little girl, I suppose. It is very sad, to lose a child by death, it must be very much more sad to have one stolen away, and never know what becomes of it, whether dead or alive; and if the mother should meet her own child in the street not to know it; but dear me, how I am running on while you are eating your supper, as though you had nothing to think of but the things that interest me so much. But if you have been able to eat while I have been talking, come up to my room and see my protégé and hear her story."

So we went up, and found the invalid almost recovered, looking so sweet, for she looked grateful, and that, when it beams out like the sunlight, will make any face look beautiful.

"I told you," said Mrs. Morgan, "about her landing here penniless and alone, and I want she should tell you—there now, there is the bell, how I do hope that is uncle—yes it is

—it is; do you hear him talking to Bridget? that is his step, now—"

Now the door opens, and now she is in his arms, and now there are more questions than answers:—

"When did he arrive? How did he find things out West. Has he been to supper? What is the news?"

"Now you are a perfect woman, you are enough to confuse a whirlwind. Sit down, and be quiet, and I will tell you all that you need to know. But first tell me who is this young lady; you forgot to introduce me."

"So I did, but of course she knows by this time that you are my uncle, and you will know directly all about her, for she was just going to tell part of her story, and I shall tell the rest before you go to bed.

"I will warrant that. Perhaps you would like to hear mine, and where I have been since I arrived."

"Yes, indeed, do tell me, and why you did not come right home?"

"I have been to jail, since I arrived; locked up in the criminal cells. It is a little singular too, how I got there. It is all owing to the newspapers."

"Owing to the newspapers, uncle, I do not understand how the papers should get you in prison."

"Very well I do. I saw an item in one of them this evening, about the arrest of a person whose name struck me very forcibly as being that of a man whom I once knew in Europe, and who I was very anxious to see, for I felt the deepest interest to know what had become of his wife. For him I cared nothing, I knew he was a villain, and felt rejoiced to think he had met his deserts at last; but his wife was a sweet good woman, a victim of unfortunate circumstances all through her life, and when I saw her last I had reason to fear that she was falling into a course adopted by many, many others, of drowning sorrow in wine. But I shall not tell my story now; I will sit down and hear yours."

"Well then, Agnes, tell what you did after landing."

At the sound of her name, Mr. Lovetree gave a little start, and said, "Agnes! oh, pshaw!" and sunk back again in his easy chair, as though he had been affected by the name, and thought it very foolish that he had been so. Agnes, said: "Indeed, ma'am, I don't think the gentlemen will be at all interested to hear anything about me."

"Yes, yes, I have promised them."

"Well, then, after my uncle died, and all my friends, I felt dreadful; it is dreadful for a young girl to be left all alone in a strange country. So when the ship landed, or rather when she came to anchor, the people from shore came aboard, and I saw how many of the poor emigrants had friends to welcome them, and that I had none; it was then that I felt the dreadful loneliness of my situation, and I sat down and cried, for I could not help it, and then a man came and spoke to me very pleasantly, and asked me where I wanted to go, and all about it, and then I told him all my troubles, and then he said it was the luckiest thing in the world that I had met with him, for he was an emigrant agent, appointed by law, and he would take charge of me and take me ashore to a boarding-house, and do everything for me. And then he asked me how much money I had, and I told him that I had but a few shillings, of my own, but that I had three gold sovereigns that were my uncle's—he had more, a great deal more, when he died, but somebody must have taken it away—and that was all I had in the world besides their chests of clothes and things. And then he said, that it was very lucky for me that I had that, for he would have to pay half a guinea head-money for each passenger, no matter how many were dead, and then he would have to pay the custom-house duty, and the wharfage and the cartage, and the week in advance for the board, and that would take all the money and more too, but he would pay that and hold the things until I could pay him back. So I gave him the money, and he got the chests, all but my trunk,. I would keep that, and took them ashore, and took me to a boarding-house, and that was the last I ever saw of him, or the money or chests either, he had robbed me of all of my poor uncle's things, and my three gold sovereigns; so the landlady said, and he never paid her a cent of board. I did not know what to do; I was willing to work, but how should I find a place. The landlady said, I must go to the 'Intelligence office.' I thought I should like to go somewhere to get intelligence of the man who had run away with my things, or any other intelligence that would be of any benefit to a poor stranger in this great Babel of a city. And I asked her to tell me the way to the 'Intelligence office,' and I went there. It was a great room, divided into two parts; one was full of men, and the other of girls, sitting on long benches. I went in and sat down among them, and I suppose, I looked sad—I felt so, and I felt worse when I heard some of the girls snickering, and overheard them say, 'there is a green one.' If that was an 'Intelligence' office, I thought it a very queer way of giving it to one so much in need of it as I was. After a while, one of the girls came and sat down by me, and spoke kindly, and asked where I came from, and a good many questions; I was almost afraid to answer her, for fear that she was 'an emigrant agent,' too, and had some plan to cheat me, or practice some deception, but I became convinced in a little while that she meant kindly; and then I told her all about myself. Then, she said, that I must get my name registered. I did not know what that was for, but I went up to the book-keeper, and told him my name, and age, and where I came from, and what I could do, and he wrote it all down in a book and then told me to give him half a dollar, and when I got a place I must give him another one; I did not know what for; he gave me no intelligence about how I was to get a place, but he told me to go and sit down again. So I did, all that day and all the three next days, waiting for somebody to pick me out of the lot. Every hour, somebody came and looked over all the girls, for all the world just as I have seen the people do in the pig-market, at an Irish fair, until they found one that would suit. One objected to me because I was 'green;' another, because I had never been at service in this country; another, because I had no recommend; and then a girl whispered to me, and told me she knew a man who would write me just as many recommends as I wanted, for a shilling a piece. If that is the way recommends are made, I don't see what good they are. At last, after being looked over day after day, like a lot of damaged goods, a lady, at least, I thought she was a lady, selected me the very first one, and for the very reason that twenty others had rejected me—because I was too good-looking. When she found that I had no friends in this country, and no father or mother in the world, she seemed still more anxious to have me, which I thought so kind of her, and then she told me that the work would be very light, only some rooms to take care of, and wait upon company a little, and she knew I should like the place; I thought I should; I did at first, but, I don't want to tell, before the gentlemen, why I did not like to live there; this one knows already."

"Well, well, you need not tell, we understand all about it. You have been treated just as a great many poor girls without friends have been treated before in this city; and you got just as much intelligence, and just as much profit from your application to the 'Intelligence office,' as a great many others have done before you."

Now, it was Athalia's turn to tell her uncle all that she knew about Agnes, and then he told about his visit to the prison.

"I found," said he, "the very man I expected, or rather hoped, it might be, and it is well that I acted upon the impulse of the moment, for if I had not, I should have been too late. It is the doctor's opinion, that he will not live till morning. It seems that he got into some difficulty with the police last night, and one of them, to prevent him from stabbing another man, broke his arm."

There was a little start of surprise on my part, and that of Mrs. Morgan; but we made no interruption, and Lovetree went on with his story. We thought, though, we could not help that.

"I expect he had been drinking hard, for he tore off the bandage from his arm in the night, and when the keeper opened his cell this morning, he found him almost dead with loss of blood and vital prostration. He cannot live. They had aroused him, and I found him quite rational when I went in, and was immediately placed beyond all doubt as to the identity of the man, for he called me by name the moment he saw me."

"I am glad you have come," said he, "I can trust you, and I want to make a clean breast of it before I die. My wife and child—my last one—are in this city, and when I am gone, I want you to go and see her, and tell her, that I shall never trouble her any more; she will be glad to hear it, for she saw me last night, and I left the old lady somewhat in a fright. I cannot tell you the exact number, but I can tell you so that you can find the house easy enough. It is in W— street."

"Oh, dear, I cannot stand it any longer," said Mrs. Morgan.

"Cannot stand it? I don't see anything that you cannot stand. You surprise me."

"Not half as much as you surprise us. We know all about it. It was him," and she pointed to me, "that knocked the ruffian down; it was him that he was about to stab when the watchman broke his arm; and it is she, uncle, Mrs. De Vrai, his wife, who is the mother of Little Katy; now, you know all about it; we know all about it."

"No, not all, for he told me, that he believed his other wife was in this city, also, married here, and he wanted that I should look her up, too; and tell her where, perhaps, she may find her child."

"Tell her," said he, "that I left it with my brother, near Belfast, an Irish farmer, by the name of William Brentnall."

"William Brentnall!" said Agnes, her eyes opening with wild surprise.

"I do think," said Mr. Lovetree, "that I have lost my senses, or else some of the rest of you have. First, one, and then the other, fairly screams out some exclamation as though I were a conjurer, and you could not comprehend my words or actions. Have you done now, shall I go on?"

"Yes, yes, uncle; I am dying with curiosity, and as for Agnes, she looks the very picture of wonder."

"Indeed I feel so."

"Well, I don't understand why, but I suppose I might as well proceed. 'Tell her,' said he, 'that he is well known and easily found, and that I left the child with him, telling him that it was mine, and that its mother was dead.' Then I was a little surprised, for I thought his name was De Vrai, 'but that,' he said, 'was an assumed one, the name by which he married the woman that I knew, because he dared not marry her by his own name. Then, I asked him what was her name, who I should look for, and who she should inquire for, to find her child? Then he took a little card out of his pocket, as though he would write her name, and then he seemed to recollect his broken arm, and said, with a groan, 'my writing days are over, and all my days nearly.' Then, he told me, to take the card and write, and so I did, here it is—'this is the mother's name, and this is her daughter's, upon the truth of a dying man—tell her so, beg her to forgive and forget the dead.' "

"What are the names? Do tell us, uncle."

"Mrs. Meltrand—Agnes Brentnall."

Now there were at least two screams and one, "Oh how wonderful!"

"Then Agnes said, "Mrs. Meltrand my mother!—that is wonderful!"

Then Mr. Lovetree looked surprised; all around him seemed to be a mass of mystery. Others began to see through it, he was now in the dark.

Athalia explained. There was one point that she was not quite clear upon, and she asked her uncle if Agnes was really De Vrai's daughter, or only Mrs. Meltrand's?

"His own. Mrs. Meltrand, was his lawful wife when he married Mrs. De Vrai."

"Oh my God! then Agnes is his own child."

None spoke—what each thought sent a thrill of icy horror to every heart. All groaned or wept, none could speak. There are moments in life of speechless agony, when the mind is completely horrified, when anything that breaks the silence comes as a relief. It came now in the sound of the door bell. It was a messenger to Mr. Lovetree. It brought relief to aching minds. It was very short. It only said, "he is dead." It is perhaps wrong to rejoice at the death of a fellow creature, but we could not feel regret.

After the first flush of excitement was over, a note was written to Agnes's mother, simply stating that if she would call at Mrs. Morgan's at her earliest convenience, she would meet with an individual who could tell her of her long-lost daughter. She made it convenient to come immediately, though it was then ten o'clock at night.

It is not reasonable to suppose that she could keep away till morning, particularly as she had heard a word or two at her first visit which left her mind uneasy.

I drop the curtain upon the scene when the mother acknowledges and receives to her arms her long-lost daughter, while I go to carry comfort to the heart of Mrs. De Vrai, the ill-treated wife—the widow of a villain—the mother of his child, soon to be an orphan.

What a load it lifted from her crushed heart, when I told her those three little words—"he is dead."

"Then my child will be safe, at least from his evil influences."

What a dreadful thing it is for a wife to feel upon the death of her husband that she is safe herself, that her child is safe, more safe among strangers than with its own father.

Why should she feel so? Why does she feel so? The answer is still shorter than that which gave her relief—which told her that her child's father was dead. That was composed of three words, this of one. That one word is—Rum!!

It was that which made a villain of him, a double villain to two wives and the children of both. It was that which made him attempt the greatest wrong that a father can do to his own child. Poor Agnes!

It was that which drove Mrs. De Vrai step by step from the paths of peaceful, youthful innocence, comfort and affluence, to —but I will not name the intermediate steps—to that wretched abode where the little girl who sold Hot Corn, and slept in the rain upon the cold stones, breathed her pure life away in prayers to that mother not to drink any more of that soul and body destroying rum.

It was that mother, who, upon her death bed, prayed me to tell the world the fruits that the traffic in rum produces. "Tell them to look at me, at my history, or a brief view of it; its details would fill a volume. Tell mothers to watch their daughters. Tell those who bring up children in hotels and public houses, that they are rearing their daughters to one chance of virtue, against ten of sin and woe. My mother was left early a widow, with a competence to raise her two daughters "at home," yet she seemed to delight in the excitement incident to a life in a hotel or great boarding-house. As children, we were petted and spoiled; as misses, we learned all that girls usually learn in such boarding-schools as fashionable mothers send them to; as young ladies, we were the flattered of fops and roués, and our mother allowed us to be in a constant flirtation at home, or out every night to parties, balls, soirées, theatres, concerts, and then to saloons, late suppers, and wines, and—oh dear!—what if I had had a home and a mother to keep me out of temptation; but I had not, and I met with the fate almost inevitable.

"Among the boarders at the hotel, where we stopped at Saratoga, was an Englishman, who claimed, and I believe rightly, to be one of the nobility, for he wrote his name, Sir Charles R——, and had a well-known coat of arms upon his seal, which he used publicly. Of course, I was flattered, proud, vain of the attentions of an English nobleman, young, handsome, full of money, and ardent in his professions of love, which I have no reason to think of otherwise than as sincere; I was seventeen, tall, straight, handsome form, face, and figure, and always dressed with taste. My eyes were black; cheeks, rosy; and hair like the wing of a crow. I was well bred, and well read, and could talk and sing to captivate. So could he, and we were both equally affected. When we left the Springs, he came with us to New York, and put up at the same hotel. Then I was innocent. Oh, mothers! mothers! how long can you answer for the innocence of your daughters who go to fashionable eating and drinking saloons, and leave them after midnight, with their young blood on fire, and in such a state of mind that they hardly know whether they go home to rest in their own room, or in some of the thousand traps for the unwary, in almost every street in the city?

"Oh, mothers, mothers, every one,
With daughters free from sin,
How can you look so coldly on
The ways from virtue daughters win?

"Late suppers and wines, and constantly seeing others, who should set the young better examples, going the road that ruins virtue, had its effect. If I had been properly restrained by my mother, had been kept at home nights, and never learned to sip fashionable intoxicating drinks, my mother would not have mourned 'a girl lost.'

"A few months after my first acquaintance with Sir Charles, I was living with him in a richly furnished house, in Eighteenth street, shamelessly passing as his wife, and treated as such by our acquaintance, although they knew that I was not. It was here that Katy was born, and received her first impressions of home and a fond father's love. Here I lived away my young womanhood in fashionable dissipation, and then Sir Charles died suddenly, and without a will. He had always said, he would make a will, and give his vast property to me and our child. But he put it off, as many others do, one day too long. Why do men defer this duty? A sacred duty to those they leave behind them, of their own flesh and blood. I knew, as his wife, I had rights; and I went to England to try and obtain them. I left my elegantly furnished house, which cost, I don't know how many thousand dollars to furnish, for my mother and my sister, and an uncle to occupy while I was gone. I found all the property in the hands of Sir Charles's brother, and he was unwilling to give up the share that rightfully belonged to his wife and child, because he said, we could not recover it by law. He did not say why, my conscience did. As a compromise, if I would give him a general release, he offered five thousand pounds. I would have taken it, but I had employed a lawyer, and he hooted at the idea; he looked for more than that for his fee when he recovered the full amount. I told him that I had no marriage certificate, and that the minister who married us was dead. So he was; Sir Charles was dead. I did not tell him that no other ever blessed our banns. I told him, that numerous persons would swear that they had heard him call me wife, and Katy his child. He said, that would do. I did not know that our opponents could produce as many more to swear, that they had heard Sir Charles say, that it was only a marriage of convenience. So, for an uncertainty of five hundred thousand as a mere prospect, I refused the certainty of five thousand, and went to law. The evidence stood so balanced that the judge could not decide. 'Let the wife be sworn. Let her say, upon her oath, that she was married to Sir Charles, and the case will be given in her favor.'

"There was a chuckling laugh just behind me, the tones of which went to my heart, and I fainted. It was De Vrai. He had known me in this city, and persecuted me with his importunities while Sir Charles was living. I had turned him off with a promise, all too common, 'when Sir Charles is dead.' Then he renewed his importunities, and I told him, to wait a respectful time. He followed me to England, and still pressed me, and I still put him off. He had hinted several times that if I recovered the suit, he well knew that he should lose his. It was him that furnished my opponent with a clue to the proof that we were never married. It was him that laughed in my ear when the case rested upon the question, whether I would swear that I was married or not. For a moment, for the sake of my child, I was tempted; that laugh recalled me partially, and I was carried away in a litter, and the case adjourned. For aught I know it still remains adjourned.

"De Vrai followed me to my hotel. I was in a state bordering upon distraction. With a foolish pride, to keep up appearances, as the wife of Sir Charles, I had exhausted all my means, and run awfully in debt. I had written to my uncle, in New York, to sell my furniture at auction, and send me the money. After a long delay I got five hundred dollars, and a very short letter, saying, that was all the nett proceeds. I felt, I cannot tell how. I knew I was cheated, and wrote a bitter letter back. Then, my own friends, those who had fawned around the rich mistress of Sir Charles, cast off the poor woman struggling to recover something for his child. In this she failed, because that child was not bo n in wedlock.

"I was now poor indeed. What could I do, alone in a strange land? I knew that De Vrai had no affection for me, only such as one animal has for another, but in my despair I married him.

"His means of living were derived from the same source

that hundreds of well-dressed gentlemen derive theirs from, in this city. He was a gambler; a genteel gambler. Such as you may find in every hotel in New York, in every public place, dressed in the very best style, living in the most expensive manner, with no trade, occupation, or exercise of mind or skill, except the skill of cheating at card playing.

"At first, we lived pleasantly; but pleasures with such men are short-lived, and must be often changed. If successful in business—that is what they call their nefarious employment—they are all smiles and affection to wife and children; but if 'luck is against them,' they are the most unhappy men in the world, and make everybody else unhappy around them. As for enduring conjugal affection, I believe the excitement of a gambler's life renders them incapable of feeling its influence. I can scarcely tell how the months passed which I lived with that man, for I drank wine to excess every day. Not to become intoxicated; only just fashionably excited. We lived in the best style of hotel life, often at the expense of the proprietors.

"A little before Sis was born, De Vrai met with 'a run of luck,' and we took a cottage out of town, and lived very comfortably for a year, upon the proceeds of that 'windfall.'

"What that run of luck was, may be guessed at from the following extract from a morning paper:—

"SUICIDE.—An American gentleman was found dead in his bed, at his lodgings, this morning, and it is supposed he died from poison, administered by himself, in consequence of immense losses at the gaming table, not only of his own money, but a sum which he had received in trust for a widow and orphans, in America. It is said, that he owes his losses to the wretched practice of drinking to intoxication, and that he was fairly robbed while in this condition, by a companion of his, one who made great pretence of friendship. He leaves a beautiful young wife, 'quite destitute,' 'tis said."

"I did not know then that this companion of his was my husband. I found that out afterwards, and that he was more than robbed.

"Soon after that event, De Vrai brought the widow of his victim to live in our house. I was the wife—she the mistress. I was blind at first, but I soon had my eyes opened. Opened not only to that fact, but that that wife had stood behind her husband's chair while he played with the villain who robbed him, and gave the signal of what cards he held; and afterwards, when he became sober enough to realize his ruin, she proposed that they should take poison, and die together.

"The result need not be told, only that he died and she lived.

"When I made these discoveries from an overheard conversation, I ordered the vile woman from my house.

"'My house, my house, ha, ha, you poor simpleton. Every article in this house and every cent of money that you or your husband has on earth belongs to me, and these are the papers.

"'Now if you behave yourself you can stay here, if not, you will have to tramp, both of you.'

"She shook the papers in my face, and laughed at my look of fear and astonishment. To finish my agony, when I began to talk something about the rights of an English wife, she coolly told me that she had just as good a right to my husband as I had, for he had one wife when I married him, and that rendered my marriage a nullity. What a shock for a wife --to hear that she is no wife, or if she is, the wife of a robber, adulterer, and murderer.

"I heard all this with a sort of indifference foreign to my very nature. It was well that I did, for it enabled me to perfect my plans, and carry them out with a degree of coolness worthy of a better purpose. I had been promising for some time to visit a friend for a week, and I set about packing up for the journey at once. I said not one word to De Vrai of what I heard, nor gave him one look of reproof. Fortune had made me acquainted with the secret hiding-place of the money this guilty pair had obtained from their poor victim, and I did not feel any compunctions of conscience in taking it from them. In three days afterwards I was in Paris. Here I lived a few months a wretched life of dissipation, and then De Vrai, tracked me to my hiding-place and I had to fly once more; this time across the ocean.

I had five hundred dollars when I arrived in this city. What might I not have done with that sum, if I had used it prudently? What I did do, I must tell, that it may be a warning to others. It would be a source of consolation to me if I knew that the follies of my life could be illuminated and set up as a beacon light to my fellow creatures, to save them from the quicksands of dissipation upon which I have been wrecked—wrecked by my own folly and foolish pride.

"It was pride, foolish wicked pride, that led me to go to a fashionable hotel, and put up, with my two children and nurse, as Madame De Vrai, from Paris. How soon five hundred dollars melt away, even with prudent living, at a New York hotel. I did not live prudently. I drank to excess, gave late suppers, and gambled. This could not last long, though many hundreds of the dollars worse than wasted in those few weeks, were won from others equally guilty of this besetting wickedness and folly with myself. Such a life could not last. My first step down was to a cheap lodging in Crosby street. I cannot tell how I lived there. I only know that my valuables, my clothes, everything went to the pawnbroker, and I went to that wretched hole where you first saw me in Cow Bay, from whence I drove my poor little Katy out in the streets at midnight, to sell Hot Corn. It was there that my poor child died. It was there that you received her dying blessing, and I her dying forgiveness for all the wrongs that I had heaped upon her poor innocent head. It was then by her death that I was awakened to consciousness and I felt and saw my own deep soul and body destroying degradation. It was through her death and translation to a home in heaven, that I have obtained a hope that my Father may forgive what my child has forgiven, and that I may yet see her again. It was Him, it must have been Him that opened your ear to that little plaintive cry of 'Hot Corn,' that rose up through your window on its way to the home of angels watching over a child whom her mother had forsaken.

"It was His power—no earthly power could have aroused my

mind from its lethargy, that awakened me one moment before it was too late. It was a bitter trial, but nothing else but the death of that sweet child would have been sufficient to save her wicked mother; I cannot mourn her loss, because I feel that she is now so much better off than while singing her nightly cry through the streets, of 'Hot Corn, Hot Corn, here's your nice hot corn!' Speaking of singing, have you seen the new song, just published, called 'The Dying Words of Little Katy, or Will He Come?'

"Oh it is beautiful. Here it is, do read it:—

"Here's hot corn, nice hot corn!" a voice was crying!
Sweet hot corn, sweet hot corn! the breeze is sighing!
Come buy, come buy—the world's unfeeling—
How can she sell while sleep is stealing?
"Hot corn! come buy my nice hot corn!"

All alone, all alone, she sat there weeping;
While at home, while at home, her sister's sleeping,
"Come buy, come buy, I'm tired of staying;
Come buy, come buy, I'm tired of saying,
Hot corn, come buy my nice hot corn!"

Often there, often there, she sat so drear'ly
With one thought, for she loved her sister dearly:
Did'st hate, did'st hate—how could she ever,
How could she hate her mother?—never.
"Hot corn, come buy my nice hot corn!"

Often there, often there, while others playing,
Hear the cry, "buy my corn," she's ever praying.

"Pray buy, pray buy, kind hearted stranger,
One ear, then home, I'll brave the danger;
Hot corn, come buy my nice hot corn!"

Now at home, now at home, her cry is changing!
"Will he come, will he come?" while fever's raging.
She cries, she cries, "pray let me see him;
Once more, once more, pray let me see him.
Hot corn, he'll buy my nice hot corn!"

"Will he come, will he come?" she's constant crying.
"Will he come, will he come?" poor Katy's dying.
"'Twas he, 'twas he, kind words was speaking
Hot corn, hot corn, while I was seeking
Hot corn, who'll buy my nice hot corn?"

"Midnight there, midnight there, my hot corn crying,
Kindly spoke, first kind words, they stop'd my sighing.
That night, that night, when sleep was stealing,
Kind words, kind words—my heart was healing;
Hot corn, he'll buy my nice hot corn!

"Will he come, will he come?"—weak hands are feeling!
"He has come, he has come—I see him kneeling—
One kiss—the light—how dim 'tis growing—
I thank—'tis dark—good bye—I'm going—
Hot corn—no more shall cry—hot corn!!!"

Drop a tear, drop a tear, for she's departed,
Drop a tear, drop a tear, poor broken hearted,
Now pledge, now pledge, the world is crying,
Take warning, warning, by Katy's dying,
"Hot corn, who'll buy my nice hot corn?"

"The music of this, as it is arranged for the piano, is one of the sweetest, plaintive things you ever heard."

"And besides that, there are a good many other songs and tales, so Agnes tells me, already written, which never would have been if my poor child had not been called away from her home of misery here on earth to one made for the innocent and good beyond the grave. Who knows how much good all those songs and stories may do in the world, to save others from the road which I took to destruction?"

"Oh, if the wretched, awful misery occasioned by rum, which I alone have seen, could be pictured to the world, it does seem to me that no sane man or woman could ever look upon the picture and live, without becoming so affected that they would foreswear all intoxicating beverages for ever afterwards."

"Oh, sir, I know that I am now on my death bed, and I feel as though I was talking from the spirit world, and I do pray you to tell my fellow creatures, one and all—tell my own sex who are just beginning this life of temptation, degradation, sin, shame, woe, and death, what it brought me to, what it will bring all to, sooner or later, who, indulge as I did, first in wine, and, finally, in anything, everything that could sink reason into forgetfulness."

Reader, have I obeyed that dying injunction?

CHAPTER XVIII.

JULIA ANTRIM, AND OTHER OLD ACQUAINTANCES.

"Should old acquaintance be forgot?"
"There is a lost sheep returned to the fold."

If those who would reform the vicious, knew the power of love and kind words towards the poor fallen creatures who abound in our city, and how much stronger they are than prison bars, how much more powerful than handcuffs, fetters and whip lashes, we should soon see the spirit of reformation hovering over us like the guardian angel sent to save a city that should be found to contain only five righteous persons.

My readers may remember the slight glimpse they had of the face of Julia Antrim, on two occasions—once as a street walker, only thirteen years old, dressed in borrowed clothes, or rather in garments furnished by one of the beldams who keep the keys of our numerous city pandemoniums, where innocence is entrapped, and virtue sold at a discount; and again a year or two later, when the fiend who said "our trade," laughed to see her dragged out of one of the underground dens where demons dwell, where rum is sold and souls destroyed, on her way to prison, and the termination of a career, to which one half, at least, arrive at, who take the first step—false step—in the same road.

In the morning she was "sent up:" a short phrase which means imprisonment for six months in the city penitentiary. Penitentiary!! What is a penitentiary? A place of repentance and reformation.

Ours is a place to harden young offenders, or rum-made criminals—to make them worse rather than better. It made Julia Antrim worse. It was the work of the missionary, and the benevolent heart of Mr. Lovetree, and the kind words of Mrs. May and Stella, that effected what dungeons, fetters whips, and harsh language could not.

"Oh!" said Mrs. Morgan to me one evening, "such a story as my uncle has been telling me; do tell him, uncle, about one of those 'Five Point girls,' rescued from one of those miserable dens."

"You remember the girl," said he, "that you saw dragged out of the cellar for picking her paramour's pocket? Come with me and you shall see her and hear her own story. Athalia, come put on your hat and go with us. You know how glad Mrs. May and Stella always are to see you."

They were so this evening. Stella was in the front shop busy with her pins and needles, threads and tapes, and all the numerous little articles of necessity which go to make up an assortment, for which she had a demand that not only kept her busy, but also a fine bright active little boy. He is on the road to wealth and manhood now. He was on the road to ruin once. He was the son of a drunken father, who taught him to "prig" and sell the stolen articles for rum. The reader has seen him before. Would you like to know where? Turn back to page 30—look at that picture of the fireman rescuing two children from the flames. This bright boy is the child of drunken Bill Eaton. How Stella's eyes did sparkle as she saw us enter; far more than they would to see her best customer, for now she saw her best friend, her kind patron, who gave her the means to gain good customers.

"Oh, mother, mother, here is Mr. Lovetree and Mrs. Morgan, and that other gentleman!"

Then Mrs. May's eyes sparkled, for "she was so glad to see us"—she was always glad to see us. She was very busy in the little back shop, working away, and she had two very neat-looking industrious girls at work with her. We have seen both of them before. One of them for the first time on the steps of the Bank of the Republic, clothed in a poor dirty ragged dress, with that same little boy, sickly and pale, leaning upon his sister for support, and keeping her company as the two wandered through the streets, making midnight melodious with that ever pealing summer cry, of, "Hot corn, hot corn, here's your nice hot corn, smoking hot, smoking hot, just from the pot, all hot, hot, hot!"

She will sing it no more. She is in a better situation now for a little girl than midnight street rambling; that is not the best school for young girls—we have seen how near the brink of ruin it led Sally Eaton.

She was rescued just in time—just before she was lost. Two great calamities fell upon her in one night. Her father was killed, and her mother's house was burned, leaving the poor widow and her two children in the street, naked, except one garment, amid the crowd that came to look upon what she then thought the wreck of all hope. It proved her greatest blessing; for in that crowd were those who took her in, and clothed and fed, and sent her children to school, and taught her girl how to work; and, finally, placed her as a help to another widow, where she will soon learn and earn enough to help herself. The other girl, who is now working with her old companion, was once her street associate in rags and wretchedness; afterwards, her envied, because better clothed, acquaintance. We saw her too, upon the same evening that we first saw the little Hot Corn girl driven away from her hard seat upon those cold stone steps—less cold than the heart of the great world towards its outcast population. We saw her again, just where we then knew that her course of life would lead her—to intoxication,—wretchedness—crime—prisons, and—no, she stopped just short of death, and returned to virtue, industry, and happiness.

After the heartfelt, happiness-giving congratulations of Mrs. May, Stella, Sally Eaton, and "Brother Willie," were over, I turned to a nice, modest-looking young girl and said, "and who is this? What is your name?"

"Julia Antrim, sir."

Did I dream? No, I did not dream, I looked upon sober reality. It was the poor outcast, whom I had seen dragged away from the underground abode of all that is bad, to "the Tombs," and from whence she went to "the Island," and as I heard, from there, at the expiration of her noviciate, to one of the lowest, most degraded, worse than beastly, abodes of those who have only the form of humanity remaining. So I told her I had heard, and she replied,

"True—where else could I go? I could go nowhere but there. I came out of prison with only the clothes they gave me there, with my hair cropped—branded, to tell all the world to beware of me—that I was a 'prison bird.' If I desired, and I really did, to return to a virtuous life, the door was for ever closed against me. I went back to Mrs. Brown's, the woman who had first tempted me, with fine clothes and jewelry, to sin—to that house where I lost all that a poor girl has on earth—her virtue—where I had sinned and profited, as the term is, by sinning; where I had left piles of rich clothing, and pretended friends. I knocked at the door, once so ready to open for my first admission, and that too was closed in my face with an oath, a horrid, wicked woman's oath, bidding me to go away or she would send a policeman—I knew the policeman would do her bidding—to take me away as a common street vagrant, coming there to disgrace a 'respectable house.' I went away, dispirited, broken-hearted, and sunk down into that wretched abode in Anthony street, where I was found by Mr. Pease, and actually compelled, much against my will, to go to the Five Points House of Industry, where I was washed, and clothed, and fed, and sobered, furnished with work, and, above all else, taught to love God and pray, and, for the first time in more than two years, to feel one moment of happiness.

When I was with those wretches in that miserable hole

where Mr. Pease found me, I really thought that my heart had got so bad, that it could not, would not, ever be good again.

"How I did use to curse and hate everybody that was good. That good man who saved me at last, I hated worse than all others. All who are like what I was then, hate him and fear him more then they do all the prisons and police in the city. If somebody would publish the truth, or only half the truth, of what I alone know of the crime and misery about the Five Points of New York, and how much good all the good men have done who have devoted themselves to the reformation of those wretched human beings, I do think that everybody with a good heart would buy the book, and thus contribute a mite to aid the good work—a work that saves from a life worse than death, scores of children and young girls, lost to every virtuous thought or action; lost to all hope in life or eternity.

"Oh, sir," and she seized me by the hands in her energy, "you can write—Stella has told me how you can write—that you have written some powerful stories; pray write more, more, more; the world will read, and it will do a world of good."

"Well, Julia, if I write, I must have characters and names, to fill up the incidents of my Life Scenes, shall I use yours?"

"Yes, yes, if it will do good, and save others."

"And mine." "And mine." "And mine." "I think," said Mrs. May, "that the incidents connected with Athalia's life, would alone make quite a volume; would you have any objection to having them written out and published, Mrs. Morgan?"

"Perhaps I might consent, if it was well done, if it would serve as a beacon to save others from being shipwrecked upon the same desolate shore where I came so near being totally lost; only escaping by the smallest chance, and by one of the most singular interpositions of Providence, and through the efforts of one of the weakest instruments. It is to Stella, first of all that I owe my present happiness. It was through her that all my friends became interested for me. In fact, if it had not been for her, my dear uncle would never have known where to find me."

"Rather give the credit to a higher power; that power which gave him the kind benevolent heart that beats in his breast; that disposition to watch over the young and guard the innocent, which led him to take an interest in my poor child. Let us be grateful to all the humble instruments of Him who giveth every good and perfect gift to man, but to Him to whom we owe all of our present happiness, be the final praise."

Now there was a little space of silence; a time for reflection; all were too full of thought, holy, happy thought, to speak. It is good to think. The world is generally too much given to act without thinking. Mr. Lovetree was not. He thought that we had agreed to visit Mrs. De Vrai, on our way home, "but before I go," said he, "I want to invite you all to dine with us next Sabbath. I want to see our little party of friends all together, for a certain purpose."

"Uncle always has a little surprise to play ofi upon his friends. I am afraid this is not a pleasant one, or else he would not have chosen Sunday."

"I chose that," said he, "because I know how difficult it is for the laboring poor to give a day from their working time, for any kind of recreation. I assure you that this will be a pleasant surprise, though not an inappropriate one for the day, for I intend to have a minister with us to ask a blessing upon our food."

"Oh," said Stella, "I can guess it."

Young girls are always ready to guess as she did. She guessed it was to be a wedding. She guessed that Mrs. Morgan was going to be married. Then the others guessed so too. Mrs. Morgan guessed not. She was sure she could not get married without somebody to have her. Of course not. But Stella thought that "somebody" would not be very hard to find. She knew a gentleman that liked her well enough to marry her."

At any rate, that the party was to be a wedding one was pretty well settled. Whether the bride will be Athalia or not we shall see So then, after lots of "good night" and "do come again soon," we parted, and went on our way to visit the sick and dying victim of fashionable dissipation, which led her through a rapid career of a few happy months, and then through years of woe, from wine at dinner, to "cobblers" at late suppers, and bitters in the morning; till an appetite was acquired which could only be satisfied by constant libations of anything that would intoxicate, procured by any means, however debasing, till she ceased to be a lady; almost ceased to be a woman; quite forgot that she was a mother; else how could she have driven that poor little innocent child out upon the streets, murky and damp, with her cry of "Hot Corn, hot corn, all smoking hot!" while the poor child was chilly, cold, and starving?

Poor girl—poor little Katy! Thy mother loves thee now. Look down from thy blest abode—it is thy mother calls, it is thy voice she hears, and she answers, "Yes, yes I will come."

"She is better, sir," said Phebe, as we entered the door. "She has been sitting up a good deal, and she talks of going over to your house to-morrow, Mrs. Morgan; she says she must go out, and take the air, or she never will get well."

This was pleasant news, and it quite elated Mrs. Morgan. Mr. Lovetree gave one of his peculiar expressions of countenance as soon as he saw her, which told as plain as though he had spoken it, that she never would go out again but once, that would be a ride which all must, none are willing, to take.

We were all very much delighted to find Mrs. Meltrand and Agnes, with Mrs. De Vrai. Mrs. Meltrand, ever since she had first seen her, had fallen in love with little Sissee, the sweet little Adaleta, and this evening Mrs. De Vrai, had made her a final promise, that if she should not get well, Mrs. Meltrand should have her for her own; and she had promised to adopt her and make her as much her child as though she was really so.

"But what is the use of talking? I don't feel any more like dying than you do. I am almost well. My cough has quite gone."

But a bright crimson spot upon each cheek had not gone, and that told its own tale. Adaleta was delighted with sister Agnes. She could hardly bear to part with her. She will not, but her mother must. How little any one would have thought, as we parted that evening, leaving the invalid so cheerful and full of hope, that we had parted for the last time. No! not the last time—may we hope for one more meeting? Let us now retire to our chambers and prepare for that meeting. Let us say to the reader, as we said to the poor sufferer, "Good night. God be with you!"

CHAPTER THE LAST.

All things must have an end.

Where there is true friendship, there needs no gloss to our deeds, no hollow welcome to real friends.

"By and by" is easy said; it means an uncertain time, but it comes at last. It came to Mrs. De Vrai, only a few hours after our last parting. Phebe came with the early morning to say, "She is gone, sir; gone to meet her poor child in the hope of the penitent. After you went away, she lay and talked and talked about you, all of you, and Mrs. Meltrand and Agnes, and how happy she should be if she was a going to die, to think that her child would have such a good mother and sister, and so many real friends; and how different it would be with herself now, here and hereafter, as well as her child, than it would have been if she had died in her former residence of wretchedness, sin, and woe. Then I asked her if she would take her medicine and go to sleep, and she said, 'by and by, not now; I feel so well, so happy, I can almost fancy that I see my poor little Katy in heaven among the angels. I often see her here in the room when I am laying with my eyes closed, but not asleep; and I often think I hear her dying words, "Will he Come!" and I say "yes, he has come; the Saviour has come, my child, to your mother."

Then she says, "then come, mother, come and live with us;" and I answer, "by and by." By and by, Phebe I shall go, but not yet, I am going to get well now.'

"So I went and lay down in the back room, and I heard nothing of her, though I got up and looked at her a good many times, but she seemed to be sleeping so sweet, I thought I would not wake her to take her medicine—the doctor said I need not. In the morning I got up, and looked in the room, and there was Sissee sitting up in the bed, trying to open her mother's eyes; then she would put her arms around her neck and kiss her, but there was no kiss in return. Then she sat back and looked at her a minute, and then called—'Phebe, Phebe, mamma does not speak, oh Phebe, is mamma dead?'"

Yes mamma was dead. She had died as calm and free from pain and full of joy as when she said "good night" to her friends. She had died full of anticipation that she was going to live to get well; that she would not join the spirit of Little Katy now, but by and by: by and by she would come.

> Drop a tear, drop a tear, for she's departed!
> Wreath a smile, for she died not broken-hearted.

This was on Friday morning. On the Sunday following, the intended party met at Mrs. Morgan's and partook of an early dinner. "For," said Mr. Lovetree, "we have a good deal to do this afternoon. In the first place, some of our friends are disposed to be united in the holy, the blessed bonds, that bind the sexes together in a union that should be indissoluble, and productive of nothing but happiness. After that we have a duty to perform, which though it is generally termed melancholy, must not be made so on the present occasion. We shall go to deposit the body in Greenwood, that lovely place of rest for the dead, of one who we have every reason to believe died a true penitent, and is now with the spirit of Little Katy, where those who are murdered by the same cause that produced her death, will seldom ever be found. Our good missionary is with us, and we will have the wedding ceremony before the funeral one, because many go from that to the grave, none come from there to the marriage feast."

Now all began to look around for the happy couple. Mrs. Morgan was dressed as though she might be a bride, but where was the groom? Mr. Lovetree whispered to Mrs. Meltrand, for she was there with Agnes and little Sis, and Mrs. Meltrand said that Frank would be there by the time.

"Now what Frank is that?" said Stella in a whisper to Mrs. May; "it must be Frank Barkley; and so it is Mrs. Morgan that is going to be married. Oh, dear, I am sorry, I was in hopes she would always live with her old uncle, as she does now."

It *was* Frank Barkley who was expected. He was an old acquaintance of Mrs. Meltrand, a little wild in his youth, and came within an inch of the precipice over which so many young men tumble. Mr. Lovetree had said, "there is something good in the fellow," and between him and Mrs. Meltrand, it was developed. He is a good fellow—a sober fellow now—and he is going to be married. Now the door bell rings.

"There that is him."

Yes, it was him. He was told that all were waiting for him, and he said "he had come to the minute agreed upon." Poor Stella shed tears. She cried to think her dèar friend, Mrs. Morgan, was about to be married. She cried without a cause.

Mr. Lovetree said to Frank, "allow me to introduce you to my niece, Mrs. Morgan."

He started back from her, rubbed his eyes, and looked again. Stella rubbed hers. She was convinced now that they were not to be married. Poor Frank looked confused and in doubt. He approached near enough to Mrs. Morgan to whisper, "Lucy," to which she replied, "Yes," and he said, "God bless you then," and turned away to meet his bride.

This was Agnes. And he took her by the hand, and led her up to the minister who was to pronounce them man and wife, and said—"Now, sir, we are ready." Then a couple, who were to act as bridesmaid and bridegroom's attendant, took their stations upon the floor. It was the opinion of all present that they would act as principals in a similar scene by and by.

Perhaps the reader would like to know who this neatly-dressed, bright couple are, for he has seen them several times before. It is one of Mr. Lovetree's oddities that you see them now. You have seen them when they would not be very fitting guests in a parlor, but they wear wedding-garments now. This is Tom, who held the cup of cold water to the lips of the dying Madalina, and this is his reward. The neat, lovely girl at his side is Wild Maggie—Miss Margaret Reagan. The fine-looking hearty man that is leading up a well-dressed woman to the altar—another couple to be married—is one of the former customers of Cale Jones's grocery. It is Maggie's father. His bride is Mrs. Eaton. We have seen her and her two children in some of the early scenes of this volume. We saw them in the street then—we see them in the parlor now. We see them much better, much happier this time, and we see them just as we might see all the laboring class, if we could abolish the traffic in rum from the world. There are two other couples here to bear testimony to that fact. It was the particular request of Reagan and Maggie that they should be present to witness and rejoice over the power of the pledge to save. We have seen both these couples stand up to be married before the same minister who is now saying the solemn words of the marriage ceremony to those before him. You may see them as they were when you first saw them, if you will turn back to the plate facing the "Two Penny Marriage."

Julia Antrim and Willie Reagan act as attendants upon this last couple, and Sally Reagan and Stella May, dressed in pure white—dresses of their own make—with wreaths of flowers in their hair, made by their own hands—served the company with cakes and fruits and tea and coffee. Then the carriages came to the door, and all went—not to a tavern, or drinking saloon for a riot, to commemorate the most serious event of life, but in all soberness due to the occasion, to consign the remains of poor Madame De Vrai to her final resting-place on the earth.

It is a pleasant drive to Greenwood Cemetery, and it is a pleasant place for the tombs of our friends. It is a good place to go to meditate, among the new-made graves in the fresh-turned earth, and among the proud monuments of those who have lain long enough beneath their marble coverings to be forgotten. I did not forget to look, as I passed along, at the rose bush which I saw planted by a widow at the grave of her rum-murdered husband. It was growing fresh and vigorously.

Now we stand around the open grave that is soon to be filled by another victim of a trade that feeds scores and starves millions—that saves one life and causes a thousand deaths—that consigns youth, innocence and beauty, equally with old age, to a premature grave. Now we lower this last victim—still young, beautiful, intelligent, full of sweetness of disposition and kindness of heart—into her grave. Now we look at the little cherub, the darling, sweet, much loved Adaleta, her orphan child, and now at her sister's grave, then at the weeping circle, who stand and sob as the falling clods bring forth that hollow sound, never heard in any other place. Now the voice of him who says: "'Tis the last of earth," "Let us pray," breaks the charmed circle of intense silence.

Why is every eye upturned at the close? Did each listening ear fancy it heard the sound of an angel's voice in the air, breathing the words,—"Will he Come?" "Will he Come?"

And did they expect to see the face of Little Katy in the

clouds, looking down upon those she loved, paying this tribute to her mother, now sleeping by her side in the grave; now with her child in the spirit land of the blest?

Now the tall corn is waving o'er the mountain and glen,
And the sickle is reaping both the corn and the men;
And the child that was sleeping where the lamps dimly shone,
Like the corn, now is with'ring, in the vale all alone.
"Hot corn!" she was crying, in the night, all alone,
"Hot corn! here's your nice hot corn!" in the grave all alone.

Where the chill rain was falling, sat the poor child asleep;
Where the lights nightly burning, city vigils help keep—
Where the ague was creeping through the blood and the bone
Of the child that was sleeping on the curb-stone alone.
"Hot corn!" she was crying, in the night all alone,
"Hot corn! here's your nice hot corn!" in the grave all alone.

In a dark room lonely, lay the child all awake,
With a voice wildly crying, "Will he come, for my sake?"
Then a good man was praying, while to her dimly shone,
Poor fading light—ceases burning—and with God she's alone.
"Hot corn!" she was crying, in the night all alone,
"Hot corn! here's your nice hot corn!" in the grave all alone.

In the dark grave sleeping, while poor Katy's at rest,
While the wild storm raging, ever sweeps o'er her breast—
While the mourners are weeping for the dead passed away,
Let us pledge by the living that the cause we will stay.
"Hot corn!" she was crying, in the night all alone,
"Hot corn! here's your nice hot corn," in the grave all alone.

A VOICE FROM KATY'S GRAVE.

Among the many poetical effusions which have been elicited by reading the story of "Little Katy," I think the following, which appeared in the New York Tribune, will be read with pleasure. It is from the pen of Mrs. B. F Foster, of New York :—

With dizzy whirl, on rushed the wheels
  Along the City's murky street,
And music's light, inspiring peals
  Rang out from folly's gay retreat;
And busy footsteps hurried past,
  And human voices, harsh and wild,
Commingling, floated on the blast;
  When the shrill accents of a child
Rose mid the din, in tones forlorn,
And cried, "Come, buy hot corn, hot corn!"

Like some sad spirit wafted by,
  A stranger to the ways of earth,
Came up that little plaintive cry—
  Sweet discord to the sounds of mirth.
Unheeded by the reckless crowd,
  There stood a girl, a pale, wan thing,
And 'neath her bosom's tattered shroud.
  There lurk'd an age of suffering;
While e'en till night approached the morn,
In feebler voice, she cried, "Hot Corn!"

The gas lamp's glare fell on her face,
But lighted not her languid eyes;
And down her pallid cheeks, the trace
Of tears, bespoke her miseries;
With hunger gnawing at her heart,
She shivered, as the night wind blew
Her soiled and ragged clothes apart;
Till all insensible she grew,
And sinking in unblessed sleep,
Forgot to cry, "Hot Corn," and weep.

Alone, so young, how came she there?
To sell hot corn so late at night;
Had she no friends, no home, nowhere
To rest, and hide her from the sight
Of the rude world? No mother? Hush!
That holy name is not the one
For Katy's parent. Woman! blush
For thy lost sister; blush to own
That thou canst ever fall so low,
To plunge thy children into woe.

Within that mother's heart, the light
Of love was quench'd, quench'd by the flood,
The damning flood, whose waters blight
All that is left of human good:
And in her breast that demon reigned,
Who "Give, give, give!" is ever crying;
Demanding still to be maintained,
While all within, around, is dying;
Outpouring in its baneful breath,
Destruction, sorrow, sin and death.

The lips which should have kiss'd away
  Her daughter's tears, dealt curses forth;
The hand which should have been her stay,
  Was but the minister of wrath;
Blind to her wants, deaf to her prayers,
  Regardless of the driving storm,
To open streets and midnight airs,
  She drove that little shrinking form,
To earn a dram! In shame and scorn
With famished lips to cry, "Hot-corn!"

"Hot corn, hot corn!"— night after night,
  More faint and feeble grew that voice—
Still fiercely burned each glaring light,
  Still music bade the town rejoice;
The ceaseless footsteps passed along,
  Up came the wild discordant tones,
The voices of the thoughtless throng,—
  The bounding wheels rolled o'er the stones,—
But midst the din, the rush, the roar,
Poor Katy's cry is heard no more.

In one of those dark, noisome cells,
  The wretched call their home, she lies
All motionless; the icy spells
  Of death, have closed those weary eyes;
She speaks not now. Alas! how dread!
  That calm reproachful silence, when
Beside the wronged and injured dead,
  We kneel in vain! Low in that den
Behold the stricken mother cower;
Grown sober in one fearful hour.

She calls her, "Katy, darling!"—peers
Into that pale and sunken face,
She bathes her senseless brow with tears,
Sees on those bruised limbs, the trace
Of her own cruelty;—again
She calls, and prays for one last word,
Of blest forgiveness;—all in vain,
The answering voice no more is heard,
The soulless clay alone is there,
And fell remorse, and dark despair.

Weep, wretched woman, weep! That face
Shall haunt thee to thy dying day;
Nor time from memory erase
Thy child's deep wrongs; for they
Shall scorch into thy guilty breast;
In mad excitement thou shalt hear
Her cries; and midst thy fitful rest,
Shall that pale phantom form appear,
And o'er thy drunken moping, stand
To curse thee with an outstretched hand.

Yet not alone with thee, abides
That curse. Oh, Men, and Christians! can
Ye robe yourse[illegible] in god-like pride,
And boast your land, the one where man
Is most exalted; yet permit
The Demon Drunkenness to roam
Unfettered through your streets; to sit
By ev'ry corner, ev'ry home—
The weak and wretched to allure
To drink, to suffer, and endure?

In mercy, then, arrest the reign
  Of this dread fiend; and Oh! protect
Man from his self-inflicted pain.
  Spare the young wife, whose hopes are wreck'd,
Whose heart is crushed, whose home forsaken,
  Whose life's a desolated wild.
To infant prayers and tears awaken,
  And from the mother save the child.
Hark to that echo!—"Save, oh, save!"
Pleads a sad voice from Katy's grave.

"Pleads a sad voice from Katy's grave—
Save, oh, save!"

Fathers! mothers! sons! daughters! husbands! wives! Christians! philanthropists! All—brothers and sisters!—hear ye that voice? If ye do not, then, indeed, are ye deaf. Then have I cried in vain. In vain I have visited the abodes of wretchedness and sin, to draw materials for my panorama of "Life Scenes in New York." In vain I have painted you dark scenes of life, instead of those which shine out in the noonday sun.

In vain have I endeavored to awaken your sympathies by relations of tales of woe, or painted vice, as I have met with it in my midnight rambles, to guard you from its snares, if I have failed to touch that chord in your heart which brings a tear to the eye, for it is that which will prompt you to action —to sleepless vigilance, to eradicate from the world the great cause of such human misery as I have depicted. It is that which will prompt you to give, if nothing more,

> "Three grains of corn,
> Only three grains of corn, mother,"

towards the redemption of the fallen, and protection of those who need a staff and a guide to hold them back from the precipice over which they have gone down to ruin.

Reader, if you have not yet done it, do not close the book until you have paid the tribute of a tear at the grave of

www.ingramcontent.com/pod-product-compliance
Lightning Source LLC
LaVergne TN
LVHW011148110826
845150LV00006B/1190

* 9 7 8 1 4 2 5 5 4 6 4 7 2 *